P9-EMQ-279

The Complete Idiot's Reference Card

Creative Writing Preparation Checklist

_____ Have I planned my writing by gathering ideas and focusing my thoughts?
- ✓ Did I consider the topic?
- ✓ Did I firm up my purpose?
- ✓ Did I analyze my audience?
- ✓ Did I take into account any special circumstances, such as deadlines, format, length, and word count?

_____ Did I shape my writing by finding the best way to organize my material?
- ✓ Did I group similar ideas?
- ✓ Did I reject nonessential ideas?
- ✓ Did I select an appropriate tone?
- ✓ Did I order ideas in a logical way?
- ✓ Did I outline key points?
- ✓ Did I select a logical method of organization, such as chronological order, order of importance, or spatial order?

_____ Did I draft by writing my ideas in sentences and paragraphs?

_____ Did I revise my draft and rethink my ideas?
- ✓ Did I add any necessary facts and details?
- ✓ Did I move anything that was illogical?
- ✓ Did I cut unnecessary words, sentences, and paragraphs?
- ✓ Did I rewrite confusing passages?

_____ Did I edit my writing?
- ✓ Did I reread for errors in spelling?
- ✓ Did I catch grammatical mistakes?
- ✓ Did I look for punctuation errors?
- ✓ Did I check for capitalization problems?

_____ Did I proofread my work by checking it for typos and illegible handwriting?

alpha
books

tear here

Creative Writing Skills Checklist
Dot the I's and Cross the T's

Commas   Use a comma to
                      ✓ separate items in a series.
                      ✓ set off interrupting words.
                      ✓ set off introductory words and phrases.
                      ✓ separate parts of a compound sentence.
                      ✓ set off a direct quotation.
                      ✓ separate the parts of an address.

Semicolons   Use a semicolon
                      ✓ to separate items in a series when the items contain commas.
                      ✓ between main clauses when the conjunction (and, but, for, or) has been left out.

Colons   Use a colon
                      ✓ before a list.
                      ✓ to separate two independent clauses when the second clause restates or explains the first clause.

Parentheses   Use parentheses to enclose
                      ✓ additional information.
                      ✓ numbers or letters.

Hyphen   Use a hyphen
                      ✓ to show a word break at the end of a line.
                      ✓ in certain compound nouns.
                      ✓ in fractions and in compound numbers from twenty-one to ninety-nine.

Quotation marks   Use quotation marks to set off
                      ✓ a speaker's exact words.
                      ✓ the titles of short works such as poems, essays, songs, short stories, and magazine articles.

Apostrophes   Use an apostrophe to
                      ✓ show ownership.
                      ✓ show that letters have been left out of contractions.
                      ✓ make plurals that could be confused for other words.

Writing Numbers   ✓ Spell out numbers from one to nine.
                      ✓ Use figures for numbers 10 and larger.
                      ✓ Spell out any number that appears at the beginning of a sentence.

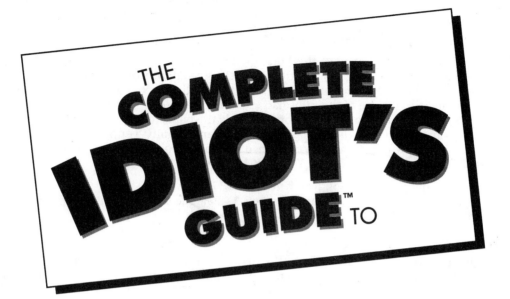

THE COMPLETE IDIOT'S GUIDE™ TO

Creative Writing

by Laurie Rozakis

alpha books

A Division of Macmillan General Reference
A Simon & Schuster Macmillan Company
1633 Broadway, New York, NY 10019

Copyright©1997 Laurie Rozakis

All rights reserved. No part of this book shall be reproduced, stored in a retrieval system, or transmitted by any means, electronic, mechanical, photocopying, recording, or otherwise, without written permission from the publisher. No patent liability is assumed with respect to the use of the information contained herein. Although every precaution has been taken in the preparation of this book, the publisher and author assume no responsibility for errors or omissions. Neither is any liability assumed for damages resulting from the use of information contained herein. For information, address Alpha Books, 1633 Broadway, 7th Floor, New York, NY 10019-6785.

International Standard Book Number: 0-02-861734-7
Library of Congress Catalog Card Number: A catalogue record is available from the Library of Congress.

99 98   8 7 6 5 4

Interpretation of the printing code: the rightmost number of the first series of numbers is the year of the book's printing; the rightmost number of the second series of numbers is the number of the book's printing. For example, a printing code of 97-1 shows that the first printing occurred in 1997.

Printed in the United States of America

Note: Reasonable care has been taken in the preparation of the text to ensure its clarity and accuracy. This book is sold with the understanding that the author and the publisher are not engaged in rendering legal, accounting, or other professional service. Laws vary from state to state, and readers with specific financial questions should seek the services of a professional advisor.

The author and publisher specifically disclaim any liability, loss or risk, personal or otherwise, which is incurred as a consequence, directly or indirectly, of the use and application of any of the contents of this book.

Publisher
Theresa Murtha

Editorial Manager
Gretchen Henderson

Editor
Nancy Stevenson

Production Editor
Michael Thomas

Cover Designer
Mike Freeland

Illustrator
Judd Winick

Designer
Glenn Larsen

Indexer
Tim Wright

Production Team
Angela Calvert
Mary Hunt
Malinda Kuhn
Christopher Morris
Maureen West

Contents at a Glance

Contents

Foreword

In 1939, an ambitious young man in California who aspired to be a writer borrowed $75—an enormous sum in those Depression days—so that he could travel to New York City for the First World Science Fiction Convention. His goal in making the days-long bus trip was to meet an agent who would represent him and his work to the various science fiction pulp magazines of the day. He made his contact, and for the next two years manuscripts traveled back and forth across the country, until one day in 1941 when the young man received a check for the sale of "The Pendulum" to one of the magazines.

Over the next few years, the young writer successfully sold seventy stories—all handled by that same agent—and established his credentials as a premier author.

His name? Ray Bradbury.

In 1946, that same agent, now working as an editor for ALL-AMERICAN COMICS, received a very precisely written, spelled, and punctuated letter from a young fan. The purpose of the letter was to inquire whether or not the editor felt its sender showed any promise as a writer. The editor replied that he thought the young fan did indeed show promise. If he continued to work at his writing, the agent told him, he would one day surely become a well-known author.

His name? Harlan Ellison.

In my career as a literary agent and as an editor at DC Comics, I have worked with countless writers. Regardless of their level of skill and ability when I first met them, they had one thing in common with Bradbury and Ellison: the desire to write and be published. Since you are reading this book, I trust that you, too, share that goal.

At the risk of stealing some thunder from the text that follows this foreword, let me share some of the "hints" I've been passing along to writers for sixty years…

1. Be original! Many of my writers referred to me as "B.O. Schwartz" because I constantly demanded that they come up with something new and different. Surprise your reader; throw out the most obvious solutions to a problem—the ones your readers will think of themselves—and come up with something innovative and interesting instead.

2. Carry a notebook and pen at all times. Science fiction award–winning writer Alfred Bester always carried something to write on, and so should you. Something you read or something you see or hear can be the spark that inspires a story. Make sure to jot your ideas down.

Keep a notepad next your bed, too. Many of my writers will attest to the plotting sessions we've had that began with the words "I woke up at 3:00 this morning with this great idea…!"

3. Use a "narrative hook." Start your story with a sentence or idea that immediately grabs the readers' attention and lures them to read on. I became a science fiction fan for life after reading this opening: "It all started when the clock on Metropolitan Tower began to run backwards." The author hooked me and made me want to know what was going on. Do the same with your own manuscripts.

4. When you finish your manuscript, put it away for at least 24 hours before looking at it again. Take time to do something else before re-reading your work. You'll be amazed at how flaws and errors jump out at you when you look at it with a fresh eye.

5. Keep writing. The only way to become a better writer is to practice. That means to keep working. As I recounted above, it took Ray Bradbury two years of writing before I sold his first story. He did not sit back and wait for the story to sell before writing a second; he continued to work until his efforts paid off.

Laurie Rozakis has put together a monumental volume here, covering an astonishingly wide variety of writing topics. I wish this book had existed years ago; I would have handed a copy to every writer who wanted to work with me. She answers virtually every question an up-and-coming writer could have.

There's plenty for experienced writers as well. Regardless of how much or how little writing you have done, you'll find invaluable tips throughout the book.

Skim the book for the areas that fit your interest or read every word. Either way, any writer who follows the paths Dr. Rozakis sets out would be a client an agent would be proud to represent and an author any editor would find a joy to work with!

That said, start reading…and then, start writing!

—Julius Schwartz

Julius Schwartz began his career as a literary agent in 1934 and continued representing a stable of prominent authors, including Ray Bradbury, Alfred Bester, Robert Bloch, and H.P. Lovecraft, until he joined DC Comics in 1944. At DC, he guided the destinies of virtually every prominent super-hero, most especially Batman and Superman, until 1986. Since then, he has served as DC's Goodwill Ambassador to numerous comic book and science fiction conventions throughout the year.

Introduction

Has your creative urge been crushed by too many know-it-alls: teachers, critics, parents, spouses, and children who offer their bone-chilling suggestions too freely? "You're not smart enough to write a book," they may have said. "Don't give up your day job," they offered not-so-kindly. Posh.

Everyone is talented, original, and has something to say. You are interesting, funny, and important. Tell it all. Let it come out on paper.

If you want to write, you can. It's as simple as that. You have my promise.

As a matter of fact, you're probably writing far more than you realize, right now. How many of these kinds of writing do you do?

➤ Advertising copy ➤ Business letters

➤ e-mail ➤ Essays

➤ Fill-in-the-blank forms ➤ Journals and diaries

➤ Legal briefs ➤ Love letters

➤ Newspaper articles ➤ Photo captions

➤ Poems ➤ Reports

➤ Stories ➤ Technical manuals

➤ School assignments ➤ Scientific papers

➤ Sermons ➤ Thank you notes

"But I'm not being creative," you claim. On the contrary, I say, the minute you put pen to paper or finger to keyboard, you're being creative. This book will help you learn to write more easily. Writing is work, but learning to write doesn't have to be.

What You'll Learn in This Book

This book is divided into six sections that take you through the process of developing your creative writing potential. You'll learn that before the actual writing comes detailed planning, analysis, and research. You'll find out that creative writing can take many different forms. Here's what the six parts of this book cover:

Part 1: Following the Writer's Trade first explores what writing is and how you can tell if you've got the "write stuff" to be a creative writer. Then I discuss the process of writing, step-by-step. Along the way, I'll teach you some of the most important secrets of writing!

Part 2: Fiction and Poetry gets into the nitty-gritty of writing novels, short stories, and poetry. Here's where you'll learn how to develop a compelling plot, realistic characters, vivid settings, and strong structure. You'll also get an overview of the conventions of poetry: rhythm, rhyme, figurative language, and poetic technique.

Part 3: Nonfiction covers biographies, autobiographies, textbooks, reference books, and magazine articles. I'll show you how to find a niche for your unique writing talents. In addition, there's an in-depth focus on hints you can really use to develop your skills.

Part 4: Drama, Scripts, and Screenplays opens with a discussion of writing plays. Then I survey the different types of screenplays you can write, including comedy, action/adventure, thrillers, and horror. You'll "toon" into the skills you need to write cartoons and the requirements for writing soap operas. Then I'll teach you all about story, structure, character, and how to write a *premise* and a *treatment*.

Part 5: Selling Your Work shows you how to support yourself while you write. You'll find out how to network for fun and profit and explore how to publish novels, short stories, plays, poems, and articles. I devote an entire chapter to literary agents so you can decide if retaining an agent is right for you. Not interested in the literary marketplace? This section also contains a great deal of information about financing your writing through grants and contests. Here's where you'll learn all about contracts and fees, too.

Part 6: Common Writing Challenges—and How to Conquer Them! describes writer's block and what to do if it strikes you. I'll teach you a series of easy methods for dispelling this affliction. Later in this section, you'll learn all about working with editors.

Last, there's the Glossary of Writing Terms, containing key words and definitions.

More for Your Money!

In addition to all the explanation and teaching, this book contains other types of information to make it even easier for you to unlock your creative abilities and learn how to write. Here's how you can recognize these features:

Bet You Didn't Know

This is interesting, useful background information that gives you even more of an "inside edge" to the writing biz. These are the facts that you can skim, but they're so nifty that you won't want to!

All the Write Stuff

Use these hints to make creative writing easier—and more enjoyable.

Wrong Turn

These warnings help you stay on track. They can help you avoid the little goofs... and the major pitfalls.

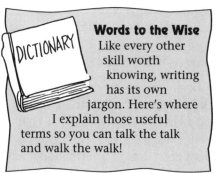

Words to the Wise

Like every other skill worth knowing, writing has its own jargon. Here's where I explain those useful terms so you can talk the talk and walk the walk!

Acknowledgments

To my family, for all their support. A special thanks to my son Charles, a real mensch, whose delightful wit, keen editing, and astonishing patience helped me enormously. (Even with this!)

Special Thanks to the Technical Reviewer

The Complete Idiot's Guide to Creative Writing was reviewed by an expert who not only checked the technical accuracy of what you'll learn in this book, but also provided invaluable insight and suggestions.

An educator for 32 years, Sharon Sorenson now works full time as a freelance writer. She has published over eighty articles in trade and professional journals; authored fifteen books on writing, the writing process, and teaching writing; and coauthored another dozen. In addition, she has written advertising copy, training manuals, industrial training film scripts, handbooks, political speeches, and magazine feature articles. When she's not on the lecture circuit, she resides with her husband in rural Indiana.

Part 1
Following the Writer's Trade

"It is wonderful that even today, with all the competition of records, of radio, of television, of motion pictures, the book has kept its precious character.

A book is somehow sacred. A dictator can kill and maim people, can sink to any kind of tyranny and only be hated, but when books are burned the ultimate in tyranny has happened. This we cannot forgive…

People…automatically believe in books. This is strange but it is so. Messages come from behind the controlled and censored areas of the world and they do not ask for radios, for papers and pamphlets. They invariably ask for books. They believe in books when they believe nothing else."

—John Steinbeck

John Steinbeck, winner of the 1963 Nobel Prize for Literature, recognized that books convey an authority that no other media can command. Plumbers may make more money, car mechanics may keep us tooling along, and fine chefs definitely make life more delicious. But writers fulfill a need that no one else can: they nurture our souls. This section of the book shows you why creative writing is so worthwhile.

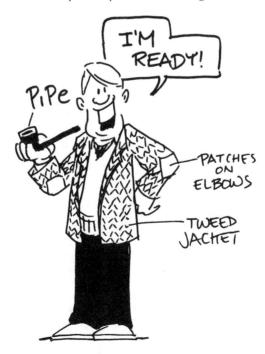

Write Away

Creative writing is easy. All you do is stare at a blank sheet of paper until drops of blood form on your forehead.

If creative writing is about as much fun as a root canal or an IRS audit, why do it? Especially in this age of phones, faxes, and FedEx; telephones, telecommunications, and tape recorders—isn't written communication as outré as girdles and guilt?

In this chapter, you'll discover what creative writing is and why people feel so compelled to do it. You'll learn that the urge to write one's innermost thoughts is as old as time itself—and as powerful. This chapter will help you discover that you're not alone in your desire to produce the Great American Novel, Essay, or Screenplay.

All the Write Stuff

A good writer is always a beginner, because writing is a process of continual discovery.

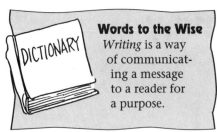

Words to the Wise

Writing is a way of communicating a message to a reader for a purpose.

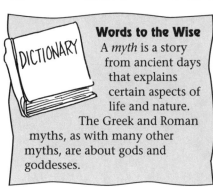

Words to the Wise

A *myth* is a story from ancient days that explains certain aspects of life and nature. The Greek and Roman myths, as with many other myths, are about gods and goddesses.

What is Writing?

We all know *writing* when we see it. Writing involves putting little marks on paper via a computer, pen, pencil, or crayon. But writing is more than mere scribbling.

When you write, you *communicate* a message to the reader. Communicating in writing means sending a message that has a destination. It takes two to tango, change a light bulb, and complete the function of the written word.

The *message* of writing is its content. You can present your message in a variety of ways. Traditionally, the forms of writing are divided into *narration, description, exposition*, and *persuasion*. Let's look at each writing form in more detail.

Narration

This is writing that tells a story. Narration that tells about real events includes *biographies* and *autobiographies*. Narrations that deal with fictional events include *short stories, myths, narrative poems*, and *novels*.

Description

This is a kind of writing that creates a word picture of what something or someone is like. Description is made up of sensory details that help readers form pictures in their minds.

Description also uses *images*, words that appeal to one or more of our five senses: sight, hearing, taste, touch, or smell. Imagery can be found in all sorts of writing (and *should* be), but it is most common in poetry.

Exposition

This type of writing explains, shows, or tells about a subject. As a result, it is the most common type of everyday writing. Exposition includes news articles; memos; business reports; and notes to the butcher, baker, and candlestick maker.

Bet You Didn't Know

Exposition can also be used to mean the opening parts of a play or story. During the exposition, the characters, action, and setting are introduced.

Persuasion

This is a type of writing that tries to move an audience to thought or action. Newspaper editorials, advertisements, and letters to the editor are all examples of persuasive writing.

What's the point of telling a story or describing something if there's no one to read it? Ditto with explaining and persuading. All four forms of writing share one crucial element—the *reader*, or *audience*. See Chapter 4, for a complete discussion of audience.

What Is Creative Writing?

But what's *creative* writing? How is it different from garden-variety white-bread writing? How is it the same? I could argue that all writing is creative. I could also argue that baseball needs the designated hitter, all colas are the same, and pizza tastes best cold. Creative writing is different from everyday-ordinary-commonplace writing.

Take a look at the following definitions of creative writing. Which ones do you agree with? Circle the best definition of creative writing.

Creative writing is...

A floor wax

A breath mint

A high-impact polymer used in food storage containers

The naughty bits

Nothing that a little Prozac wouldn't cure

Writing that uses language imaginatively

Go for the last one: *Creative writing* is a kind of writing that uses language in imaginative and bold ways. So you're sure you'll know creative writing when you see it, I've charted some examples of creative and non-creative writing:

Creative Writing	Usually Not Creative Writing
Novel	Your tax return (unless you claim the lawn as a deduction because it would die without you)
Short story	A grocery list
Play	The check for a decaf mocha latte and a low-fat bran muffin
TV script	An excuse note (with the possible exception of "I didn't make it to work because I spent the night on a spaceship with Elvis.")
Poem	A losing lottery ticket
Autobiography	A report card (but we have some leeway here)
Biography	A toe-tag
Article	Your boss's memos
Love letter	Your on-line profile (well, it shouldn't be)

Prime Time Players: Fiction and Nonfiction

Creative writing falls into different categories. This means that there's something for everyone to read—and to write.

Words to the Wise
Creative writing is a kind of writing that uses language in imaginative and bold ways.

Creative writing falls into two main categories: *fiction* and *nonfiction*. *Fiction* is writing that tells about made-up events and characters. Novels and short stories are examples of fiction. Fiction that contains imaginary situations and characters that are very similar to real life is called *realistic fiction*. *Nonfiction* is a type of writing about real people and events. Essays, biographies, autobiographies, and articles are all examples of nonfiction.

Bet You Didn't Know

Prose is all written work that is not poetry, drama, or song. Examples of prose include articles, autobiographies, biographies, novels, essays, and editorials.

Creative Writing Superstars

Here are the main types of creative writing, the heavy hitters.

Top Ten Types of Creative Writing

1. *Article.* An *article* is a short work of nonfiction. You can find articles in magazines, newspapers, and books.

2. *Autobiography.* An *autobiography* is a person's story of his or her own life. An autobiography is nonfiction and describes key events from the person's life.

3. *Biography.* A *biography* is a true story about a person's life written by another person. Biographies are often written about well-known people, such as O.J., Di, and Sting, and important people, such as Thurgood Marshall, Jonas Salk, and Eleanor Roosevelt.

4. *Drama. Drama* is a piece of literature written to be performed in front of an audience. The actors tell the story through their actions. Dramas can be read as well as acted.

Bet You Didn't Know

Although the term "drama" is often used to describe serious plays, "comedy" is actually a subcategory of this genre. (I would lie to you?) A subcategory of comedy is *farce,* a humorous play that is based on a silly plot, ridiculous situations, and comic dialogue. The characters are usually one-dimensional stereotypical figures. They often find themselves in situations that start out normally but soon turn absurd. Often, humor is created through an identity switch and the other characters' reaction to it.

5. *Essays*. An *essay* is a brief writing on a particular subject or idea.

6. *Fantasy*. *Fantasy* is a kind of writing that describes events that could not take place in real life. Fantasy contains unrealistic characters, settings, and events. *Science fiction* is fantasy writing that tells about make-believe events that include science or technology. Often, science fiction is set in the future, on distant planets, or among alien races.

7. *Novels*. A *novel* is a long work of fiction. The elements of a novel— plot, characterization, setting, and theme— are developed in detail. Novels usually have one main plot and several less important subplots.

8. *Poetry*. *Poetry* is a type of writing in which words are selected for their beauty, sound, and power to express feelings. Traditionally, poems had a specific rhythm and rhyme, but such modern poetry as *free verse* does not have a regular beat, rhyme, or line length. Most poems are written in lines, which are arranged together in groups called *stanzas*.

9. *Short stories*. A *short story* is narrative prose fiction shorter than a novel that focuses on a single character and a single event. Most short stories can be read in one sitting and convey a single overall impression.

10. *Song lyrics*. *Songs* are poems set to music. All songs have a strong beat, created largely through the 3R's: rhythm, rhyme, and repetition.

    A *ballad* is a story told in song form. Traditional ballads were passed down by word of mouth from person to person; the words are simple and have a strong beat. Like their older relatives, newer ballads often tell stories about adventure and love.

How Can You Tell If You've Got the Write Stuff?

If you're 8' tall, odds are you're going to end up on the basketball court sooner or later— even if you have two left feet. Are you built like a Buick? People will assume you're a sumo wrestler, gridiron star, or earth mother.

Got red hair? You *must* have a flaming temper. Do you pierce, tattoo, and dye various portions of your body? Then it's as plain as the ring in your nose that you're the creative type.

But is it? Sometimes the assumptions people make do have some basis in fact. Some tall people *do* play basketball; some muscular types *do* move pianos. Other times, however, you can't judge a book by its cover or a Madonna wanna-be by her pierced navel.

How can you tell if you're cut out to be a creative writer? Here, your fat-to-muscle ratio doesn't provide a clue. Some writers are deliciously buff; others, appallingly broad in the beam. Could *you* pick a creative writer out from the crowd? Take this simple true/false test to see how much you know about being a creative writer. Write true for every statement you think is correct and false for every one you think is hooey.

_____1. Only really smart people can be creative writers.

_____2. You have to suffer to be a writer.

_____3. Writers must smoke pipes, but cigars will do in a pinch.

_____4. All writers have agents.

_____5. All writers make a lot of money.

_____6. You need special training to be a creative writer.

_____7. If you don't start writing when you're young, forget it.

_____8. All writers are sensitive and usually temperamental.

_____9. You can't write without inspiration.

_____10. Writers are born, not made.

Bonus: _____Writers drink scotch, rye, or dry white wine.

Answer Key

All true: Your 11th grade teacher really did a number on your head, didn't she?

7–9 true: Don't try to pick up a writer in a bar. You'll end up with a used car salesman, computer programmer, or a circus rouster.

4–6 true: You've read too many bad novels and watched too many TV mini-series. Put down that clicker and pick up that pen!

1–3 true: You're on the write track.

None true: Write now, write here.

Every answer is false. If you write, you're a writer. It's as simple as that.

Why Write?

Several years ago, my local school district held a "Celebrate the Arts" day. I was invited to be a guest speaker on the "writing process." Because it had been a while since I had shaved both legs on the same day, I decided to spiff up a bit and get a free lunch.

The first speaker on the panel, a local novelist with two published books to his credit, stood straight and tall. "Writing is a tremendous amount of fun," he proclaimed. "The words flow like honey," he said. Writing was as easy as falling off a log, shooting fish in a barrel, or stealing candy from a baby.

"Liar, liar, pants on fire," I thought. The previous week I had fallen off a ladder trying to get some leaves out of the gutter, and that was not fun. And many days, neither is writing. It is often lonely, hard, and as mucky as leaf removal. The words seldom flowed like honey. I eat too much candy and clean too many cabinets to avoid writing. But still I keep at it. Why?

Creative writers have a story to tell. The story may be fiction or nonfiction. It may be a play, a script, a poem. Whatever form the writing takes, it must be expressed. Creative writers have a need to write, as much as they have a need to breathe, eat, and sleep. And their task is equally important to humanity.

Creative writing is as crucial today as it was to the Egyptians sweating over their papyrus and the medieval monks hunched over their illuminated manuscripts. Perhaps the very qualities that would seem to make writing passé are the reasons it's more important than ever. As we litter the Information Superhighway with embarrassing, poorly written trash and communicate in itty-bitty sound bites, we need a medium that allows us to communicate, think, discover, and learn—creatively.

What, Me Write?

As any good ball player will tell you, you can't steal second base and keep one foot on first. So what stops most people from writing? It's not lack of talent, whatever "talent" is. It's fear. "Who am I?" most beginning writers think. "What right do I have to think I can be a writer? Besides, no one will listen to me."

Nonsense. You are a person with a unique story to tell. I've been teaching creative writing for more than (gulp) 25 years. I've been publishing my work for nearly 20 years. And I tell you that everyone has a story that should be told. Take this quick quiz to learn why *you* should be writing.

I write because…

____ 1. I want to communicate ideas.

____ 2. I have a story to tell.

____ 3. I am a unique person.

____ 4. It satisfies my soul.

____ 5. I speak with passion.

____ 6. I want to learn something.

____ 7. I need to fulfill a dream.

____ 8. I have information to share.

____ 9. I want to be famous.

____ 10. I want to make money.

Let's take a look at each reason in greater depth.

Reason #1: Convey a Message. How can you know what you mean until you write it? The act of writing allows you to make unexpected connections among ideas and language. Creative writing helps you get your ideas across in fresh, new ways.

Reason #2: Tell a Story. "I have an ordinary life," you say. "Nothing special ever happens to me." But you don't need special events to be a writer; it's what you do with the everyday that matters. That's the beauty of writing— it allows you to make the mundane into the magical.

Reason #3: Express My Individuality. Writer John Updike compares being a creative writer to a sailor who sets a course out to sea. A creative writer is an explorer, a groundbreaker. Creative writing allows you to chart your own course and boldly go where no one has gone before.

Reason #4: Gain Personal Satisfaction. It is a delicious thing to write, to be no longer yourself but to move in an entire universe of your own creating. Today, for instance, as man and woman, both lover and mistress, I rode along a beach on a summer morning by the crashing surf. I was also the horses, the wind, the words my people spoke, even the blazing sun that made them almost close their love-drowned eyes. When I consider the marvelous pleasures I have enjoyed, I am tempted to offer a prayer of thanks.

Reason #5: Express Emotion. See Reason #4.

Reason #6: Gain Knowledge. We are poised on the brink of the most exciting time in the history of the world. It's a happening place, baby. One day's issue of *The New York Times* contains more information than a citizen of the Renaissance would encounter in his or her entire life. How do people process all these bits and bytes? The smart ones write.

Writing is a way of thinking and learning. Creative writers have a unique opportunity to explore ideas and acquire information. Writing allows you to:

➤ Know subjects well

➤ Own the information

➤ Recall details years later

➤ Gain authority and credibility

➤ Organize and present ideas logically and creatively

Reason #7: Fulfill a Dream. Writing creates a permanent, visible record of your ideas for others to consider and ponder. Writing gives you a taste of immortality.

Reason #8: Share Information. Writing is a powerful means of communication because it forms and shapes human thought. In an open society, everyone is free to write and thereby share information with others. And beyond sharing information, writing helps change ideas and attitudes through persuasion.

Reason #9: Become Famous. Want to become the head weenie at the roast? Writing is a legal and accessible way to leave your footprint in the sands of time.

Reason #10: Earn a Living. I make a very handsome living from my labors; you can, too. With the explosion of information, there are more markets than ever before for writers in all fields. Not all writers are rich, but many do support themselves by their pen. It's a nice feeling to ply the writer's trade.

The Least You Need to Know

➤ *Writing* is a way of communicating a message to a reader for a purpose.

➤ Traditionally, the forms of writing are divided into *narration, description, exposition,* and *persuasion.*

➤ *Creative writing* is a kind of writing that uses language in imaginative and bold ways.

➤ You can be a creative writer. I promise.

Chapter 2

In Your Write Mind

In This Chapter

➤ Discover why it's crucial to get in your "write mind"

➤ Learn how writers really feel about writing

➤ Find out how to see yourself as a writer

When I was six years old, I announced to anyone who would listen that I was going to be a writer. Half my friends laughed; the rest sneered. "Don't be a dope," people said. "Only a genius can be a writer. And you're no rocket scientist." I was so upset that I burst into tears. Later that night, I blew my nose, squared my shoulders, and decided to get even. I was going to show them! I would become a successful writer. And I did.

Later on, I met many supportive teachers, friends, editors, and fellow writers. "You can write a book if you want to," they said. "Even if you're really busy, you can find the time." As a matter of fact, I wrote my first book while my first child napped. Fortunately, the book was fairly short and his naps were fairly long! My husband and children have offered unfailing support to my career in countless ways, but I never forgot that initial rejection.

As a result, I have great sympathy for people who want to be writers but feel that they can't because they don't have the education, brains, proper equipment, or talent. I wish they had friends like the ones I met later who said, "Yes, you can be a writer! Believe in yourself and you can reach your dream."

In this chapter, you will learn how important it is to see yourself as a writer. Writing is easy—anyone can do it. But believing that you can be a writer is another kettle of fish entirely. The first step is having the *write attitude*. That's what this chapter is all about. Here, you'll learn how to develop a successful attitude and successful writing habits.

Writing: A Love/Hate Relationship

I love super-premium chocolate ice cream, luxury vacations, and video games. But each of my passions has a downside: ice cream is fattening, vacations are expensive, and video games rot my brain. I love to write, but it has its downside, too. Writing can be lonely, frustrating, and just plain hard. After a full day of writing, my brain and butt hurt. I'm not alone in my love/hate feelings about my vocation. All writers experience this ambivalence toward their life's work.

Now it's your turn. Complete the following list with reasons why you—or someone you know—doesn't like to write:

Writing: The Downside

1. _____

2. _____

3. _____

4. _____

5. _____

What are the most frequently mentioned feelings? Many people dislike writing because they worry about making mistakes in spelling, grammar, and punctuation. You don't have to share that fear—there are plenty of good reference books on the market. You might even want to check out my upcoming book, *The Complete Idiot's Guide to Grammar and Style.*

Other people dislike writing because they don't know how to get started. I've taken care of that, too; it's the topic of Chapter 3, "Putting a Toe in the Water: Getting Started."

Still other writers dislike writing because it's essentially a lonely occupation. Speech, in contrast, gives instant gratification: your audience is right there to urge you on if you falter. But writing is a solitary occupation. Most of the time, a writer's only companions are paper, pencil, computer, and m&ms. When you finish writing, you may have to wait for feedback. And many times, you don't get any feedback at all. Your story sells, but there are no fan letters; your mother/father/significant other/co-workers read your article and may never say anything about it. That's the nature of the beast.

All the Write Stuff
Graffiti found in New York City: "Bad spellers of the world, untie."

But writing can't all be bad, you protest. If it were, no one would ever write. You are completely correct: with the right attitude, writing can be one of the most glorious experiences on earth. Complete the following list with the good things about writing:

Writing: The Upside

1. _____

2. _____

3. _____

4. _____

5. _____

As you learned in Chapter 1, "Write Away," creative writers have a story to tell. Writing allows you to communicate, think, discover, and learn—creatively. It also allows you to make your own thoughts clearer or even to discover new thoughts and new ideas that help you understand yourself and others. This makes your life fuller and more enjoyable. Sometimes, these new thoughts and ideas can also make other people's lives richer.

Writing also allows you to record the key events in your life. You know valuable things that no one else knows. By writing down your experiences as well as your thoughts, you can communicate what you learn to others.

The first step in getting the "write attitude" is recognizing that all writers have positive and negative feelings about their craft. So don't beat yourself up if some days you say, "Why am I doing *this*?" Other days you'll say, "How could I ever do anything else?"

Top Ten Excuses People Use to Avoid Writing

If this were the best of all possible worlds, realizing that writing offers rich spiritual (and sometimes material) rewards would be enough to set us all 'a working on our opus. But this is not the best of all possible worlds and we have a million other things to do before we can get started writing. Every day it's the same routine: car repair, laundry, dishes, gardening, cleaning, cooking, taking care of the kiddies—and let us not forget that little matter of earning a living. In most cases, you have to meet all your responsibilities before you can even consider sitting down to write.

Besides, we know that writing is lonely, hard work. Often, writers with the best of intentions find themselves sidetracked. Before they know it, time has slipped by and nothing has been written. "I'm too busy," they wail. "I'm too tired at the end of the day" or "I'm too wired to sit down that long," they moan.

Below are the top excuses people use to avoid applying their fanny to the chair and their pencil to the paper. After the list, I describe what you can do to make sure you don't need any of these excuses when you're getting ready to write. I also provide cross-references to later chapters of the book where you can find detailed information to help you overcome each excuse. See which excuses you've used yourself.

Top Ten Excuses to Avoid Writing

1. I don't have anything to write.

2. I'll make a fool of myself by failing.

3. I have writer's block.

4. I don't have time to sit down and write.

5. I'm embarrassed about my poor grammar and spelling.

6. I don't have the right tools, such as a word processor or computer.

7. It's been too long since I've written anything.

8. I'm not creative at all.

9. No one will buy my writing anyway, so what's the point?

10. Everything good has been written already.

Extra Credit: Fill in your personal favorite excuse. Try the one you used in 12th grade English.

Let's take a look at some of these excuses and see how you can make sure that you don't fall into these traps.

Excuse #1: *I don't have anything to write*. Sorry—this one won't wash. *Everyone* has something to write. In fact, everyone has a lot to write…even you. *Especially* you. If you don't believe me, try this strategy.

> **All the Write Stuff**
> You might find it easier to do this writing exercise on a laptop or notebook computer. However, this is not cause to use Excuse #6!

For one week, carry around a notepad and a pen. Every few hours, take out your writing tools and jot down your ideas. Don't worry about spelling, grammar, and punctuation. Just get those ideas down on paper. Write about people, places, things, ideas, and memories. Jot down flashes of conversation, too.

Part of your list might look like this:

I will always remember my first view of Prince Edward Island where we lived when my family left the mainland. It was sunset when we arrived. The lighthouse looked down on us like a tall, black-capped giant.

Idea for a story:

It's dress-down Friday at the brokerage house. Mr. Fitzpatrick, the big boss, is wearing an open-necked sports shirt. Brian, the new guy in accounts, comes walking down the hall—in a suit and tie.

"It's Friday," Mr. Fitzpatrick said. "You're not supposed to wear a tie."

Brian (crushed), "But it's not silk."

Idea for a science article:

Is there any truth in the saying, "Liquor before beer, never fear; beer before liquor, never sicker"?

Writers call this technique keeping a *Journal* or a *Commonplace Book*. Down through the ages, many famous writers have kept journals in which to record their ideas for later writings. You'll learn more about journals in Chapter 3, "Putting a Toe in the Water: Getting Started."

Excuse #2: *I'll make a fool of myself by failing*. Actually, just the opposite is likely to happen; people will respect and admire you for having the courage to write that book, article, or script. The vast majority of people in this country harbor the dream of writing The Great American Novel. You might be the one to actually do it. So cross this excuse off your list, too.

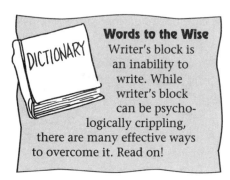

Words to the Wise
Writer's block is an inability to write. While writer's block can be psychologically crippling, there are many effective ways to overcome it. Read on!

Excuse #3: *I have writer's block.* No matter how much you may want to write, you may get blocked. Even the best of the best get blocked. So take comfort from the company you'll be keeping: Ernest Hemingway, Ralph Ellison, and Joseph Heller, to name just a few.

What can you do if you get writer's block? Here are some ideas:

➤ First, recognize that there are times when it really won't matter whether you write or not. You can set aside your manuscript for a few days, or even for a few months. Your work might be better for a breather. Give yourself a break.

➤ Start a different project or turn to something entirely physical. This might be the time to finish your holiday shopping, clean the garage, or visit your mother-in-law.

➤ Be honest with yourself. Assess why you're blocked. Do you hate the project? Do you have serious problems on your mind that are interfering with your concentration? Are you ill?

➤ Enlist a friend's help. Have your friend look over your work and suggest some possible directions for the plot, research, or dialogue.

➤ Find out more about writer's block in Chapter 22.

Excuse #4: *I don't have time to sit down and write.* Ha! Attorney/writer Scott Turow wrote his first few best sellers, those taut courtroom thrillers, on the train on the way to and from work. Toni Morrison won a Pulitzer prize for her novels—almost all of them written while she was an editor in Manhattan. Poet William Carlos Williams was a pediatrician; poet Wallace Stevens sold insurance.

In the nineteenth century, Harriet Beecher Stowe wrote her great bestseller, *Uncle Tom's Cabin,* between scrubbing floors, cooking, and raising her scores of children. Nathaniel Hawthorne? He worked in the Salem Custom House during the day and penned *The Scarlet Letter* at night. Lewis Carroll wrote *Alice in Wonderland* while he worked as a mathematician. Few writers—even the biggies—have the luxury of giving up their day jobs.

When can you get a chance to write? Fill in this log to see when you can carve out some time. Put a check next to each time that seems a good possibility.

6:00–8:00 AM

_____ Before work

_____ At breakfast

_____ While traveling to the job

_____ At the office, before work starts

9:00–11:00 AM

_____ During my coffee break

_____ Between meetings, clients, or patients

_____ Between sales calls and visits

12:00–5:00 PM

_____ At lunch

_____ As my computer boots up

_____ During my coffee break

6:00–8:00 PM

_____ On the way home, on the subway, bus, or train

_____ Before dinner

_____ After dinner

9:00–12:00 PM

_____ Before bed

_____ In place of TV, bowling, or surfing the Net

_____ So who needs sex anyway?

Wrong Turn
Set aside the same writing time every day and stick to it. It doesn't have to be a huge block of time—even half an hour will do—but carve that time in granite. Don't let anyone chip away at your writing time!

Excuse #5: *I'm embarrassed about my poor grammar and spelling.* Better living through technology: spell-checkers and grammar programs can help you correct most of your writing problems. You'll also find any number of good ol' fashioned reference books available at your local bookstore. They'll help you find out everything you always wanted to know about grammar but were too shy to ask.

Bet You Didn't Know

William Shakespeare spelled his own name several different ways. And what harm did it do *him*?

Want more help? That's why editors and proofreaders were invented. A good editor is a beautiful thing, a better friend to a writer than a sharp pencil, cup o' java, or souped-up computer. In Chapter 21, I take you step-by-step through the process of working with an editor.

Excuse #6: *I don't have the right tools, such as a word processor or computer.* There's no denying that a computer or word processor can make writing easier. Both tools enable you to edit and revise with ease. A computer also enables you to get on-line assistance from research software. You can take a drive on the Information Superhighway, too. It's a great place to get facts and aid and comfort.

But let us not forget that the *Bible*, the *Iliad*, the *Odyssey*, Shakespeare's plays, Dante's *Inferno*, and Milton's *Paradise Lost* (all 12 books) were written long-hand. So were *Pride and Prejudice, Frankenstein* (in one weekend), and *Moby Dick*. All you need is a pen and paper, bunky.

Excuse #7: *It's been too long since I've written anything.* No dice, here either. In Chapter 3, "Putting a Toe in the Water: Getting Started," I'll take you through the writing process from start to finish. You'll get an instant refresher course!

Excuse #8: *I'm not creative at all.* That's what you think. You don't have to wrap a national monument in aluminum foil, cut off your ear, dye your hair fuchsia, or grab your crotch on stage to be considered creative. Millions of seemingly ordinary everyday people, people like you and me, are deeply creative. The proof? Their writing. Remember the *Wizard of Oz*? You have the heart already. Stick with me and you'll get the courage and brain as well. See especially chapters 3, 4, and 5.

Excuse #9: *No one will buy my writing anyway, so what's the point?* So who says they have to? No one bought Emily Dickinson's poems. She wrote more than a thousand poems. During her life, only seven were published—all anonymously. Edgar Allan Poe never made enough from his writing to rub two dimes together; Henry David Thoreau published *Walden* with his own money. You can write for the pleasure of writing, just as you may jog, cook, or garden for the sheer joy of it.

"But I want to make money from my writing," you say. Not to worry. Right now there are more publishing opportunities than ever before. Sometimes identifying the right markets for your work can take as much time as writing itself! But you can't win it if you're not in it. You've got to search if you want to publish. I'll show you how in Part 5, "Selling Your Work."

Bet You Didn't Know

More than 250,000 writers and editors are currently holding staff jobs. Nearly a third of these writers work for newspapers, magazines, and book publishers. More on this in Part 5.

Excuse #10: *Everything good's been written already.* This is lame, kid, really lame. It's also an easy excuse to refute. First off, while all the common themes and plots have been written, they have never been written from your point of view—and that makes all the difference! When *you* write the stories, they become unique, because they are yours.

And just check out the shelves of any book store. You'll see that there's an explosion of good writing. Surf the channels on your TV and you'll see that there's *really* a need for good writers *there!*

Now you know that these excuses won't hold any Perrier or even tap water. So it's time to buckle down and...

Put Your Nose to the Grindstone

Scene: Ms. Cheery Writer and I were sitting in on a seminar together. "What do you do on days when your writing isn't going well?" a member of the audience asked my ebullient compatriot. "First and foremost, I'm in sales," she said. "That's how I make my living, so my writing doesn't matter that much. I write when I feel like it. It's not like my writing really matters or anything."

The audience turned to me. I didn't want to be crabby, just honest. "My writing matters to me," I answered. "It matters a whole lot. Whether or not I earn money from my craft, I see myself as a writer. I'm also a full-time university professor, a community activist, scout leader, and a parent, but I see myself as a writer. If I didn't, I would not be able to write."

All the Write Stuff
Join a writers group. These groups offer invaluable support and suggestions. No writers group in your area? Start your own by advertising in local newspapers and on bulletin boards. I started a writers group about five years ago.

I said that a dedicated writer must establish a schedule and stick to it. If you want to be a writer, you must write. There will be plenty of days that you *have* to take off. There will be the day that Johnny stuffs his sister into the dryer, the dryer repairman comes, and you go to Sears to buy a new dryer. But there will be even more days that you can devote to writing.

Schmoozing with the Literati

Fantasy: Famous writers spend their days doing lunch with their publisher at trendy Big City/Bright Lights bistros.

Reality: Famous writers spend their days writing.

Fantasy: Famous writers spend their days making kissy-face with people so famous they are known only by their first names: Cindy, Dave, Ivana.

Reality: Famous writers spend their days writing.

Fantasy: Famous writers spend their days networking with other famous writers.

Reality: Famous writers spend their days writing.

This is not to say that I haven't had my share of nice Manhattan lunches. I have—but most of the time I'm too busy trying to cut a better deal with the publisher to worry if my fettucini alfredo is really a heart attack on a plate. Most of the time I rarely even taste what I order.

Put your nose to the grindstone and your fingers to the pencil. Become determined to write. And then, write you will.

Get the Write Attitude

Start by getting the "write attitude." By this I mean to think of yourself as a writer. To make sure that you don't chicken out, tell everyone that you're a writer. Believing in yourself—and having others believe in you—is the first step to success. Here are some more ideas to try:

➤ *Read*. Read everything—not just the type of writing you want to do. The more you read, the more you learn about writing. I recommend newspapers, magazines, fiction, and nonfiction.

➤ *Consider taking writing classes*. If your local adult education center offers a writing course, sign up. Try the local community college and library, too. In addition to learning more about writing, you'll become part of a circle of fellow writers.

➤ *Sharpen your skills*. Review spelling, grammar, and usage.

➤ *Become computer literate*. Learn how to use a computer and a standard word processing program. Increasingly, computers are the primary way to access reference materials in libraries. Being computer literate is especially important if you want to publish later on because many editors won't accept manuscripts that aren't on disk.

➤ *Get on the Net*. The Internet is a great way to meet other writers. It's also a super source for ideas. In addition, cyberspace is fast becoming an important venue of publication.

➤ *Buy personal letterhead*. Get yourself some nice stationery. Have it printed with your name, address, telephone number, fax, and e-mail address. You'll use these supplies to contact editors as well as other writers.

➤ *Get business cards*. Under occupation, list "writer." You'll find that business cards are very useful for helping you network.

➤ *Get working!* You can't be a writer if you don't write. When you finish reading this chapter, take a break and write for an hour.

All the Write Stuff
Having trouble thinking of stuff to write? Start by writing some letters, journals, diaries, and lists. These types of writing can all provide invaluable story ideas down the road.

Chip off the Old Shoulder: The Writer's Temperament

The temperamental "difficult person" has become a rarity in the writing biz. The writers who quit a job after hurling an inkwell at their boss are few and far between. Nowadays, almost no one throws a temper tantrum over an editor's excision of some objectionable language, as Hemingway once did.

No one likes to work with a prima donna. Getting the "write attitude" means thinking of yourself as a writer, not as a gifted person entitled to special dispensation. Don't use your new identity as an excuse to trample on the rights of others. If you decide to publish, recognize that your words will be changed and your ideas will be rearranged. Sometimes the changes will be for the better, but sometimes they won't be. More on this in Chapter 21, "A Writer's Best Friend: Editors."

Wrong Turn
Your spouse and friends might be threatened by your determination to become a writer. "Maybe she won't love me when she's a big success," they think. Your boss might worry that you'll quit your day job when you make the best-seller list. Ignore them. Follow your heart and become a writer.

The Least You Need to Know

➤ All writers feel ambivalent about writing. Some days they love it; other days they hate it.

➤ As a result, people make excuses to avoid writing. (Not you, however!)

➤ To get in the "write attitude," start seeing yourself as a writer.

Putting a Toe in the Water: Getting Started

All writers are optimists—whether they see themselves that way or not. Otherwise, how could any person sit down to a pile of blank sheets and decide to write?

But writers are also notorious for using any reason to keep from writing: there's always too much researching, retyping, rethinking. In a pinch, cleaning the drawers or changing the oil will do—anything to avoid plunging into that manuscript. But writing is a lot like cooking, auto repair, and sex—no matter how you do it, you have to start *somewhere*.

In this chapter, you will learn how to get started writing. I'll teach you different methods to make it easier for you to get your ideas down on paper. You'll learn proven techniques used by writers in all different fields, from fiction to nonfiction, poetry to prose. I'll show you how to select the routines that work best for you and your individual writing style. Now you've tested the water, so it's time to kick off the high board, speedo.

Writing vs. Speaking

We all know how to talk. In fact, you probably can't remember a time when you didn't know how to talk. It's easy to talk to our friends... so why is it so hard to write to them?

To answer that question, we must analyze how writing differs from speaking. Take a few minutes to write down all the differences you can brainstorm between these two vital activities.

Use the spaces provided below to compare speaking and writing.

Speaking	Writing
_____	_____
_____	_____
_____	_____
_____	_____
_____	_____
_____	_____

As you can see from your chart, writing and speaking differ in several important ways. First of all, speech vanishes faster than yesterday's media darling. This is not necessarily a bad thing: for one, it means that any mistakes we make as we speak are likely to glide right by before they register in our listener's consciousness. In contrast, any mistakes we make when we write tend to stick around like an especially vile hangover. This gives people a chance to comment on our faux pas.

In addition, speech is immediate. There is a good point to this: the message gets across fast. But there is also a bad point to this: sometimes we jump start our mouths before our brains have had a chance to kick in. The immediacy of spoken communication gives people a chance to respond right then and there. If our message is garbled, our audience can say, "Huh?" and give us a chance to clarify our words. But when we write, our words may not be read for hours, days, months, or even years. As a result, a great deal of time may pass before we know if we have communicated successfully. Sometimes, we may not even remember what we intended to write and so cannot straighten out any miscommunication.

Nonetheless, speech and writing are similar in one important way: both methods of expression have patterns, such as accent, speed of delivery, and repetition. But writing has several unique conventions not shared by speech, such as spelling, punctuation, and capitalization. If we do not master these customs, our written communication will be flawed. People may judge us harshly as a result of our written errors.

> **All the Write Stuff**
> Want to capture the cadences of speech in your written dialogue? Use a tape recorder to record an actual dialogue, then study the speech patterns.

Whether you realize it or not, you've worked to master the conventions of speech. You can do the same to master the conventions of writing.

Because of all these differences between writing and speech, you cannot simply write the way you speak. Instead, you have to learn to use those features of written communication that will allow you to communicate your ideas clearly and powerfully. That's what you'll learn next in this chapter.

The Right Way to Write?

Certain processes have a right way and wrong way. We *all* know that to eat a chocolate Easter bunny properly, you start by biting the head off. Even a toddler knows that you put the cereal in the bowl first, *then* you pour in the milk. What car owner doesn't know that you take off the lug nuts *before* you change a tire? (Actually, changing a tire is an entirely different matter, of course. That's why we have road service.) Need I get into lather, rinse, repeat?

But what about getting started writing? Is there a right way and a wrong way with this all-important procedure? Take this true/false quiz to see how much you know about starting the process of writing.

Write *true* if you think the answer is true; write *false* if you think it is a bold-faced lie.

How Does the Typical Writer Write?

_____1. Sometimes, writers don't have difficulty coming up with ideas. Their words flow as effortlessly as cheap white wine at a holiday office party.

_____2. Some equally good writers agonize over every single word, even those itty-bitty prepositions.

_____3. Some writers set to work every day at 8:00 A.M. sharp.

continues

---

continued

_____4. There are times that writers get crackin' after lunch rather than at the crack of dawn.

_____5. Some writers, like bats and disco queens, do their best work when the sun goes down.

_____6. There are times that writers must have total silence to do their best work.

_____7. Other writers can't write without the radio or stereo blaring, preferably with oldies, show tunes, or opera.

_____8. Many writers do their best work on a computer.

_____9. Some writers sprawl on their stomach and write parts of their first drafts in longhand.

_____10. All writers write the same way.

Answer Key

Items 1–9 are true; only item 10 is false.

What does this quiz prove? It shows that there isn't a "right" way to write. Writing is so intensely personal that there are all kinds of methods that accomplish the same aim. But all writers are vulnerable and tense. Driven by a compulsion to put the best of themselves down on paper, they are terrified by their audacity.

Wrong Turn
Don't be taken in by those people who try to force you into using a specific writing method. Write the way that feels most comfortable to you.

Even though anyone who's ever written knows that creative writing is a high-wire act performed without a net, many people assume that writers can just sit down and start writing any old time. Some writers *can* sometimes start cold, but most writers can't pen glittering prose first thing in the morning. Experienced writers know that writing is a series of activities, a process as much as a product. The writing process is described in detail in Chapter 4, "The Process of Writing, Part I." But like plants, all writers need the same things for their creativity to germinate. Let's look at some of these tools now.

Space, the Final Frontier

Nearly all experienced writers find that they compose most easily in a quiet and calm place, free from distractions. To paraphrase the famous British writer Virginia Woolf, every writer needs a "room of their own" in which to compose. I agree, but nowadays this isn't always possible. Few worker bees today have the luxury of having their own personal offices, dedicated to nothing but creative writing.

However, it usually isn't impossible to carve out a small space for yourself somewhere in your home. Your "office" can be a desk in the corner of the kitchen, bedroom, or hall. It can be an unused closet converted to a writing "room" or an attic finished off with a desk, light, and coffeemaker. I know aspiring writers who made over part of the garage or shed as their offices. A close friend created an office in her mother's house. With the kids grown and flown the coop, there's plenty of room in the old split-level homestead. Mom even makes lunch sometimes.

Try to avoid writing in the kitchen, dining room, or family room. Aside from the natural distractions in these high-traffic areas, you'll have to sweep aside your papers every time someone walks in and wants to eat. And if your house is like mine, someone is *always* eating something. Your family might very well have to sprawl on the floor with their pizza... which may not be a bad thing to teach the buggers a little respect. If you use a crowded place in your house, you also run the risk of having your manuscript used to wrap fish and your floppy disks becoming props for uneven table legs.

Wrong Turn
Avoid using office time and materials for your personal writing. At work, your time belongs to someone else. If you absolutely must write at work, be sure it's before your shift starts, during lunch, or after your day is formally done. And never, never, never use your office computer for your personal writing.

Smashing the Sound Barrier

Some writers require absolute pin-drop silence. Others like a little background noise while they write. I write my very best with the radio on. The music matters, too. I can't write to "lite" feel-good elevator music; it turns my prose to sludge. Hard rock makes me twitch; opera makes me doze off faster than Uncle Harry's war stories.

Experiment with different noise levels as you start off. Find your comfort zone. But don't delude yourself: aside from Edward R. Murrow, no one writes his or her best in the middle of a war zone. It stands to reason: you cannot concentrate if people are distracting you with bullets, bongos, or burgers.

Performance Anxiety

If you have ever had trouble getting started, er, *writing,* rest assured that you are in very good company. *Very* good company. Let me get real here—I dare you to name a writer who hasn't had *some* trouble putting down those first words. The only nonstop modern writer I could find was the late Isaac Asimov, but I'm convinced that he was really a robot... which could explain why he wrote about robots so convincingly. The rest of us mere mortals often experience times when we just can't jump start the writing machine, no matter how many pots of coffee we down.

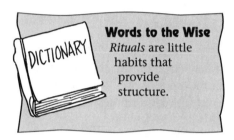

Words to the Wise
Rituals are little habits that provide structure.

Beginning writers often fail to realize that even the most experienced writers occasionally may have difficulty putting pen to paper. Many professional writers have devised little *rituals* to help them overcome their hesitation and make it easier for them to get into their work.

Ritual Behavior

Some writing rituals are as simple as turning on the radio and sharpening a pencil. Some are silly, like using the same coffee mug every day or eating three jelly beans before setting down to work. Other rituals involve hard boiled eggs, whipped cream, and olives, but let's not go there.

Instead, let me give you this checklist to use as you create your own rituals to help you get started being a creative writer.

Check each ritual to see which habits make it easier for you to get started writing.

_____1. I can't start writing until I've had a cup of coffee, preferably from the donut shop.

_____2. I have to pour the coffee into a thermal mug. Can't drink the coffee from Styrofoam or cardboard.

_____3. I have to sharpen my pencils before I start writing, even though I write on a computer.

_____4. I have to have a fresh notebook before I start.

_____5. I can't start writing anything until the mail carrier comes.

_____6. I have to exercise for precisely half an hour before I start writing.

_____7. I have to read the morning paper, cover to cover, first.

_____8. I have to set up my CD player with precisely three sets of oldies.

_____9. I write best by first reading a favorite poem.

_____10. Meditating always helps me relax enough to get my ideas flowing.

_____11. I can't start writing until the fat lady sings.

_____12. I have to spill a little chicken blood first.

Patterns Plus

Okay, so now we know that we're all creatures of habit, never more so than when we're involved in deeply creative endeavors. Go with it because it works.

It's vital that you discover your optimal work time and work habits so that you can make it as easy as possible to get started writing. How can you isolate your best time and place to write? Try filling out the following worksheet.

Answer each question to see what work patterns make it easier for you to get started writing.

1. At what time of day do I write *best*?

_____

2. At what time of day do I get the *least* writing done?

_____

3. Where do I get the *most* writing done?

_____

4. Where do I get the *least* writing done?

_____

5. What writing tools work *best* for me?

_____

6. What writing tools work *least* for me?

_____

continues

continued

7. How long can I write at one sitting without tiring or running dry?

_____

8. What music do I play when I get the most writing done?

_____

9. What light source do I use when I write the most easily?

_____

10. What do I wear when I write best?

_____

On Your Mark, Get Set... Go!

All the Write Stuff
Writing is a deliberate act; you have to make up your mind to do it.

Here are some tried-and-true methods that professional writers use to get started. These methods are not designed to produced final, polished drafts. Rather, they are intended to help you get your ideas down on paper. The key to all these suggestions is kindness: be nice to yourself. Suspend your criticism until you have enough words on the page to do some serious revision. Evaluating too soon can stall even the most self-assured writer. So use these ideas as a springboard rather than as a truncheon.

Top Ten Ways to Get Started Writing

1. *Assume the position.* Get yourself ready to write by doing the writing things. This is not the time to be running to the deli for a donut. Instead, sit at your writing station. Get your weapon of choice: computer or pen. Remember: it's almost impossible to start writing if you're pumping iron, cleaning the venetian blinds, or attending the Tuesday morning staff meeting. You can think, but you can't put those thoughts down on paper.

2. *Make the mind-body connection.* I guarantee you that I'm not a UFO abductee, but I do believe the scientific studies that link the movement of the hand to the movement of the brain. It seems that scientists have discovered that mimicking the action of writing by "air writing" can actually trigger your brain into leaping to attention. The action of writing while thinking can spark your brain to churn out some usable material.

To get started writing, relax your mind and allow your hand to move across the page or the keyboard. If words won't come, draw pictures. If pictures won't come, scribble. Give yourself at least fifteen minutes with this technique.

All the Write Stuff
Are you intimidated by the empty computer screen staring at you like something from a bad sci-fi flick? Turn off the screen and keep writing. Then turn the screen back on and check out your ideas.

3. *Fill the paper.* To a writer, nothing is more intimidating than a blank sheet of paper: not Butch the Sixth-Grade Bully, the IRS, or even your ex. Overcome this fear by writing. Write anything, but be sure to fill the entire sheet of paper. At least you'll have one sheet filled. Even if it's nonsense, you will have leaped one big hurdle.

4. *Visualize yourself writing.* Many professional writers say that they can write more easily if they first imagine themselves writing successfully. When you step in the shower in the morning, imagine yourself later in the day writing a few pages of your manuscript. Keep that picture as you brush your teeth, eat breakfast, and board the bus. Refer to it throughout the day. Keep the picture of yourself successfully writing in the back of your mind.

"What kind of new age nonsense is this?" you may be thinking. "Are we back to the mind-body connection? What comes next—nuts and berries?" Try it, you doubting Thomas: Close your eyes and sit in a comfortable chair. Imagine yourself watching a movie and wanting to try your hand at a screenplay of your own. Visualize yourself making a list of notes, placing them in order, and writing. Imagine the writing flowing smoothly and easily. Then sit down and write for fifteen minutes. Evaluate the results. And stick with the method; it usually takes a few tries until you see progress.

5. *Change point of view.* When you start writing, try putting yourself in someone else's Gucci loafers for a change. It's a very effective way to rev the writing engines. For example, write from the point of view of your sister, spouse, or supervisor. Cross gender. If you're a man, try writing as a woman; if you're a woman, try writing as a man. William Faulkner wrote *The Sound and the Fury* from four different points of view—one female. It took a while for people to figure out that the Brontës were women, not men. (Okay, so they were a little slower about that stuff back then.)

Cross species. Assume the personae of your pet. Once you assume a mask, you will feel less inhibited about starting to write.

Bet You Didn't Know

Some writers take literary cross-dressing one step further and adopt pen names from the opposite gender. How many of the writers behind these pseudonyms can you identify?

Pen Name	Real Name
Acton Bell	Anne Brönte
Currer Bell	Charlotte Brönte
Edith Van Dyne	L. Frank Baum
Ellis Bell	Emily Brönte
George Eliot	Mary Ann (or Marian) Evans
P.D. James	Phyllis Dorothy James

Extra Credit: *Gender Blending.* What two writers adopted the pen name Ellery Queen?

Answer: Frederic Dannay and Manfred B. Lee

6. *Switch writing methods.* If you usually write with a computer, try pen-and-paper. If your favorite method is pencil-and-paper, try a computer, word processor, or typewriter. Often the change in writing method is enough to help you get started. Novelty is a wonderful thing.

7. *Use a brainstorming method.* Professional writers know a variety of "brainstorming" strategies to help them over the initial hump. Here's one of my favorites.

All the Write Stuff
If you like to write longhand, treat yourself to some good-quality writing paper and a top-notch pen. The sensuous feel of expensive writing tools can make it easier for you to get started.

Think of a topic. Write nonstop for ten to fifteen minutes on your topic. If you're writing longhand, try not to lift your pen. If you're keyboarding, try not to stop typing. Don't worry about grammar, spelling, or punctuation. Instead, concentrate on getting your ideas down on paper. Then go back and read what you wrote. Pick out one or more sentences that look promising. You can always find at least one nice, juicy sentence, I promise. Start again with these sentences. You'll have warmed up and gotten your writing pointed in a promising direction. See Chapter 4, "The Process of Writing, Part I," for more brainstorming techniques.

8. *Picture a scene.* Some people are intensely visual. How can you tell if you're one of these lucky people? Try these simple tests. Are you able to tell how much furniture will fit in a room, how many people you can pack around a holiday table, and how much room is left in the freezer? Can you pack a suitcase with everything you need for a week's trip and close it without having to hire an elephant to jump on the lid? Do you have a reliable sense of direction?

   If so, this writing method will likely work for you. Close your eyes. Now imagine being back at the circus you attended as a child or the one you took your children to last year. Listen to the happy crowds roaring, smell the rich odor of peanuts roasting, feel the sticky cotton candy on your fingers and taste it melting on your tongue. See the clowns packing into the car. Start your writing by describing what you perceived with your five senses.

9. *Frame your material as a letter.* Creative writing is a pressure situation. Curiously, many people don't think of writing to a friend as tense at all. Even though it's still writing, people imagine it as an easy chat between friends, a pleasant tête-à-tête. Take advantage of this perception by starting to write as though you were addressing a friend. Use this writing event as an opportunity to chat with a friend. You'll relax and your ideas will flow.

10. *Don't start at the beginning.* Julie Andrews in *The Sound of Music* aside, who says you have to start at the very beginning? You can just as easily (and often much more easily) start at the middle or even at the end. This method works especially well if you don't know how you want to start your writing. Compose your writing from the middle out or from the end to the beginning.

    As a nice bonus, this method makes it unlikely that you'll end up with the hackneyed *Peanuts* opening, "It was a dark and stormy night."

What method has worked well for you in the past? Fill it in here and then share your ideas with a friend.

The Least You Need to Know

➤ Like breaking up, starting to write is hard to do.

➤ Writing and speaking are not the same. You can't write the way you speak.

➤ Writers have rituals and habits they use to help them get started. Identify and develop the ones that work best for you.

➤ You can't win it if you're not in it: you have to get your ideas down on paper (or tape recorder) if you want to be a writer.

➤ Talk is cheap; write already.

ON YER MARK!

Chapter 4

The Process of Writing, Part I

In This Chapter

➤ Learn how writing is a *process* as much as a *product*

➤ See which planning methods work best for you

➤ Discover how to shape, order, and arrange your ideas

Creative writing is easy; you just jot down ideas as they occur to you. The jotting is simplicity itself—it's the *occurring* that's difficult.

In this chapter, you will delve into the nature of creative writing, what has been called the *writing process*. To greater and lesser extents, all writers go through the stages you will learn about here. I'll teach you why this method of composing your thoughts into words can make the "occurring" stage of creative writing—and all that comes after—less like a root canal and more like a day at the races. I'll also show you how to adapt the writing process to suit your own needs and style.

Six Easy Pieces

Lunch at a large deli poses numbing choices. White or rye? Pastrami or roast beef? Mayo or butter? In the same way, creative writing is an ongoing process of considering alternatives and making choices. Some choices you make when you write can be as delicious as a juicy corned beef on rye—while some can be as quirky as peanut butter and bologna. But no matter what writing choices you make, they all involve some serious thinking.

When you write, your "bread" is your choice of writing style and subject. The "fillings" are your sentences and paragraphs. The "condiments" are the different styles of punctuation you select. With so many choices, how can you know what to do?

Start by recognizing that creative writing is a *process* as much as a *product*. Understanding that writing is a process with several stages allows you to write most efficiently. It enables you to focus on one task at a time rather than trying to juggle many different aspects of writing simultaneously.

So what is the writing process? Different writing theorists divide the steps in different ways. Below, I've worked out a division that will help you write anything, no matter what your audience, purpose, and task.

Writing Process Overview

1. *Plan.* Gather ideas and focus your thoughts.

2. *Shape.* Find the best way to organize your material.

3. *Draft.* Write your ideas in sentences and paragraphs.

4. *Revise.* Revisit your draft and rethink your ideas. Here's where you add, cut, move, and rewrite. In some cases, you may rework your draft as drastically as plastic surgeons have revised Michael Jackson's face; in other instances, you'll be more along the lines of a Goldie Hawn brush-up.

5. *Edit.* Reread for errors in technical areas: spelling, grammar, punctuation, capitalization, and so on.

6. *Proofread.* Check the draft for typos and illegible handwriting.

It's tempting to look at the writing process as a kitchen-tested recipe or a reliable Rand McNally map, but unfortunately it ain't so. Writing is just not a linear process. You can't always trip merrily down the yellow brick road—especially when you write creatively. That's why I haven't attached times next to each step, as in "You should prewrite for no more than five minutes" or "Drafting should take 2.456 hours."

It takes some writers a lifetime to produce a masterpiece; others can churn them out faster than a farm bride can make butter. Ralph Ellison wrote only one book, *Invisible Man*, but it was a whopper; Stephen King and Joyce Carol Oates write so fast that they're in danger of flooding the market with their tomes. In fact, each of these modern writers has adopted a pen name to avoid overexposure.

Sometimes, you may spend only a few minutes planning and then go right into shaping; other times, you may find yourself circling back to previous steps. I revise and edit as I draft. Not to worry; this is how it works. Take the writing process as an analysis of how writers compose, not as a hard-and-fast, dyed-in-the-wool command from the Writing Maven.

Now that you've got the overview, it's time to apply the writing process to planning and shaping your own creative writing. Let's look at each step in detail. I'll discuss planning and shaping in this chapter, then continue in the next chapter to delve into the other four phases of the process.

All the Write Stuff
Successful writers under-stand that they must convince the reader that they've given some serious thought to the idea they're trying to communicate. Good writing may look as effortless as Fred Astaire swirling Ginger Rogers around the dance floor, but just as the audience can sense the hours Fred and Ginger toiled over those steps, so readers will be able to tell you've given serious thought to your ideas and their expression.

The Gang of Four

All planning begins with thinking about four key elements:

➤ Topic

➤ Purpose

➤ Audience

➤ Special circumstances

Genre is not a factor with these four key players. No matter what you write—a novel, short story, drama, screenplay, poem, biography, autobiography, or article—you must consider all four elements as you plan. It's what Edgar Allan Poe did when he planned his thriller chillers and what Shelby Foote does when he plans his epic histories. So come plan along with me; the best is yet to be. Zoom in on topic, purpose, audience, and special circumstances to see how they affect your creative writing.

Topic

Your *topic* is what you will write about. Also known as the *thesis, theme,* or *subject,* the topic comes from everything you have ever known, seen, dreamed, experienced, remembered, read, and heard. Creative writers draw on this rich storehouse of experience to spark their imaginations and make their vision come alive for their readers.

Where can you get topics from? Fill out this web to see some of the sources of effective writing topics. I've filled in several balloons to get you started.

Complete this web to spark ideas about writing.

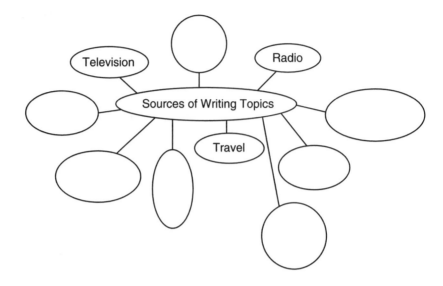

The Author's Purpose

An *author's purpose* is the author's goal in writing a selection. Common purposes include to entertain, instruct, persuade, or describe. Nearly all creative writing has the same purpose: to entertain. Nonetheless, an author may have more than one purpose for writing a particular selection, but one purpose is often the most important. For example, the main purpose of this book is to instruct, even though I try to entertain along the way! Study the following chart to see the purposes behind the most common types of creative writing.

All the Write Stuff
Effective writing has a point—the main idea the writer wants to communicate to the reader.

Remember: Some pieces you write will have more than one purpose.

Type of Writing	Purposes
Article	Entertain, instruct, persuade, describe
Autobiography	Entertain, describe
Biography	Entertain, describe
Drama	Entertain
Novel	Entertain, describe
Poetry	Entertain, describe

Type of Writing	Purposes
Screenplay	Entertain, describe
Short story	Entertain, describe
Textbook	Instruct

Say Goodnight, Gracie: Audience

Your audience is your readers. Sometimes you know who your audience is. For example, my previous books in this series include *The Complete Idiot's Guide to Speaking in Public with Confidence* and *The Complete Idiot's Guide to Buying and Selling Collectibles*. The people who buy the first book are professionals called upon to give speeches in pressured settings; the audience for my second book is a far wider range of people interested in everything from antique jewelry, coins, and stamps to zebra-striped chaise lounges.

But other times, your audience isn't as clear cut. You may be sending an outline and a sample chapter of your novel to an editor you have never met. In still other cases, you know who your readers are but the group may be so broad that it's hard to identify specific characteristics. For example, you may be writing a biography for a "young adult" reader. What's the typical "young adult" like?

Writing without first considering your audience is like mailing a letter without a stamp, cutting wallpaper without measuring it, or buying a pair of pants without trying them on. How do you know it will arrive? How do you know it will fit? You're too smart for that. (I'm not, but that's why there are MailBoxes, handymen, and professional shoppers.) Audience influences your choice of topic, language, sentence length, punctuation, and allusions. It can even influence your choice of form, such as novel, article, or poetry.

> **Words to the Wise**
> An *allusion* is a reference to a well-known place, event, person, work of art, or other work of literature. Allusions enrich a novel, story, or poem by suggesting powerful and exciting comparisons.

It's easy to overestimate your audience's level of knowledge and interest. If you're writing nonfiction, people outside your field of expertise may not have the slightest idea what you're talking about. If you're writing fiction, they may be fed up to there with historical settings, heroines with heaving breasts, and heroes with tawny limbs. So, as you plan, you're going to think about your audience and how they feel about your topic. That's why I've included this audience analysis worksheet.

It's crucial to know where you stand—before you go somewhere you don't want to be. As you plan your writing, analyze your prospective audience by asking yourself the following questions:

1. How old are my readers?

_____

2. What is their gender?

_____

3. What is their sexual orientation?

_____

4. How much education do they have?

_____

5. Are they mainly rural, urban, or suburban folk?

_____

6. In which country were they born? How much do I know about their culture and heritage?

_____

7. What is their socio-economic status?

_____

8. What are their primary interests?

_____

9. How much does my audience already know about my topic?

_____

10. How do they feel about the topic? Will they be neutral, arch-enemies, or will I be preaching to the converted?

_____

Practical Considerations

In the best of all possible worlds, we'd all have time and money enough to write, unfettered by reality. Unfortunately, reality bites. Here are some of the constraints that all creative writers must face sooner or later:

➤ Readership

➤ Budget (for screenplays and dramas, especially)

➤ Deadlines

➤ Format (especially if the work is part of a series)

➤ Length, word count

➤ Purpose

➤ Staging constraints (if the work is a drama)

A Man, a Plan, a Canal: Panama

You wouldn't dig the Panama Canal without planning, would you? Actually, none of us would even consider *visiting* the Panama Canal, much less digging it, but the comparison holds because any big project—like a canal or a book—requires a surprising amount of advance planning.

In Chapter 3, "Putting a Toe in the Water: Getting Started," you learned about diving into the creative writing process. In that chapter, I explain how to use the focused freewriting method of brainstorming ideas. Here are four more methods you can use to plan your writing: *listing, webbing, diaries and journals,* and *the 5 W's and H.*

Listing

This is a no-brainer: just think of a topic and list all the ideas that come to mind about it. You can list the ideas as words or phrases. As with the freewriting strategy you learned in the previous chapter, listing works best when you let your mind free-associate. List a bunch of ideas before you start scrutinizing them. Work in one concentrated burst of energy. You can always add as many ideas as you like later on, but your mind will kick in faster if you set aside five to ten minutes to get cooking.

Charlotte's Webbing

Also known as "clustering" and "mapping," this is a more visual means to plan your writing. A web looks different from a list of words, and so it helps some writers branch off in exciting new directions.

43

To start a web, draw a circle in the middle of a sheet of paper. Then draw lines radiating out from the circle. If you want, you can label each line with a major subdivision of your topic. At the end of each line, draw a circle and fill it in with a subtopic. If you filled in the web at the beginning of this chapter under the heading "Topic," you've already experimented with this method.

A Journal by Any Other Name...

Creative writers are always on the lookout for topics and details to spark their imaginations. Like eternally hopeful beachcombers with their metal detectors, we writers comb the sands of time for fragments of written gold. Literary mining spans the ages: Shakespeare took the ideas for many of his great tragedies, including *Hamlet*, *Julius Caesar*, and *Romeo and Juliet*, from other sources; Leonard Bernstein recast *Romeo and Juliet* as *West Side Story*. Nobel Laureate William Faulkner summed it up when he said: "If a writer has to rob his mother he will not hesitate; the 'Ode On a Grecian Urn' is worth any number of old ladies."

Think about actors observing human activity so they can mimic it, even picking up mannerisms or inflections from other actors. At this point, Kelsey Grammar does a better Jack Benny than Benny did!

For this reason, many writers carry a journal with them at all times so they can jot down ideas that spring to mind, fragments of conversation, and passing observations. Whether I call it a "diary," a "journal," or an "idea book," this planning aid is usually a bound volume, notebook, or booklet in which authors write freely for themselves and sometimes others. A journal can even be a collection of electronic correspondence between writers who communicate via computer and modem.

How does writing in a journal help you plan your writing? Journals provide creative writers with a record of their own thoughts, ideas, and observations and so invite them to reread, revisit, and perhaps revise past thoughts. Keeping a journal can help you in both the creation and expression of thought.

Bet You Didn't Know

Samuel Pepys (1633–1703) is one of the most curious figures in English literature because his fame rests on only one work that he never intended for publication: his diary. Could that man dish the dirt! Pepys's diary is a vivid portrait of seventeenth-century life, filled with candid, private revelations and keenly observed public scenes.

Just the Facts, Ma'am: The 5 W's and H

Brenda Starr and her fellow journalists have been using this clever planning method for years. That's a good tip-off that the 5 W's and H work great with nonfiction, but they can also help you narrow down your characters, plot, and setting in fiction. I cover this type of writing in depth in Part 2, "Fiction and Poetry."

The six letters stand for *Who? What? When? Where? Why?* and *How?* Asking these questions as you plan forces you to approach a topic from several different vantage points.

Shape Up!

The next step in the writing process, *shaping*, helps you bridge the gap between planning and drafting. Shaping your ideas is really no different from shaping your body—both require a lot of hard work and sweat, but both can yield impressive results.

Shaping your writing involves five steps:

All the Write Stuff
In effective writing, all the ideas are presented in an organized, logical manner.

➤ Grouping similar ideas

➤ Rejecting nonessential ideas

➤ Selecting a tone

➤ Ordering ideas

➤ Outlining key points

Time to whip your planning ideas into shape with Miss Laurie, but I promise no physical exertion in *this* class. The heaviest thing you'll lift here is a verb or two.

Groups

When you group ideas, you make connections and find patterns. Sort ideas into two piles: *general* and *specific*. Then place all the specific ideas under the general ones. Thinking about levels of abstraction also helps you realize that powerful writing starts with **general statements** backed up by **specific details**. More on that in Part 2.

Elimination Derby

It's time to be ruthless, kiddo. If an idea doesn't fit, set it aside. Thanks to the wonders of computers, you can safely stash it in another file and return to it later if you change your mind. No computer? Make two piles of paper. If you're having trouble separating the gold from the dross, try several different variations to see which ideas follow each other most logically.

And while you're in the cleaning mode, you could take a look at your closet, too. I don't think that powder blue polyester leisure suit is coming back into style in our lifetime.

Tone Deaf

The *tone* of a work of literature is the writer's attitude toward his or her subject matter. Generally speaking, tone can be *formal* or *informal*. An article in a technical journal, for example, has a more formal tone than a letter to the lovelorn. For most audiences, your tone will be more informal than formal.

All the Write Stuff
Are you unwilling or unable to eliminate ideas at the shaping stage? Try this idea: underline or boldface any idea that doesn't fit. Then you can see at a flash what should be cut later on.

The tone of a piece of writing can also have shades of feeling. For example, the tone might be *angry, bitter, sad,* or *frightening.* Compare the tone of a Stephen King novel to the tone of Louisa May Alcott's *Little Women.* King's novels usually convey a tone of horror and terror; Alcott's novels, in contrast, have a gentle, sweet tone.

Decide what tone you want to use in your work based on these three criteria:

➤ Subject matter

➤ Purpose

➤ Audience

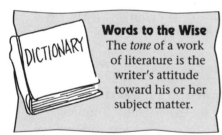

Words to the Wise
The *tone* of a work of literature is the writer's attitude toward his or her subject matter.

In this book, for instance, I use an informal tone, friendly and hip. I created this tone with contractions, pronouns, everyday language, sentence fragments, and humor. For example, notice that I address the reader directly by using the informal pronoun "you," rather than the formal pronoun "one." Since my subject matter is serious and even a little intimidating, an informal tone best accomplishes my purpose—to help unlock your creativity.

Order on the Page!

When you *order* ideas, you put them in a logical sequence. You decide what you want your audience to read first, second, third, and so on. If your ideas aren't in a logical order, your readers won't understand your purpose, main idea, or message. A logical order or structure to ideas also makes it easier for you to proceed through the work. There are several different ways you can order your ideas. Here are three of the most common ways material can be ordered:

➤ Chronological order (order of time)

➤ Order of importance (most important to least important)

➤ Spatial order (left to right, right to left, and so on)

Select the type of order that matches the type of writing you're doing. Fiction, such as novels and short stories, often follow *chronological order*. Essays and articles, in contrast, may use *order of importance*. With this type of writing, you may want to place your most persuasive ideas first. Descriptions, such as those found in novels, usually follow *spatial order*. You set the scene by describing the objects and people in the room and their relation to each other.

Outline, Inline, Circle Line

Many writers find *outlining* a useful way to order their ideas at the shaping stage of the writing process. I'm a big fan of outlines because they help me see the overall plan of the work. They are especially helpful for breaking big writing tasks like this book into manageable chunks.

Outlining is a projection, an educated guess—sorta like my monthly budget. Like my household finances, consider your outline as a work in progress, a frame around which to fashion your finished work. Here's a template for an outline you can use for nonfiction writing that explains or proves a point. Expand or contract it to meet your needs.

All the Write Stuff
Many editors and publishers require outlines as part of a book proposal. While there are many similarities among these proposals, always get the "Proposal Guidelines" from each individual publisher to satisfy specific requirements for proposal submission.

Use this outline as a starting point to order your ideas.

Title: _____

I. First main idea _____

_____

  A. Detail _____

    1. Reason or example _____

      a. Detail _____

      b. Detail _____

    2. Reason or example _____

      a. Detail _____

      b. Detail _____

  B. Detail _____

    1. Reason or example _____

      a. Detail _____

      b. Detail _____

    2. Reason or example _____

      a. Detail _____

      b. Detail _____

II. Second main idea _____

_____

  A. Detail _____

    1. Reason or example _____

      a. Detail _____

      b. Detail _____

2. Reason or example _____

    a. Detail _____

    b. Detail _____

B. Detail _____

1. Reason or example _____

    a. Detail _____

    b. Detail _____

2. Reason or example _____

    a. Detail _____

    b. Detail _____

In Chapter 7, I cover different methods for organizing your ideas in fiction.

The Least You Need to Know

➤ Writing is a six-step, non-linear process: *planning, shaping, drafting, revising, editing,* and *proofreading.*

➤ *Planning* involves considering your topic, purpose, audience, and any special circumstances.

➤ *Shape* your writing by grouping similar ideas, cutting extraneous ideas, selecting a tone, ordering, and outlining.

➤ Do your groundwork; it pays off in the end.

Chapter 5

The Process of Writing, Part II

In This Chapter

➤ Learn how to write your first draft

➤ Revise and edit like a pro

➤ Proofread to make your writing letter-perfect

We've put it off as long as possible, but now it's the moment of truth. You've planned and shaped your ideas. The place is a mess and your brain hurts. It's time to start writing a first copy. That's what this chapter is all about.

First, I'll help you whip your ideas into sentences and paragraphs. Then I'll show you how to *revise* your draft and rethink your ideas. To do so, you'll learn to add, cut, move, and rewrite. This is followed by *editing,* rereading your writing for errors in technical areas: spelling, grammar, usage, punctuation, and capitalization. Finally, it's time to *proofread,* to check your draft for surface errors such as typos and illegible handwriting.

Is There a Draft in Here? Hope So!

Fortunately for readers, one size *doesn't* fit all when it comes to creative writing. No single writing process works for all writers all the time. However, effective creative writers tend to follow more steps in the writing process than less-productive writers. Successful writers are more likely to

➤ Have a clear understanding of purpose

➤ Analyze their audience fully

➤ Divide huge writing tasks into manageable chunks

➤ Accept that their first draft won't be perfect

➤ Understand the writing process

➤ Revise ruthlessly

➤ Edit and proofread thoroughly

➤ Write all the time

When you write, you arrange words to create meaningful sentences and paragraphs. First drafts are not meant to be perfect. Don't think of them that way, or you might stifle your most fertile time of experimentation. You know from previous chapters that creativity is an idiosyncratic beast—it can be pushed and prodded just so far without balking.

Different creative writers compose in different ways, each guided by his or her style, purpose, and audience. According to your individual style, you may wish to try any of the following ways of writing your first draft: with the notes you made while planning your writing, without them, or a combination of the two. Let's look at each method in detail.

Using Notes

Arrange your planning notes and outlines and use them as a scaffold for your first draft. Work through all your material in the order you have established. Obviously, if some-

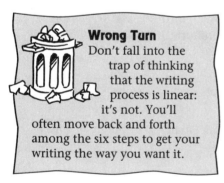

Wrong Turn
Don't fall into the trap of thinking that the writing process is linear: it's not. You'll often move back and forth among the six steps to get your writing the way you want it.

thing isn't working, you'll want to revise your outline to take this change into account. For example, if you find a major loose thread in the story—as in "Why *did* she marry him in the first place?"—you're going to have to resolve the issue before it unravels the entire plot. You may also wish to go back and add new ideas to your planning list.

Try to write at a steady pace until you reach a natural breaking point, such as the end of a chapter, act, or scene. This method often works well for Type A writers, those driven folks who like the security of structure.

Working Without a Net

You can try the opposite method: set aside all the notes you made when you planned and shaped your ideas. You still have all the information in your head, but writing without notes allows you to be more open to discovering new ideas as you draft. As you write, try to forge connections among ideas. Remember, you're not under any obligation to use all or even part of this first draft. This realization can free you to explore new directions.

Consider trying this method with poetry or other descriptive writing that calls for bursts of inspiration. Some novelists avoid this method because it tends to result in sprawling novels and rambling short stories. Free spirits, those souls who shop for Christmas presents on December 24th, often report good results with this method.

Combo Platter

With this approach, you can use your planning notes as a framework, but if you find yourself running dry, feel free to set aside your notes and let your imagination take you where it will. Don't feel constrained by your notes; rather, try to use them as you need them.

Bet You Didn't Know

Your personality type may affect your writing method. Extroverts tend to do little planning, preferring to work out their ideas as they write. Introverts, in contrast, tend to work out their ideas fully before they put pen to paper.

The 3 R's: Readin', 'Ritin', Revisin'

So there it sits: your beautiful first draft. Bravo! Now it's time to revise—to evaluate—what you wrote. When you revise, you change what you need to better satisfy your purpose and audience. Revising is the essence of writing. Most professional writers rewrite their sentences, rewrite their sentences, and then rewrite them again. Sainted writers E.B. White and James Thurber were known for rewriting their pieces eight or nine times each.

But creative writers tend to be an anal retentive lot. Professional as well as novice writers have been known to hold on to their ideas more dearly than toddlers to a lollipop. Oh, we know we should slash and burn, but we're often unwilling to touch a single word. Take the case of three of the giants of twentieth-century fiction: Thomas Wolfe, Ernest Hemingway, and T.S. Eliot.

➤ Wolfe knew he was in trouble when he had to rent a hand-truck to get his manuscripts to his publisher, Charles Scribner's and Sons. The legendary Scribner editor Maxwell Perkins cut more than 1,000 pages from Thomas Wolfe's masterpiece *Look Homeward, Angel*. Max was right.

➤ Mr. Roaring Twenties himself, F. Scott Fitzgerald, advised Ernest Hemingway to lop off the entire beginning of Ernie's *The Sun Also Rises*. Hemingway grudgingly took Fitzgerald's advice, which made for a much better book. Hemingway repaid the favor by maligning Fitzgerald in print and in person every chance he got.

➤ Ezra Pound made T.S. Eliot's 1922 epic poem "The Waste Land" almost readable by offering suggestions for major revision.

All the Write Stuff
Does working on a computer give you a headache? The remedy may be as simple as a blink of the eye. That's right, try blinking. It moistens your eyes and helps prevent headaches. Even better, take a break every fifteen minutes to stand and stretch.

Like breaking up, revising is hard to do. As you revise, remember what the bartender said to the brokenhearted Judy Garland in *Easter Parade*: "For every rose that withers and dies, another blooms in its stead." You may have to cut *that* sentence, but there will be an even better one to replace it. I promise.

Revise Like a Pro

When you revise, you do four things:

➤ *Cut* material

➤ *Replace* material

➤ *Add* material

➤ *Rearrange* what's already there

As you revise, you work to change your writing on all levels: word, sentence, paragraph, and entirety. Don't be surprised if a revised draft looks radically different from a first draft. Here's how English poet William Blake revised his poem "The Tyger."

WILLIAM BLAKE
The Tyger

[First Draft]

What differences and similarities do you see among these drafts?

The Tyger

1   Tyger Tyger burning bright
In the forests of the night
What immortal hand or eye
~~Dare~~ ~~Could~~ frame thy fearful symmetry

         Burnt in
2   ~~In what~~ distant deeps or skies
~~The cruel~~ ~~Burnt the~~ fire of thine eyes
On what wings dare he aspire
What the hand dare sieze the fire

3   And what shoulder & what art
Could twist the sinews of thy heart
And when thy heart began to beat
What dread hand & what dread feet

    ~~Could fetch it from the furnace deep~~
    ~~And in thy horrid ribs dare steep~~
    ~~In the well of sanguine woe~~
    ~~In what clay & what mould~~
    ~~Were thy eyes of fury rolld~~

    ~~Where~~   ~~where~~
4   ~~What~~ the hammer ~~what~~ the chain
In what furnace was thy brain

                       dread grasp
What the anvil what ~~the arm arm grasp clasp~~
~~Dare~~ ~~Could~~ its deadly terrors ~~clasp grasp~~ clasp

6   Tyger Tyger burning bright
In the forests of the night
What immortal hand & eye
        frame
Dare ~~form~~ thy fearful symmetry

[*Trial Stanzas*]

Burnt in distant deeps or skies
The cruel fire of thine eye,
Could heart descend or wings aspire
What the hand dare sieze the fire

dare he <s>smile laugh</s>

5 ~~3~~ And <s>did he laugh</s> his work to see

ankle

<s>What the shoulder what the knee</s>

Dare

4 <s>Did</s> he who made the lamb make thee
1 When the stars threw down their spears
2 And waterd heaven with their tears

[*Second Full Draft*]

Tyger Tyger burning/bright
In the forests of the night
What Immortal hand & eye
Dare frame thy fearful symmetry

And what shoulder & what art
Could twist the sinews of thy heart
And when thy heart began to beat
What dread hand & what dread feet

When the stars threw down their spears
And waterd heaven with their tears
Did he smile his work to see
Did he who made the lamb make thee

Tyger Tyger burning bright
In the forests of the night
What Immortal hand & eye
Dare frame thy fearful symmetry

[*Final Version*, 1794]

The Tyger

Tyger Tyger, burning bright,
In the forests of the night;
What immortal hand or eye,
Could frame thy fearful symmetry?

In what distant deeps or skies
Burnt the fire of thine eyes!
On what wings dare he aspire?
What the hand, dare sieze the fire?

And what shoulder, & what art,
Could twist the sinews of thy heart?
And when thy heart began to beat,
What dread hand? & what dread feet?

What the hammer? what the chain,
In what furnace was thy brain?
What the anvil? what dread grasp,
Dare its deadly terrors clasp?

When the stars threw down their spears
And water'd heaven with their tears:
Did he smile his work to see?
Did he who made the Lamb make thee?

Tyger, Tyger burning bright,
In the forests of the night:
What immortal hand or eye,
Dare frame thy fearful symmetry?

Follow these five steps when you revise:

1. Let your writing "cool off" for at least a day before you touch it.

2. Look at your writing from a critical standpoint.

3. Read your draft once all the way through.

4. Decide whether you want to revise this draft or start again.

5. If you revise, go step by step. Concentrate on one issue at a time.

For example, first read for organization, then for tone, and finally for mechanics like spelling.

> ## Bet You Didn't Know
>
> There are several useful products available to relieve back and wrist problems caused by too much keyboarding. Start with an ergonomically designed computer chair. Spend the bucks; it will more than pay off in less back strain. Then consider a wrist support bar. Check your local computer store for the models that suit your needs.

Transitions

All good writing is coherent. We say that speakers are *coherent* if they make sense. In the same way, effective writing has coherence if the ideas are related to each other in a logical manner. When you revise for coherence, look over your writing to see if the ideas cling to each other like high-priced plastic wrap. If they don't, you may need to add some *transitions*.

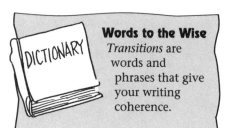

Words to the Wise
Transitions are words and phrases that give your writing coherence.

A transition can be a whole paragraph of text or simply a transitional expression, a word or phrase that shows a logical relationship between ideas. Different transitional expressions signal to the reader how one idea is linked to the others. Using the appropriate transitions helps you convey your ideas smoothly and clearly.

Table 6.1 Use These Transitions to Help Link Ideas

Signal	Transitions
Addition	also, in addition, too, and, besides, further, furthermore, next, then, finally, moreover
Example	for example, for instance, namely, specifically
Chronological Order	first, firstly, second, secondly, third, fourth, next, subsequently, immediately, later, eventually, in the future, currently, now, during, meanwhile, before, soon, afterwards, at length, finally, then
Contrast	nevertheless, nonetheless, yet, in contrast, on the contrary, still, however, on the other hand
Comparison	in comparison, similarly, likewise, in the same way
Concession	naturally, granted, certainly, to be sure, of course
Place	nearby, in the distance, here, there, at the side, next to, adjacent, in the front, in the back

Signal	Transitions
Result	due to this, so, accordingly, consequently, as a result, therefore
Summary	finally, in conclusion, in summary, in brief, as a result, hence, on the whole, in short

Check It Off

I find revising much easier if I use a checklist. This helps me remember which elements to consider as I evaluate my work. I have an all-purpose, one-size-fits-all checklist that I'll share with you now, but I also create individual checklists to fit special writing tasks. For example, I have a different checklist for short stories than I do for poetry because each writing event requires specific considerations. For short stories, I try to create a compelling plot and memorable characters, while in poetry I strive for compression of language and strength of imagery.

Wrong Turn
Transitional expressions are usually set off from the rest of the sentence with commas.

Adapt the following revision checklist to meet the needs of each creative writing event.

Use this checklist when you revise to make sure your writing is as good as it can be.

Revision Checklist

_____ Is your purpose clear?

_____ Is your language and topic suited to your audience?

_____ Is your writing organized in a logical way?

_____ Have you cut all material that's off the topic?

_____ Are your sentences concise and correct?

_____ Is your writing fluid and graceful?

_____ Have you used descriptive and precise words?

_____ Is your writing entertaining and fun to read?

_____ Is your writing free from biased language?

_____ Have you corrected all errors in grammar, usage, spelling, punctuation, and capitalization?

Edit

When you *edit*, you make surface-level changes so your writing is grammatically correct. Editing is the creative writing equivalent of polishing your shoes, tacking up your hem, or splashing on a little Brut before a big date.

To become a skilled editor, you need to know what to look for when you read over your work. Overall, you're checking for mistakes in GUMs: grammar, usage, and mechanics (spelling, punctuation, and capitalization).

All writers have their favorite editing bloopers, the writing errors that drive us batty. I go off the deep end when I see "its'" or, even worse, "hero'es." However, I reserve a special place in my Hall of Shame for the wrought iron "Ninty-Nine" that was marking a neighbor's house number.

Check and Double-check

In the following checklist, I've isolated the most common and annoying writing errors. Each one is considered a hanging offense in certain writing circles. Use the editing checklist to see if you're guilty of committing these errors and so deserve to be flogged. Keep this checklist handy when you edit your work.

The 25 Most Annoying Writing Errors

Sentences

_____ 1. Fragments (parts of sentences)

_____ 2. Run-ons (two sentences incorrectly joined)

Spelling

_____ 3. Missing letters

_____ 4. Extra letters

_____ 5. Transposed letters

_____ 6. Incorrect plurals

_____ 7. Errors in homonyms (such as *their/there/they're*)

Usage

_____ 8. Errors in pronouns, such as *who/whom*

_____ 9. Problems with subject-verb agreement

_____ 10. Lack of clarity

_____ 11. Wrong verb tense

_____ 12. Double negatives

_____ 13. Dangling modifiers

_____ 14. Misplaced modifiers

_____ 15. Unnecessary words

_____ 16. Misused adjectives and adverbs

_____ 17. Sexist language

_____ 18. Incorrect voice (active vs. passive voice)

_____ 19. Lack of parallel structure

Punctuation

_____ 20. Missing commas

_____ 21. Missing quotation marks in dialogue

_____ 22. Misused semicolons and colons

_____ 23. Missing or misused apostrophes

Capitalization

_____ 24. Proper nouns and adjectives not capitalized

_____ 25. Errors in titles

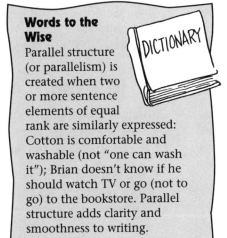

Words to the Wise
Parallel structure (or parallelism) is created when two or more sentence elements of equal rank are similarly expressed: Cotton is comfortable and washable (not "one can wash it"); Brian doesn't know if he should watch TV or go (not to go) to the bookstore. Parallel structure adds clarity and smoothness to writing.

All the Write Stuff
It's easier to see errors in typed copy than in a handwritten manuscript.

A Nitpicker's Guide to Editing

As you'll learn in later chapters, a skilled editor is more wonderful than a bag of Oreos and a glass of cold milk. But you may not always be blessed with an editor, much less the eagle-eyed ones like the gems who catch my bloopers. (That's a special thank-you to Nancy Stevenson and Michael Thomas, who've made me seem a lot more logical and intelligent than I am!)

If you're flying solo, you must be extra-special careful to go over and over your manuscript looking for errors. You might want to photocopy the checklist above and run your work through it more than once. I cover this later on in the book as well, so stay tuned.

Remember, writing flaws such as errors in spelling, punctuation, and grammar might cause an editor to throw your manuscript out the window—without reading it all the way through. Actually, since most windows in the big Manhattan publishing companies don't open, your manuscript will be tossed into the circular file instead. That's true even if your book ranks as the Great American Novel in content. Busy acquisitions editors have no patience with silly editing flaws. These types of errors mark you as careless.

Proof It! Proofreading

Just as you wouldn't go out without checking yourself in a mirror (Okay, maybe you would, but we don't want to go *there*), you wouldn't let anyone see your writing without having first checked it completely.

When you proofread your writing, look for those embarrassing errors in spelling, punctuation, grammar, and usage. For example, a friend of mine saw a brochure for a training company that offered "Pubic" Workshops rather than "Public" Workshops. Fortunately, all your writing errors won't be so embarrassing, but they can be just as lethal. That's why it's so important to proofread thoroughly.

To proofread effectively, you have to slow your reading speed so that you see each individual letter. It's a difficult process because writers tend to see what they know should be there rather than what is really there—sort of like love. Proofreading is about as exciting as watching linoleum curl, but it's crucial to the success of your finished product.

Bet You Didn't Know

In metropolitan areas, skilled proofreaders earn between $12 and $15 an hour, on average. If you don't have the cash, run your manuscript by a friend or spouse's critical eye.

Playing with the Big Kids

Here are some tricks that professional proofreaders use. See which techniques work best for you in each writing situation. Vary the techniques to keep yourself from dozing off as you proofread.

> ➤ *Read backwards.* Start at the end of the essay, proofreading the last sentence. Then proofread backwards, one sentence at a time from the end of the essay to the beginning. Reading backwards allows you to concentrate on the errors in mechanics and usage without being distracted by the ideas in the writing.

➤ *Take me to your ruler.* Use a ruler or a blank piece of paper to cover everything on the paper except the sentence you're reading at the time. This method helps you focus all your attention on finding the mistakes in that sentence.

➤ *See and say.* One of the best ways to proofread is to read your writing aloud while another person follows along on a typed copy. Say the punctuation marks and spell out all names. This is a very effective method, but it's as slow as watching paint flake and just as dull.

Wrong Turn
The larger the type, the easier it is to assume that it's correct. Be extra careful with titles and headings; that's where some of the worst boo-boos occur.

➤ *Double Dutch.* Read the paper twice. The first time, read it slowly for meaning and to see that nothing has been left out. Then read it again. If you find an error, correct it and then reread that line. You tend to become less vigilant once you find a few errors. "There can't be any more errors here," novice proofers think. Guess again. Double- and triple-check numbers, names, and first and last paragraphs.

➤ *Switch hitter.* Since it's always easier to proof something you haven't written, you may wish to beg a friend, relative, or co-worker to proofread your writing. Get someone who's both brutally honest and too slow to run away when you ask.

Marvels of the Electronic Age

So what about on-line grammar and spell-checkers? If you write on a computer, by all means use the handy-dandy built-in checkers. But that doesn't let you off the proofreading hook.

Even when you use a spell-checker and a grammar-checker, you still need to proofread your writing. That's because spell-checkers work by matching words: they call out any group of letters that is not listed in their dictionary. However, they cannot tell you if a word is missing or that a specific meaning is called for in a specific situation.

Writers with a handle on grammar and usage still do much better than the grammar programs currently available. If you're a little shaky on grammar, the grammar checker can bail you out now and again. But I find that they're usually not worth all the effort. They call out just about everything, until I feel that my writing has been frappéd in the blender.

P.S.

A few final words to remember about the writing process:

1. Some writers do not follow all the steps I've described here. It's likely that you will use more of these steps when you try a type of creative writing that's new to you.

2. The activities do not have to come in this order. You may be more comfortable revising as you draft, for example.

3. You don't have to finish one step in the process to start another. Some writers plan one short section and write it, plan another short section and write it, and so on.

The Least You Need to Know

➤ *Drafting* involves arranging words to create meaningful sentences and paragraphs.

➤ *Revising* is evaluating your writing by cutting, adding, replacing, and rearranging what you wrote.

➤ *Editing* is making surface-level changes so your writing is grammatically correct.

➤ *Proofreading* helps you catch errors in typing and handwriting.

Chapter 6

The Secrets of Writing

In This Chapter

➤ Learn how to use words in fresh, new ways to spark your reader's imagination

➤ See how *parallelism, repetition,* and *diction* can help you find your *voice* and create an individual *style*

The late author Truman Capote once said, "Writing has laws of perspective, of light and shade, just as painting or music does. If you are born knowing them, fine. If not, learn them. Then rearrange the rules to suit yourself."

You say the dishes are done, the kids are in bed, and there's nothing on TV? Good. This is your chance to take a few minutes to discover the secrets of writing—and I don't mean "onomatopoeia" and "foreshadowing." *They're* for high school sophomores. We're into the big leagues here. In Chapter 4, you learned about *topic, purpose,* and *audience.* Now it's time to meet the rest of the gang: *parallelism, repetition, diction, style, voice,* and *wit.*

I Know It When I See It

Can you recognize great writing when you see it? There are a lot of myths and half-truths about good writing. Take this snap quiz to see how much you know about the Real Thing.

Write T if you think the statement is true or F if you think it's false.

If it Walks Like a Duck and Quacks Like a Duck...

_____ 1. We all know good writing when we see it.

_____ 2. Good writing is the novel you stay up all night to finish.

_____ 3. Great writing is the short story you insist on sharing with all your friends.

_____ 4. It's the play you want to see over and over.

_____ 5. Excellent writing is the movie that makes you laugh and cry at the same time.

_____ 6. You can find great writing in song lyrics that you can't get out of your head.

_____ 7. Great writing is the poem that comforts you when times are tough.

_____ 8. Good writing can be poetry or prose.

_____ 9. Good writing can be fiction or nonfiction.

_____ 10. Only geniuses can create great writing.

Answers

Items 1–9 are true; only item 10 is false.

Below are three examples of great writing. The first is dramatic poetry, the second is the opening of a novel, and the third is part of an essay. See if you can identify each piece and explain why it is good.

Go Figure: Figures of Speech

Passage #1: Who said it? What makes it so beautiful?

> But, soft! what light through yonder window breaks?
> It is the east, and Juliet is the sun.
> Arise, fair sun, and kill the envious moon,
> Who is already sick and pale with grief,
> That thou her maid art far more fair than she:

Be not her maid, since she is envious;
Her vestal livery is but sick and green
And none but fools do wear it; cast it off.
It is my lady, O, it is my love!
O, that she knew she were!

Source: _____

Outstanding qualities: _____

_____

This is an excerpt from Shakespeare's *Romeo and Juliet,* of course. You know it's good writing because everything Shakespeare wrote is worshipped. But look a little closer to see why his writing *deserves* to be revered—and used as a model.

Shakespeare uses a number of *figures of speech* (or *figurative language*)—words and expressions not meant to be taken literally. Figures of speech use words in fresh, new ways to appeal to the imagination. Figures of speech include *similes, metaphors, extended metaphors, hyperbole,* and *personification.* Here are just two examples that you can find in this soliloquy from *Romeo and Juliet*:

All the Write Stuff
Reading is one of the best ways to learn good writing. Read everything—trash, classics, the good, bad, and the ugly—and see how other writers do it.

➤ *Metaphors.* These figures of speech compare two unlike things, the more familiar thing describing the less familiar one. Metaphors do not use the words "like" or "as" to make the comparison. "It is the east, and Juliet is the sun" is a metaphor.

➤ *Personification.* Here, a nonhuman subject is given human characteristics. Effective personification of things makes them seem vital and alive, as if they were human. Shakespeare personifies the sun and moon when he writes: "Arise, fair sun, and kill the envious moon,/ Who is already sick and pale with grief,/That thou her maid art far more fair than she."

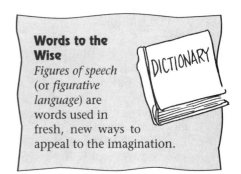

Words to the Wise
Figures of speech (or *figurative language*) are words used in fresh, new ways to appeal to the imagination.

Using figures of speech in your own writing enables you to describe people, places, and things with precision and lyric beauty. This helps you create memorable images that stay in your readers' minds long after they have finished reading your words.

On the Straight and Narrow: Parallelism and Repetition

Passage #2: Can you identify this creative writing?

> It was the best of times, it was the worst of times, it was the age of wisdom, it was the age of foolishness, it was the epoch of belief, it was the epoch of incredulity, it was the season of Light, it was the season of Darkness, it was the spring of hope, it was the winter of despair, we had everything before us, we had nothing before us, we were all going direct to Heaven, we were all going direct the other way—in short, the period was so far like the present period, that some of its noisiest authorities insisted on its being received, for good or for evil, in the superlative degree of comparison only.

Source: _____

Outstanding qualities: _____

This is the opening from Charles Dickens' classic novel of revolution, *A Tale of Two Cities*. Here, Dickens uses two other writing secrets to create powerful, memorable writing: *parallelism* (or *parallel structure*) and *repetition*. Much of the power of formal prose like this novel comes from the repetition of words and phrases and the connections between them.

All the Write Stuff
When you use parallelism, repeating or adding words creates emphasis and rhythm; leaving out conjunctions creates tension. Dickens creates tension by leaving out the coordinating conjunction *and* between the following two complete sentences: "It was the best of times, it was the worst of times." The sentence should read: It was the best of times, *and* it was the worst of times."

Parallel Bars

You can create balance by pairing two related words, such as "men and women," or two related compounds, such as "best of times and worst of times." This balance in construction is called *parallelism*. Notice how Dickens begins each sentence with the same phrase, "It was the..." and follows with an adjective, preposition, and noun.

Dickens also uses parallelism to create humor: "...we were all going direct to Heaven, we were all going direct the other way...". Dickens' use of parallelism creates memorable phrases; it's no surprise that the opening of *A Tale of Two Cities* is one of the most famous passages in literature.

Speaker of the House

Parallelism and repetition are key elements in many of our most famous speeches, such as John F. Kennedy's inaugural address. Here, parallelism and repetition capture the cadences of natural speech to create one of the most memorable lines of the twentieth century: "And so, my fellow Americans, ask not what your country can do for you—ask what you can do for your country."

Abraham Lincoln built the "Gettysburg Address" on parallelism and repetition, drawn from his deep knowledge of Biblical rhythms: "But in a larger sense, we cannot dedicate—we cannot consecrate—we cannot hallow—this ground." Notice the repetition of the parallel phrase *we cannot.*

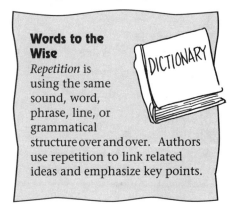

Words to the Wise
Repetition is using the same sound, word, phrase, line, or grammatical structure over and over. Authors use repetition to link related ideas and emphasize key points.

Proper Words in Proper Places: Diction

Passage #3: What makes this essay so effective?

> These are the times that try men's souls: The summer soldier and the sunshine patriot will in this crisis, shrink from the service of his country; but he that stands it NOW, deserves the love and thanks of man and woman. Tyranny, like hell, is not easily conquered; yet we have this consolation with us, that the harder the conflict, the more glorious the triumph. What we obtain too cheap, we esteem too lightly:—'Tis dearness only that gives everything its value. Heaven knows how to put a proper price upon its goods; and it would be strange indeed, if so celestial an article as freedom should not be highly rated.

All the Write Stuff
In Chapter 4, you learned about *tone.* Notice how Paine opens with a reasonable tone but quickly progresses to an incendiary, fiery attitude.

Source: _____

Outstanding qualities: _____

_____

You've heard it, maybe even quoted it, but can you identify it? It's the opening of Thomas Paine's *The American Crisis,* a series of essays to convince people to support

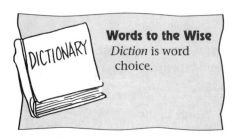

Words to the Wise
Diction is word choice.

Wrong Turn
Don't discount the importance of context and connotation. Words carry different connotations depending on how they are used, especially where gender is concerned. For example, an aggressive man and an aggressive woman are often perceived as two different animals: the former as an achiever; the latter as a word that rhymes with "witch" and "rich."

American independence from English rule. Before the Revolution, Paine had lived an inconspicuous life, working at a series of unimpressive jobs ranging from corset-maker to grocer. The revolution called forth his brilliant prose. *The American Crisis* was a colonial best-seller, and with good cause. It's great writing.

Paine selects the precise words he needs to make his point and reach his audience. For example, notice the implications in the descriptions "summer soldier" and "sunshine patriot." Paine's words suggest that these are the people who support you only when it is convenient. Using "celestial" to describe *freedom* conveys the priceless quality of independence.

The words you select make up your *diction*. Your diction affects the clarity and impact of your message. Diction is measured from high to low, high being multisyllabic tongue-twisters and low being slang and vernacular. Neither is intrinsically good or bad; rather, each is appropriate in different writing situations.

➤ *Elevated diction.* Here's some elevated diction from philosopher Ralph Waldo Emerson: "Whoso would be a man, must be a nonconformist. He who would gather immortal palms must not be hindered by the name of goodness, but must explore if it be goodness."

➤ *Vernacular.* Here's some plain speaking from Mark Twain: "I do wonder what in the nation that frog throw'd off for—I wonder if there ain't something the matter with him—he 'pers to look mighty baggy, somehow."

How would you describe the level of Paine's diction in the preceding essay?

Connotation and Denotation

To be successful at choosing exact words for each particular context, you have to understand the *denotation* and *connotation* of words. Every word has a denotation, its explicit meaning. You can find the denotation of a word by looking it up in a dictionary. For example, if you look up the word "fat" in the dictionary, it will say, "having too much adipose tissue."

Some words also have *connotations,* or emotional overtones. These connotations can be positive, negative, or neutral. For example, "fat" has a negative connotation in our fitness-obsessed society. Being sensitive to a word's denotation and connotation is essential for clear and effective creative writing. It can also help you use the right word and so avoid getting your nose punched out because you insulted someone. Finally, you can use these connotations to create an emotional response in your reader.

> **Words to the Wise** 
> The *denotation* of a word is its exact meaning. The *connotation* of a word is its emotional overtones.
>
> DICTIONARY

Chart It!

Check out your understanding of connotation and denotation by completing the following chart. Write a plus (+) next to any word with a positive connotation or a dash (-) next to any word with a negative connotation.

When would you use each of these words? Why?

Word	Connotation
1. paunchy	
2. chubby	
3. cheap	
4. thrifty	
5. stubborn	
6. loyal	
7. reckless	
8. bold	
9. gaunt	
10. slender	

Answers

All odd-numbered words have a negative connotation; all even-numbered words have a positive connotation.

How to Write Well: Get Some Style

"Every style that is not boring is good," wrote French writer Voltaire. All good writing shares one common quality: it has *style*. Some modern American writers celebrated for their lucid style include Truman Capote, James Thurber, Dorothy Thompson, Joan Didion, John McPhee, Tracy Kidder, and E.B. White. Mr. White, a long-time essayist and short story writer for *The New Yorker*, oozed so much style that he even coauthored a famous little writing manual called *The Elements of Style*. It's the ne plus ultra of style.

Style is a series of choices—words, sentence length and structure, figures of speech, tone, voice, diction, and overall structure. A writer may change his or her style for different kinds of writing and to suit different audiences. In poetry, for example, a writer might use more imagery than he or she would use in prose. Style depends on purpose, audience, and appropriateness.

Don't confuse *style* with *stylishness*. The latter is faddish; the former, eternal. Stylishness is go-go boots, hula-hoops, and spandex; style is wing-tips, baseball, and pure wool. Stylish writing doesn't make it in the long haul: choose-your-own-ending novels, snuff fiction, and nonfiction fiction are the literary equivalent of the Edsel, Olestra, and the new-formula Coca-Cola.

Words to the Wise
An author's *style* is his or her distinctive way of writing.

Also, don't confuse style with bizarreness or eccentricity. Style is not something you do to a text to tart it up, like slapping whipped cream over a sagging cake. Style is a beginning, not an end unto itself. Unless you're James Joyce, avoid making up words, running ideas together, and dragging out stream of consciousness.

Thrift, Thrift, Thrift

In every fat book there is a thin book trying to get out. Your job is to write the thin book that says it all. Often, as much gets left out as put in. A fine writing style shows an economy of language.

Conciseness describes writing that is direct and to the point. This is not to say that you have to pare away all description, figures of speech, and images. No. It *is* to say that wordy writing annoys your readers because it forces them to slash their way through rainforest verbiage before they can understand what you're saying. Hard and lean sentences, like hard and lean bodies, require far more effort than flabby ones. And they are so much nicer.

Follow these three easy rules to create taut, effective sentences.

1. Eliminate unneeded words.

2. Don't say the same thing twice.

3. Make passive sentences active.

Let's look at each of these rules in greater detail.

Eliminate Unneeded Words

Combine sentences to achieve clarity. Cut any words that just take up space like an unwanted house guest. Here's an example:

Wordy: *The Chamber* was a best seller. It was written by John Grisham. *The Chamber* was a courtroom thriller.

Better: *The Chamber,* by John Grisham, was a best-selling courtroom thriller.

Here are some words and phrases that weigh down your writing. They can always be eliminated to better effect.

Words and Phrases to Cut

as a matter of fact	because of the fact that
factor	for the purpose of
in a very real sense	in light of the fact that
in the case of	to get to the point
that is to say	what I mean to say
the point I am trying to make	

Wrong Turn
Repetition is a good thing, redundancy is not. When you use repetition, you deliberately repeat words and phrases to create rhythm and emphasis. Redundancy, in contrast, adds unnecessary bits and pieces that need to be trimmed like fat from the federal budget.

Don't Say the Same Thing Twice

Phrases such as "revert back," "cover over," "circle around," and "square in shape" are redundant—they say the same thing twice. Cut! Cut! Cut!

Redundant: The editor was looking forward to the book's final completion.

Better: The editor was looking forward to the book's completion.

Make Passive Sentences Active

In the *active voice,* the subject performs the action named by the verb. In the passive voice, the subject receives the action. The *passive voice* is often far wordier than the active voice. How many unnecessary words were cut by rewriting the following sentence from the passive voice to the active voice?

Passive: Ten pages were completed in one day by the writer.

Active: The writer completed ten pages in one day.

A Voice in the Dark

According to Philip Roth, a writer's voice is "something that begins around the back of the knees." Voice lets you tell stories that are uniquely your own. Good writing has a sense of life that forces the reader to keep going. There's the sense that a real person wrote the text. That's voice. It's a part of a writer's style.

Novice writers are often afraid to let their voice emerge. They start with someone else's voice and hope it will yield original material. It rarely does. Getting to know your voice can be a perilous process, because in so doing you are revealing much of yourself. But you cannot adopt another personae until you find your own.

You can turn off all the lights, sacrifice a few goats, and wait for your voice to come to you. Or you can try a few of the following suggestions to see if you can cultivate voice without angering the ASPCA.

Find Your Voice!

1. Be outrageous. Experiment. The more freedom you feel, the more willing you will be to release your voice.

2. Write in the dark or with your eyes closed.

3. Dress all in one color and write.

4. Activate odors that move your spirit. Try cinnamon, pine, vanilla.

5. Try writing outdoors.

6. Surround yourself with special, evocative objects as you write.

7. Play music as you write. Change the music and see what happens.

8. Lose yourself in colors and shapes. Draw pictures; finger paint.

9. Write with the opposite hand.

10. Write fragments—dialogue, description, poetry. Don't worry about how everything will fit together.

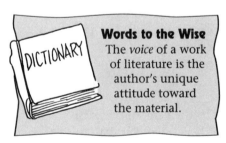

Words to the Wise
The *voice* of a work of literature is the author's unique attitude toward the material.

Wit

Wit is like a Ginsu knife: fast, sharp, and merciless. Wit stays sharp, too, even when it's cut a hundred times. Like an Armani suit, you know wit when you see it: Oscar Wilde, Dorothy Parker, and Tom Stoppard are witty. Groucho Marx, Jay Leno, and Rosie

O'Donnell are funny, maybe even acerbic—but not witty. Joan Rivers is too nasty; Dave Letterman is too idiotic. (Sorry, Dave, but you did it to yourself with those stupid pet tricks). *Vanity Fair* has moments of wit; so does *The New Yorker*.

Here are some examples from Dorothy Parker's "Pig's Eye View of Literature." The first poem turns on Wilde's reputation for creating memorable epigrams; the second, on Carlyle's temper.

Oscar Wilde

If, with the literate I am
Impelled to try an epigram,
I never seek to take the credit;
We all assume Oscar said it.

Thomas Carlyle

Carlyle combined the lit'ry life
With throwing teacups at his wife,
Remarking, rather testily,
"Oh, stop your dodging, Mrs. C.!"

Wit comes from an Anglo-Saxon word that means "mind, intelligence, and reason." By the Renaissance, it referred to a clever remark, especially one that was unexpected or paradoxical. By the 1700s, *wit* came to mean eloquence and precision. Writers in the 1800s didn't much go for wit. They preferred the term *imagination* and all its connotations.

Today, saying it fast and funny is back. Like rock-hard abs and overpriced goat cheese, wit is in. See if it works for you.

The Least You Need to Know

➤ *Figures of speech* use words in fresh, new ways to appeal to the imagination.

➤ *Parallelism* and *repetition* create powerful, memorable writing.

➤ Select the precise words (*diction*) you need to make your point and reach your audience. Watch for the *connotation* (implied meaning) of words.

➤ Create *style* through your choices: words, sentence length and structure, figures of speech, tone, voice, diction, and structure.

➤ Be *concise*—direct and to the point.

➤ Cultivate your writer's *voice,* through *wit,* if you choose.

Part 2
Fiction and Poetry

Once upon a time there was fiction and nonfiction and everybody knew which was which: fiction told stories and nonfiction reported facts and opinions. But now, all that has changed—twentieth-century writing has fogged the distinction between the forms.

For more than thirty years now, nonfiction writers have been swiping tasty morsels from the fiction writer's table. Not to be outdone, fiction writers have been using some of the techniques traditionally associated with nonfiction. This is a good thing, for it allows much greater freedom in writing. In addition to good ol' fiction, we also have faction, metafiction, *and* literary journalism.

No matter what "fiction" is called today, you'll learn how to write it in this section of the book. I'll take you step-by-step through the elements of fiction, including plot, conflict, characterization, setting, and point of view. You'll also find out how to write fiction's kissing cousin, poetry.

TWAIN   GINSBERG SHAKESPEARE

A Novel Idea

"Oh! It is only a novel!" exclaims a character in Jane Austen's novel *Northanger Abbey*. In short, it's only "some work in which the most thorough knowledge of human nature, the happiest delineation of its varieties, the liveliest effusions of wit and humor are conveyed to the world in the best chosen language." It is a creed that all modern novelists (down to our own Sidney Sheldon and Anne Rice) have tried to live up to. And now the mantle has passed to you.

All books are a monument to the human spirit, but the novel is a particularly admirable feat because of its length and breadth. The story of a good novel resonates within us as something more real than life itself. Who can forget Oliver Twist's wrenching plea for a little more gruel, Rhett Butler's slamming the door on Scarlett, and Huck Finn's "lighting out for the territory ahead of the rest." And even though novelists may sometimes use real-life people as their inspiration, successful characters end up as unique creations, greater than the sum of their parts. Fierce Captain Ahab, proud Hester Prynne, and sinister Michael Corleone are among the most notable.

In this chapter, you'll find out how to get your novel down on paper. First, I'll list and describe the different kinds of novels so you can discover which types you would like to write. Next, you'll discover how to plot your story, create memorable characters, and craft fast-paced dialogue. You'll also learn about point of view, foreshadowing, and length.

Always a Bridesmaid, Never a Bride?

According to the family legend, James Fenimore Cooper was reading a new English novel one night when he suddenly threw the book down in disgust. "I could write a better book than that myself!" he shouted in a fury. His wife Susan challenged him to make good on his boast. The following year he completed a novel he called *Precaution* (1820). The critics objected that it was little more than another echo of English fiction, so Cooper once again rose to the taunt, this time producing two undeniably American books: *The Spy*, a tale of the American Revolution, and *The Pioneers,* a runaway bestseller about the frontier. The latter sold 3,500 copies on the morning of its first day in print.

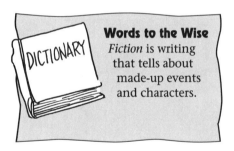

Words to the Wise
Fiction is writing that tells about made-up events and characters.

Cooper's determination to write a better novel resulted in a number of astonishing firsts: the first American adventure story, the first American novel of manners, and the first American novel of the sea. With all of this, Cooper became the first successful American novelist. His macho frontiersman, Natty Bumppo, is one of the best-known characters in world literature. Cooper's fame rests largely on *The Leatherstocking Tales*, a series of five novels about Natty Bumppo. If Fenimore Cooper could do it, so can you.

Fiction is writing that tells about made-up events and characters. Novels and short stories are examples of fiction. There is no specific required length that sets the novel apart from its cousin the short story (see Chapter 8) or the *novelette*, a story usually between 50 to 100 pages.

If you're going to push me to the edge, as a general rule, a novel is more than 50,000 words.

Bet You Didn't Know

Do-It-Yourself Cooper Novel

Take one or more phrases from each column to create your own Cooper plot in one sentence.

SETTING	HEROES
Amidst virgin forests,	manly pioneers
Amidst heaving oceans,	manly Indians
Amidst besieged forts,	demure blond debs
Amidst Lake Glimmerglass,	brunette spitfires

VILLAINS	WEAPONS
confront dastardly sailors	armed with swords.
confront dastardly Indians	armed with muskets.
confront dastardly soldiers	armed with bows and arrows.

Like new-age lovers, fiction comes in many forms. Which type (or types) do you want to write? Use this checklist to make note of them. Starred entries are explained below.

Fiction offers something for every writer! Check off the types that you want to write.

_____ adult novels   _____ realistic fiction

_____ Bildungsroman*   _____ roman à clef*

_____ children's storybooks   _____ romance novels*

_____ comic novels   _____ satiric novels

_____ epistolary novels*   _____ science fiction

_____ gothic horror novels*   _____ transgressive fiction*

_____ historical novels   _____ young adult fiction

_____ mysteries   _____ westerns

_____ picaresque novels*

Let's take a closer look at some of the different forms that a novel can take. See which ones suit your unique interests and abilities.

"Bildungsroman"

So you want to describe how the hero escaped his lousy childhood to become a mensch? Then the "Bildungsroman" is the form for you. German for "novel of development," this fictional form deals with maturation, wherein the hero becomes civilized. No, this does not mean that he finally puts his socks in the hamper and remembers that the treadmill is not an extension of his closet. Rather, in these novels, the hero becomes aware of himself as he relates to the objective world outside of his subjective consciousness. Famous examples include Thomas Mann's *The Magic Mountain*, Samuel Butler's *The Way of All Flesh*, and James Joyce's *A Portrait of the Artist as a Young Man*.

All the Write Stuff
Writing Mysteries, a handbook by the Mystery Writers of America (edited by Sue Grafton), offers detailed advice for writing gripping whodunits.

Take a Letter, Maria: The Epistolary Novel

If you've read Alice Walker's *The Color Purple*, you'll recall that Walker used letters between her characters to advance the story. By using this form of the novel, Walker is drawing on a long literary history. The 1700s were the heyday of the epistolary novel. Samuel Richardson's staggeringly long novel *Clarissa* (over a million words, which makes it the longest novel in English), concerns a young woman of virtue and her seducer. Most epistolary novels depend on an exchange of correspondence: you write to me, I write back, and so on. But the rule is carved in sand, not granite. Mary Shelley's *Frankenstein*, for example, is a one-way letter.

Here's Johnny!

We have the Gothic tradition to thank for such gems as *Sorority Girl Slashers at the Bowl-a-Rama* and *Abbott and Costello Meet the Bride of Frankenstein*. First popular in the late eighteenth century and the early nineteenth, Gothic lit is chock full of mystery, horror, violence, and terror. Gothic writers accomplish this through:

➤ Decapitations

➤ Undead dead

➤ Premature entombment

➤ Spooky castles

➤ Rattling chains

➤ If you're really lucky, even a little perverted sex

Long before Stephen King, the trendsetters were the following shockmasters:

➤ Horace Walpole (*The Castle of Otranto,* 1764)

➤ Clara Reeve (*The Champion of Virtue,* 1777)

➤ Ann Radcliffe (*The Mysteries of Udolpho,* 1794)

➤ Mary Wollstonecraft Shelley (ol' Zipperneck himself, *Frankenstein,* 1818)

➤ Edgar Allan Poe ("The Raven" 1845)

Read these novels for a good look at how it should be done.

All the Write Stuff
Notice that I keep citing all these classic writers? There's a method to my madness. To write the best, you have to read the best. Fortunately, they're not all dead white guys. The classic honchos come in all varieties and offer something for everyone.

Picaresque Novel

A travelogue with a twist: the picaresque (pronounced *pick-are-ESK,* not *picturesque*) novel describes the exploits of a rogue. "Picaresque" comes from the Spanish word *picaro,* which means "rogue." Not surprisingly, it's a Spanish genre (there are more rogues in Spain than there is coal in Newcastle). The form originated in sixteenth-century Spain as a kind of parody of tales of chivalric adventures. As a result, the picaresque novel has an episodic structure, as the hero experiences a series of wild adventures.

Among the most famous picaresque novels are Henry Fielding's *Tom Jones* and Mark Twain's *The Adventures of Huckleberry Finn.* The movie *Goodfellas* can also be considered a picaresque story because of its portrayal of mobster Henry Hill.

All the Write Stuff
Little green men with large stun guns set your blood a tingling? Then sci-fi may be your bag. If so, you may wish to consult *How to Write Science Fiction and Fantasy* by Orson Scott Card for a step-by-step description of writing this type of fiction.

> ## Bet You Didn't Know
>
> All novels have a fairly specific setting (the time and place of the action). If the setting includes real historical figures and becomes as a character in the story, you're dealing with a historical novel. Charles Dickens's *A Tale of Two Cities* and Robert Grave's *I, Claudius* are both historical novels.

Novel with a Key

A *roman à clef* uses contemporary historical figures as its chief characters, but they are cloaked with fictitious names. The most recent and notorious example is Joe Klein's *Primary Colors*, a thinly disguised account of the Clinton administration. Reaching a little further back through the curtains of time, there's *Valley of the Dolls*, Jackie Susann's account of pill-popping among Hollywood's leading ladies. On a less sensational plane, the main character in Aldous Huxley's *Point Counter Point*, Mark Rampion, is modeled on fellow novelist D. H. Lawrence.

Love Makes the World Go 'Round: Romance Novels

Put an innocent young woman in an isolated mansion. Throw in a devilishly handsome, brooding young man. On page 22, have the hero say, "Good morning." For the next ten pages, the heroine wonders what he meant. Add some heaving breasts, flowing hair (male and female), and passionate whoopee. Don't you wish it were that easy to write a romance novel?

> ## All the Write Stuff
> To figure out what pseudonym you should use if you decide to write a romance novel, take the name of your first pet + your mother's maiden name.

Romance novels have come a long way, baby. Perhaps in the entire history of book publishing, there has never been such a phenomenon as the apparently limitless success of romance novels. They total nearly forty percent of all paperback novels sold in America. *Harlequin Publishers* alone sold nearly two hundred million romances in 1996, averaging a book per second.

Because the romance novel follows a *formula* (a set of strict guidelines about characters, plot, setting, and length), it may be easier for the first-time author to write. If you're interested in this type of novel, you can get more information from these resources: *How to Write Romances* (Phyllis Taylor Pianka), *Writing and Selling the Romance Novel* (Sylvia K. Burack), *How to Write Romance Novels that Sell* (Marilyn M. Lowery), and *You Can Write a Romance and Get It Published!* (Yvonne MacManus).

Transgressive Fiction

The term "transgressive fiction" was coined less than five years ago by a writer in the *Los Angeles Times* to describe fiction that graphically explores nasty stuff like aberrant sexual practices, urban violence, dysfunctional family relationships, and drug use. Words used as compliments to describe these novels include "subversive, avant-guard, bleak, and pornographic."

Transgressive fiction has its roots in the novels of William Burroughs and the Marquis de Sade. Its practitioners include Dennis Cooper, the author of *Try*, a novel whose main character is a sexually abused teenager with a heroin-addicted buddy and an uncle who makes pornographic videos. The genre is also characterized by distinctive visuals, such as undersized formats, the whole text set in italics, and bizarre cover art. Write at your own risk.

> **Wrong Turn**
> If you decide to write a romance novel, send for the author's guidelines *before* you start writing. Otherwise, you could end up trashing a whole lot of manuscript. You can get the publisher's address from *Literary Marketplace* (in the reference section of the library) or from the inside cover of any romance novel.

> **All the Write Stuff**
> Remember, you can always publish your novel under a pseudonym if you're afraid of hurting someone's feelings, damaging reputations, or otherwise wreaking havoc.

A Force Is a Force, of Course, of Course: Plot

Now it's time to get a story—the *plot*—in place for your novel. *Plot* is the arrangement of events in a work of fiction. Successful writers arrange the events of the plot to keep the reader's interest and convey the theme.

In many stories and novels, the events of the plot can be divided as follows:

➤ *Exposition*. Introduces the characters, setting, and conflict.

➤ *Rising action*. Builds the conflict and develops the characters.

➤ *Climax.* The highest point of the action.

➤ *Denouement.* Resolves the story and ties up all the loose ends.

Bet You Didn't Know

What you'll learn about plot in this section applies to writing all fiction—novels, short stories, and drama. You'll also find information about plot, character, and conflict in other chapters in this book, so read it all!

According to writer Peter De Vries, "Every novel should have a beginning, a muddle, and an end." How can you avoid having a "muddle" in the middle of your novel? I recommend that you start by plotting the basic idea of your novel with a simple diagram. These diagrams can help you establish causation—having each event build to the one that follows.

Here are two diagrams that work well. Select the one that best suits your novel's Big Three considerations: audience, purpose, and tone.

This diagram gives you a simple way to plot your novel. You may wish to use this diagram when you're brainstorming the basics of your novel.

Jot down ideas in each of these boxes to arrange the events in your novel.

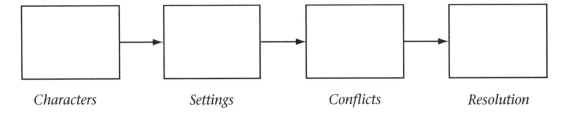

   Characters   *Settings*   *Conflicts*   *Resolution*

Let's take it one step further.

Complete the following worksheet to arrange the framework of your novel.

Working title: _____

Main Characters:_____
_____
_____

Minor Characters: _____
_____
_____

↓

Settings: _____
_____
_____

↓

Conflict:_____

Events

_____
_____
_____
_____

↓

Resolution:
_____

In Literature as in Life

So you're stuck in a cab and the driver offers you a plot idea. "I'd rather chew glass than take his idea," you mutter deep into your collar. Later that week, your hairdresser offers you another intriguing plot idea. Because she's holding a sharp pair of scissors, you are exceedingly polite. Nonetheless, you're thinking, "Don't give up your day job."

Conventional wisdom sneers at novel ideas drawn from ordinary people. Don't sneer so fast. I believe that you should listen to everyone. Many of the best plots come from suggestions and everyday events.

For example, famous novelist Joseph Conrad (1857–1924) drew many of the plots of his novels from his own experience. His novel *Lord Jim* is based on the story of the pilgrim ship *Jeddah,* which set out from Singapore in 1880 with 950 passengers bound for the holy lands. Conrad heard the story (probably from a rickshaw driver) when he disembarked in Singapore in 1883, although he didn't write the novel for another fifteen years.

Theodore Dreiser's classic *An American Tragedy* is based on the true story of Chester Gillette, who murdered his pregnant girlfriend when she stood in the way of his ascension into high society. Dreiser read the story in the newspaper. Truman Capote got the idea for his "nonfiction novel" *In Cold Blood* from another real life murder case.

"Call Me Ishmael": First Lines

First impressions count. Great first lines have entered our consciousness like first kisses. So now you're thinking, "If I can't write the perfect beginning, how am I going to make it through the next 299 pages?"

If you're stuck for an opener, skip it. You heard me, just skip it. Draw some lines in your manuscript and move on. By the time you're halfway through your novel, you'll have come up with a great opening.

Rebel with a Cause

"Write about what you know," is classic advice for beginning novelists—and with good reason. The richest source for ideas is your own life. Unfortunately, it's also the most sensitive.

Most novelists want to write about their own lives. Brutal childhoods, not-so-brutal childhoods, painful teen years, prom queen thrills, lost loves, found loves—they all make good pickings for the creative writer. But no one wants to read 300 pages of moaning about how your parents made you walk 10 miles to school, uphill both ways, in the snow, barefoot, and so on *ad nauseum.*

By far the most common experience is a novelist who tries to entertain and move readers without taking any personal risks. Some experts will advise you to spill your guts as freely as you spill ink. I don't agree with either of these viewpoints.

Only you can judge your level of comfort. There's a not-so-fine line between truth and dare. I question the motives of novelists who claim to "tell the truth" about their lives. It often seems to me that they are doing little more than getting revenge. My advice: Mine your own life freely, but mind your motives, too.

Foreshadowing

Foreshadowing is a novelistic technique used to prepare the reader for future events. The Russian writer Anton Chekhov advised writers that if they used a gun as a prop in their writing, the gun had better go off by the end. Mysterious incidents in a novel can increase dramatic suspense by leading readers to anticipate strange events. In *Jane Eyre*, for example, the author foreshadows the novel's terrible secret: the crazy wife whom Rochester keeps in his attic. (Oops! You *have* read *Jane Eyre*, right?) Bronte used strange howls in the night, the brother's mysterious visit, and a near-tragic fire to foreshadow Rochester's entanglement. You can do the same thing to build suspense in your novel.

Wrong Turn
Foreshadowing is like garlic: a little goes a long way. Select and plant events carefully to hint at—not hammer home—further plot twists.

Point of View

Point of view is the position from which a story is told. Here are the three different points of view you will encounter most often in novels:

➤ *First-person point of view:* The narrator is one of the characters in the novel and explains the events through his or her own eyes, using the pronouns *I* and *me*. For example, it was vital to Poe's fiction that he use the first person point of view as the narrator about being buried alive and murdering people. This point of view increased the horror and terror. Check out Holden Caulfield (Salinger's *Catcher in the Rye*) and Huck Finn, too.

➤ *Third-person omniscient point of view:* The narrator is not a character in the novel. Instead, the narrator looks through the eyes of all the characters. As a result, the narrator is "all-knowing." The narrator uses the pronouns *he, she,* and *they*. Stephen King often uses the third-person point of view to delve into each character's motives.

➤ *Third-person limited point of view:* The narrator tells the story through the eyes of only one character, using the pronouns *he, she,* and *they*. William Faulkner used this point of view in the final section of his audacious novel *The Sound and the Fury* to show a rational interpretation of events (the other three first-person narrators were one sandwich short of a picnic).

All the Right Stuff

If you do decide to switch point of view midstream, be sure to leave a one-line break for every switch in narrator. This way, your reader will have a guidepost to follow.

In multiple viewpoints, the author chooses two or three characters from whom readers learn what is happening. Each character can only know what he or she learns by witnessing something or being told. John Fowles' novel *The Collector*, for example, is written half from the kidnapper's point of view and half from the victim's. Point of view is crucial because it determines what events you will present in your novel (or other work of fiction). When you select a point of view, consider what plot events you want revealed—and which ones you want the readers to infer. Whenever possible, I always urge new writers to stick with the third-person point of view in the beginning. It is the easiest point of view to master.

Does Length Matter?

I'm often asked, "How long should a chapter be?" This question makes me think of the reporter who poked fun at Abraham Lincoln's height. "Mr. Lincoln," the reporter said, "how long should a man's legs be?" "Long enough," Lincoln replied, "to reach from his hips to the ground."

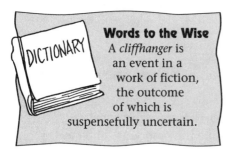

Words to the Wise

A *cliffhanger* is an event in a work of fiction, the outcome of which is suspensefully uncertain.

This is true about the length of chapters. They should be long enough to convey the message and leave the reader anxious to turn the pages for more. As a general rule, strive for about ten pages per chapter. Few people read an entire novel at one sitting, so it is best to give them natural places to break.

Many novels break at an especially tense point, called a "cliffhanger." This suspenseful event propels the story and urges readers to continue.

Round up the Usual Suspects: Characters

First of all, keep the usual suspects to a minimum. We don't have to meet the whole family. Use only as many characters as you need to tell the story.

Some writers begin with plot and find characters who fit the story. Other novelists, in contrast, begin with characters and let them interact as the plot unfolds. Still others begin with a theme and seek plot and characters to address that truth about life. There are even some writers who begin with a setting and let the plot and characters unfold from there.

Select the method that works best for you. Remember, though, that the method may vary from novel to novel. Experiment with different techniques until you find the one that works for you at that particular point in your writing career.

What's in a Name?

What's in a name? A lot. Look what happened to Romeo and Juliet because of *their* names. The significance of names is deeply embedded in our consciousness. Some Native Americans believe that knowing a person's name gives you power over them; some Christians take a new name when they are confirmed. As a novelist, you should pick your characters' names carefully because readers relate to characters according to their names.

Find names that convey a sense of each character's personality. Think how the names sound, their connotations. For example, "Daisy" suggests flower-like vulnerability, while "Butch" conveys a hulk. "Dexter" is a geek, "Amber" is a beauty queen, "Martha" is virtuous but dull. Margaret Mitchell originally planned to call the protagonist of *Gone with the Wind* "Pansy," but wisely decided that "Scarlett" (as in scarlet woman) certainly described her strong-willed heroine much better.

Wrong Turn
In general, avoid using the names of real people. There are too many lawyers in the world who don't have enough work and would love to sue your butt off. If you get your characters' names from a telephone book, use the first name of one person and the last name of another.

They Talk Alike, They Walk Alike: You Could Lose Your Mind

Dialogue not only draws you immediately into the story, but it's one of the best ways to reveal character. Dialogue helps you show your characters'

➤ Educational level

➤ Geographic background

➤ Ethnic background

➤ Emotional state

➤ Motives

Wrong Turn
In general, name only your main characters. Identify the one-shot gas station attendants as "gas station attendant" and the walk-through store clerk as "store clerk." Most of us have filled up our brains already, so why clutter them with unnecessary details?

You reveal these characteristics by the level of diction, slang, accent, euphemisms, jargon, and punctuation you use.

Dialogue should be easy to read. For this to work, don't run several characters' dialogue all in one paragraph. Begin a new paragraph for each exchange or reply. This also helps eliminate the repetitive "he said" and "she replied."

It should also sound like real speech. You can accomplish this by using your ear. Read the dialogue aloud. Does it sound realistic? Would real people talk like this? If not, change the words until it *does* sound realistic. You should be able to identify each character by his or her dialogue—without mentioning who is speaking.

Effective dialogue can also help you further the plot. It's usually more interesting to listen to a character describing something than to explain the same thing in a long block of copy. A clever novelist, afraid his or her ideas may be foolish, slyly puts them into the mouth of some other fool and reserves the right to disavow them.

> **Wrong Turn**
> Among writers of fiction, literary critics occupy a particular region of hell, for they are capable of making or breaking a novelist's reputation without ever having written fiction of their own. Check the *New York Review of Books*, *The New York Times*, and the *London Times* for the names of the literary ballbreakers or makers du jour.

You Can Get There from Here

Okay, so you've decided what type of novel to write. Perhaps you'll start with a romance; maybe sci-fi is your bag. No matter: now it's time to get crackin'. "I don't have the time to write a novel," you whine. Not to worry; the journey of ten thousand words starts with a single sentence.

Follow these suggestions to get started on your novel—*today*.

1. *Make yourself a "writing appointment."* Set aside a block of time during which you will write—and only write. Start with ten minutes a day and build up. As your novel takes shape, you'll want to write more and more.

2. *Schedule breaks.* Breaks help you clear your mind and generate ideas. Keep the breaks brief. I recommend a half-hour walk or jog.

3. *Delegate, delegate, delegate.* One way to give yourself more time is to pay someone else to do the things that are keeping you from writing. Obviously, this only makes sense if you can afford it. You don't need a staff of seven. Instead, consider getting someone to mow the lawn, clean the place, and watch the kids.

4. *Set priorities.* Let the houseplants die. A little dust never hurt anyone. Who needs home-baked cookies?

5. *Reward yourself.* Reward yourself for finishing a certain number of pages, for writing for a specific length of time, or just for work well done. Do lunch with a friend, buy a silly trinket, stop and plant the flowers.

6. *Avoid isolation.* Writing a novel is not the same as taking religious vows. You don't have to become the life of the party as you write, but neither do you have to go native in greasy sweatpants and ratty slippers.

> **All the Write Stuff**
>
> Get an answering machine (if you don't already have one). Use the answering machine to monitor your calls. Take the call only if it's really important. For example: your agent calls to say your novel has been sold—and optioned for a movie.

> **Bet You Didn't Know**
>
> The people who write novels are not necessarily the most witty, brilliant, or well-educated. They aren't even the most deserving, compassionate, or likable. They are, however, the most relentless, patient, and thick-skinned. Stick with it!

The Least You Need to Know

➤ Fiction is writing that tells about made-up events and characters. Like frozen desserts, fiction comes in many forms.

➤ *Plot* is the arrangement of events in a work of literature. Successful writers arrange the events of the plot to keep the reader's interest and convey the theme.

➤ *Point of view* is the position from which a story is told.

➤ Create and use only the *characters* you need. Give them names that convey their personalities.

➤ *Dialogue*, the character's speech, should reveal the character's important traits, be easy to read, and further the plot.

Chapter 8

The Long and Short of It: Short Stories

> ### In This Chapter
>
> ➤ Learn the definition of a short story
>
> ➤ Create *conflict*
>
> ➤ Learn more about creating realistic *characters*
>
> ➤ Build an effective *setting*
>
> ➤ Establish the story's *structure*

I've heard novice writers declare that they plan to write short stories for a few years before they tackle a novel. They figure a short story is easier to write than a novel because it's shorter. "I'll learn to walk before I learn to dance," they argue. Bad move. It's like saying you're going to learn the cha-cha before attempting pole vaulting.

Learning to write a short story isn't easier than learning to write a novel—it's just different. As a result, it doesn't necessarily take more time to become a proficient novelist than it does to become a proficient short story writer.

Here, you'll learn what a short story is—and isn't. Then I'll teach you how to create conflict and how to resolve it. You'll also discover more about creating realistic *characters*. This is followed by a discussion of setting and structure. Finally, I'll get into style, endings, and titles.

Inquiring Minds Want to Know

So what *is* a short story? You know they're shorter than novels, their weightier first cousins. In general, a short story is a prose narrative that has fewer than 30,000 words. On average, a short story tends to run between 2,000 to 7,000 words.

As with designer water, we even have specialized kinds of short stories today. A *short short* story can be between 1,000 and 1,500 words. There's even a micro-mini story, called a *flash,* that runs about 750 words. So how long should *your* short story be? Make it just long enough to tell what you need it to tell. No more, no less.

But even more important than the length of a story is its *content.* When he wasn't busy marrying jail bait and ingesting every controlled substance short of plutonium, Edgar Allan Poe created the modern short story. In a review of Nathaniel Hawthorne's *Twice-Told Tales*, Poe defined the short story this way:

> A skillful literary artist has constructed a tale. If wise, he has not fashioned his thoughts to accommodate his incidents; but having conceived, with deliberate care, a certain unique or single effect to be wrought out, he then invents such incidents— he then combines such events as may best aid him in establishing this preconceived effect...In the whole composition there should be no word written, of which the tendency, direct or indirect, is not to the one preestablished design.

The key here is "single effect" and "preconceived design." A short story, like a good outfit, is all of a piece. Because it is brief when compared to a novel, a short story has:

➤ A limited time frame

➤ One to two main characters

➤ One main event

In a short story, one thing happens to one person. Everything else in the story exists to support that event. In many cases, the event leads the character to a self-realization. For example, O. Henry's ironic chestnut "The Gift of the Magi" had only two characters (husband and wife), one major event (selling the combs and watch fob to buy Christmas gifts), and one setting (the apartment). Both characters come to realize the true meaning of Christmas: love and self-sacrifice (are you sobbing yet?).

What's Love Got to Do with It? Conflict

In fiction, a *conflict* is a struggle or fight. Conflict makes a short story interesting because readers want to discover the outcome. The conflict sets up action and leads to suspense. Both are necessary to make a successful short story.

There are two kinds of conflict. In an *external conflict*, characters struggle against a force outside themselves. In an *internal conflict*, characters battle a force within themselves. Short stories often contain both external and internal conflicts.

Conflict does not necessarily mean violence. In your stories, your main character will have a specific need, goal, or purpose that he or she wants to attain, but something is standing in the way. The main character struggles to overcome the opposition. He or she may win—or lose. It's the struggle that engages your readers.

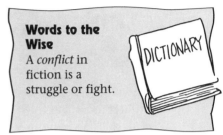

Words to the Wise
A *conflict* in fiction is a struggle or fight.

Do you live a calm life without conflict? If so, call me and we'll swap lives. I'll gladly give you the neighbor from hell, the teenage son panting for his driver's license (and for every teenage girl in town), and the leaky puppy on the new carpet.

In the meantime, here are some broad categories of conflict you can adapt for your short stories. Narrow each of these to target your audience, purpose, and tone.

➤ Food

➤ Health

➤ Clothing

➤ Physical safety

➤ Shelter

➤ Approval and esteem

➤ Friendship

➤ Love

➤ People vs. nature (storms, earthquakes, and so on)

➤ Philosophical conflicts (crises of conscience)

➤ Spiritual conflicts (religious faith)

Bet You Didn't Know

Folktales and fairy tales often use conflicts about unfulfilled wishes. Think of Cinderella and her Prince. Think of Pinocchio longing to be a real boy.

Contemporary short story writer Garrison Keillor focuses on deceptively simple, everyday conflicts in a small town in Minnesota (whether the men of the family will watch football on TV at Thanksgiving or not, for example). Shockmeister Edgar Allan Poe, in contrast, wrote about a crisis of conscience over a murder in "The Telltale Heart." Lots of juicy internal conflict there.

Guess Who's Coming to Dinner? Developing Realistic Characters

Who are the people in your story? Why do they act as they do? Most short stories have a main character, also called a *protagonist*. The *protagonist* is the most important character in your story. He, she, or it is at the center of the conflict and the focus of the reader's attention. The *antagonist* is the force or person in conflict with the main character. An antagonist can be another character, a force of nature, society, or something within the character.

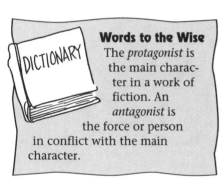

Words to the Wise
The *protagonist* is the main character in a work of fiction. An *antagonist* is the force or person in conflict with the main character.

If your story is to come alive on the page, your characters must seem to be alive. Your reader has to be able to visualize your characters. This doesn't mean that your characters have to be based on real people; neither does it mean that we have to like your characters. But if your readers aren't interested in your characters, they won't want to read your story.

The more you know about your characters, the easier it will be for you to make your readers feel like they know them as well. Below are two ways that you can create realistic, believable characters that will hook your readers so you can reel 'em in.

Getting to Know You

One of the best and easiest ways to flesh out your characters is by creating a "character trait web." Photocopy the following graphic organizer so you have one for each character. Feel free to modify the number of traits as necessary to fit the character and the story.

Examples can come directly from details you will include in the story or be based on inferences that readers will make.

Start by writing the character's name in the middle of the web. Then add details and examples.

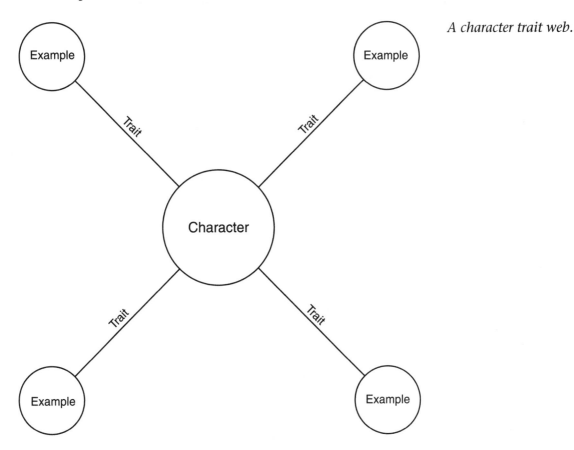

A character trait web.

Just the Facts, Ma'am

Another effective way to create boffo characters is by constructing a character chart. Here, you profile your characters by inventing their history. The following worksheet is a handy way to build their lives. Photocopy this worksheet and use one for your protagonist and one for your antagonist.

Fill in as many details as you can to help you create three-dimensional characters.

Character Worksheet

Name: _____

Physical description:

Age: _____

Height and weight: _____

Eyes: _____

Hair: _____

Special abilities: _____

_____

Personal data:

Education: _____

Occupation: _____

Social class: _____

Religion: _____

Ethnicity: _____

Hobbies: _____

Marital status: _____

Children: _____

Friends: _____

_____

Ambitions: _____

_____

Family:

Place in family: _____

Immediate family members: _____

_____

Pets: _____

Personality:

Main personality traits: _____

Disposition: _____

Self-image: _____

Location, Location, Location: Setting

The *setting* of a story is the time and place where the events take place. Sometimes you will state the setting outright: "It was a dark and stormy night." Other times, however, you will have readers infer it from details in the story. You'll plant clues in the characters' speech, clothing, or means of transportation. To quote from Edgar Allan Poe, it depends on what "single effect" you want to create in your story.

A story's setting is always important, but some settings are more important than others. That's because in some cases the setting plays a leading role in the story; it becomes another character in the action. Certain short stories remain the same no matter where they take place. For example, almost every country in the world has a version of the Cinderella story.

But other times, the story has to take place during a specific time and place. This is true of the short stories of Jack London, where the frozen north is as important a character as the prospectors. It's also the case with Nathaniel Hawthorne's interminable stories of Puritan sin and guilt and John Updike's angst-filled stories of suburban infidelity.

Even when it doesn't play a leading role, setting can be used to create mood—even if the location isn't specific.

All the Write Stuff
Stuck for character traits? Here are some to get you started:

ambitious	lazy	brave
cruel	generous	gloomy
honest	loving	selfish
humble	dishonest	shy
loyal	patriotic	bold

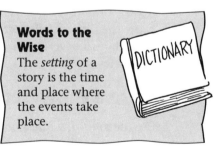

Words to the Wise
The *setting* of a story is the time and place where the events take place.

How can you tell how important the setting should be in your short story? The setting will be a major player if the main character is

➤ Challenging the elements

➤ Attempting to conquer the environment

101

➤ Escaping from a specific place

➤ Staying alive in a dangerous place

Build Me Up, Buttercup: Structure

Once you figure out who your character is and what he wants, you have to figure out why he or she can't get it. A character not getting what he or she wants also leads to conflict! That leads us to the next big decision you have to make, *structure*.

The structure of a story can be as loose as modern morality, but there must be something there to keep the reader reading. There has to be something more than the mere list of events or the writer's deep insight into the human condition. What makes us keep reading, what holds the words together, is like the melody in music. It's the structure.

Traditional short stories follow a very specific structure. They open by introducing the *setting* (time and place), *characters*, and *conflict*. As the story unfolds, the action builds (or rises) to the point of highest interest, the *climax*. Next, the events wind down through the falling action. Notice that the rising action is longer than the falling action. That allows the writer to eke out that last drop of suspense and tension. Last, the writer ties up all the loose ends in the *denouement*. Here's how a well-made story looks:

The structure of a well-made story.

Setting, Characters, Conflict

Climax

Denouement

This three-part structure—beginning/middle/end—dominated short story writing for centuries before experimental writers began to shake it up. As a result, in contemporary fiction, the structure of a short story can vary. For example, a single story can be narrated by several different characters. The story can begin with the end and end with the beginning. But whatever the arrangement of parts, there has to be a structure to hold it all together.

Asked and Answered

Use the following questions to narrow down your story and build its structure:

Answer each of these questions to structure your short story.

| Who? Characters _____ |
| What? Conflict _____ |
| When? Time _____ |

Where? Place _____

Why? Characters' motivation _____

How? Resolve the conflict _____

Story Triangle

The "story triangle" is another creative way to generate story ideas. Like the story maps that you used in Chapter 7, the story triangle helps you describe characters, events, and problems.

Follow these directions.

1. Name of main character

2. Two words describing the main character

3. Three words describing the setting

4. Four words describing the main problem

5. Five words describing first problem

6. Six words describing second problem

7. Seven words describing third problem

8. Eight words describing the solution

Now complete the worksheet to get your story humming.

1. _____

2. _____ _____

3. _____ _____ _____

4. _____ _____ _____ _____

5. _____ _____ _____ _____ _____

6. _____ _____ _____ _____ _____ _____

7. _____ _____ _____ _____ _____ _____ _____

8. _____ _____ _____ _____ _____ _____ _____ _____

Closing Arguments

So far, your story has plot, characters, and setting. You're almost home, bunky. Now it's time to do a little polishing to turn your wannabe into a winner. Submitted for your approval: style, titles, and endings. Let's look at each one in turn.

Show, Don't Tell

Make this your story-telling mantra. Bring the characters, conflict, and setting alive in your short stories by using sensory details. Describe how things taste, smell, look, feel, and sound. Use concrete details that help readers form vivid mental images. Here's an example:

> **No:** Nick enjoyed walking through country graveyards on fall afternoons. He enjoyed looking at the marble tablets with their ornate, old-fashioned inscriptions. They made him remember how sad he felt when his grandfather had died last year.

> **Yes:** I remember my grandfather's funeral, the hurried cross of sand the minister drew on the coffin lid, the whine of the lowering straps, the lengthening cleanly cut sides of clay, the lack of air forever in the close, dark lined pink satin.

The second example is more vivid because it appeals to the senses. Which ones? Read this chart to see:

Sense	Description
Sight:	"the lengthening cleanly cut sides of clay"
Sound:	"the whine of the lowering straps"
Smell:	"the lengthening cleanly cut sides of clay"
Touch:	"cross of sand the minister drew on the coffin lid," "the lack of air forever in the close, dark lined pink satin"

What's in a Name? Titles

Like a sign above the door, a title is your first chance to grab your readers. It should tantalize your readers and leave them panting for more. The famous British mystery writer Agatha Christie once used a snatch of overheard conversation for a title. What did she hear? "Why Didn't They Ask Evans?" So keep your ears open. Take this as your license to snoop.

There are five main types of short story titles:

➤ Labels

➤ Statements

➤ Questions

➤ Commands

➤ "Combo Platters" (such as a statement that functions as a label)

Wrong Turn
Some writing czars argue that a title should be no more than six words long. Pish-posh, I say to that. A title should be as long—or as short—as it takes to do the job.

It All Comes Out in the End

Your readers will hate you if your story's resolution isn't logical. Don't depend on coincidence to resolve the conflict. None of this "Thank goodness we won the lottery and saved the farm!" stuff. Nix also on "So you're the long-lost cousin I've been searching for all this time?"

And none of this "And then they woke up and it was all a dream" stuff, either. It's just plain lazy.

Are We There Yet?

Are you ready to write your short story? Ready or not, here you go. Use this checklist to make sure you've included everything you need to pen a prize-winning short story.

_____ 1. Have you decided what type of short story you're writing? (a short story, a short short story, or a flash)

_____ 2. Have you worked out the conflict?

_____ 3. Do you have a protagonist and an antagonist?

_____ 4. Have you established the time and place for the action?

_____ 5. Have you structured your story with a clear beginning, middle, and end?

_____ 6. Is the conflict resolved in a logical way?

_____ 7. Have you identified your audience?

_____ 8. Did you "show, not tell" by using description?

_____ 9. Did you create a tantalizing title?

_____ 10. Did you revise and edit your work as you learned in Part 1 of this book?

Must you be as prepared as a Boy Scout when you write a short story? No. You don't have to do all this preparation every time you sit down to write a short story. If you're going somewhere you've been many times before, you won't need a detailed map. But if you're exploring uncharted regions, you'll want to prepare. If you have all the time in the world, by all means enjoy yourself writing. But if you have to meet professional and personal obligations, doing the advance work can save you a great deal of time, effort, and frustration.

Some short story writers claim they never know where the story will go when they start it. I don't doubt this technique works well for them, but then again, I also believe Richard Nixon wasn't a crook, the check is in the mail, and there's another train right behind this one. I'll argue that writers who claim they don't plan *on paper* have done a great deal of planning *in their heads* before they started putting pen to paper. They also tend to gloss over all their false starts and wasted time.

I suggest that you experiment with the suggestions I've given you. See what works for your personal style. Here's the key: roll with the punches. Be flexible. Don't get yourself boxed into your planning notes. Think about what you want to achieve in your story and then choose the best way to accomplish your aim.

The Least You Need to Know

➤ In fiction, a *conflict* is a struggle or fight.

➤ The *protagonist* is the main character; an *antagonist* is the force or person in conflict with the main character.

➤ The *setting* of a story is the time and place.

➤ Character + conflict + resolution = story.

➤ Show, don't tell; create logical endings; and look both ways before crossing the street.

Chapter 9

For Better or Verse: Poetry

In This Chapter

➤ Define poetry

➤ Learn about the different poetic forms

➤ Pick the poetic techniques you need

➤ Write a poem

Poetry is one of the oldest arts, and until very recently, one of the most important ones. In olden days, poetry was as crucial as food, shelter, clothing, and super-premium ice cream (even though the latter hadn't been invented yet). Poetry was recited at important public occasions and learned by educated people as a part of their basic intellectual equipment.

A century ago, anyone aspiring to become a writer would, as a matter of course, practice writing poems, for they were considered the best way for a writer to learn order and discipline. To learn how to write an acceptable poem was to learn how to create art.

Today, poetry's place in the world has changed more radically than Dennis Rodman's hair color. In the past seventy-five to one hundred years, poetry has declined from a noble art to become the bailiwick of small-time academics jostling each other for tenure. Poetry has lost its importance and much of its audience. Fortunately, large and small publishing houses still publish some poetry and a humble, hardy, and faithful band still read it.

In this chapter, I'll first teach you the basics of poetry. Then comes a detailed description of different poetic forms so you can decide which ones are right for your taste and talent. Throughout the chapter, I provide specific examples of famous poems that you can use as models. Finally, I'll have you write a little poem to get those creative juices flowing.

What Is Poetry and Why Should I Write It?

Poetry is like sex appeal: it's hard to define, but we know it when we see it. Edgar Allan Poe believed that poetry was "the rhythmical creation of beauty"; to Robert Frost, poetry was "a reaching out toward expression, an effort to find fulfillment." Percy Bysshe Shelley wrote that "Poetry is the record of the best and happiest moments of the best minds, the very image of life expressed in its eternal truth."

Try these definitions of poetry. See which suits your vision of your craft. Poetry is a type of literature

➤ In which words are selected for their beauty, sound, and power to express feelings

➤ That uses a kind of language that is more intense and expressive than everyday speech

➤ That presents the speaker's emotions as they are aroused by beauty, experience, or attachment

➤ That provides a fresh, unexpected way of looking at things

➤ That gives pleasure, whether it appeals to the senses, emotion, or intellect

Bet You Didn't Know

The word "poem" comes from an ancient Greek word meaning "to make, compose." The implication is important: poetry is made and the poet is the maker. The word *made* suggests materials; the word *maker* suggests effort.

To Emily Dickinson, poetry was

> ...my letter to the World
> That never wrote to Me—
> The simple News that Nature Told—
> With tender Majesty
> Her Message is committed
> To Hands I cannot see
> For love of Her—Sweet—countrymen—
> Judge tenderly—of Me.

A Real Slugfest: Poetry vs. Prose

"Prose," claimed Samuel Taylor Coleridge, "consists of words in their best order. Poetry consists of the *best* words in the *best* order." The primary difference between poetry and prose is *concreteness*. A single word of poetry says far more than a single word of prose. That's because the language in poetry resonates worlds of other meaning. In a sense, the poet distills meaning in brief and vivid phrases. The poet's use of economy and suggestion evoke response in the reader.

Taking the Road Less Traveled By: Becoming a Poet

It's not easy to write poetry (especially in today's world!), and most people aren't willing to do that much work for what seems like so little reward. But if you can write a single sonnet to equal one of Shakespeare's, you can forever call yourself a writer.

But regardless of what poems you eventually produce, writing poetry is crucial to your progress as a creative writer. Learning to work within strict forms, finding effective rhythms, selecting and using words properly, and constructing poems carefully will make you a better writer in any genre.

Walk the Walk and Talk the Talk

Since poetry comes in a wide range of forms, from haiku to rock lyrics, it's not a simple genre to define. Fortunately, we *can* put our finger on the elements that distinguish poetry from prose, so you can tell what you're writing and learn to write it with more precision.

Studying the following Big Three poetic terms and their definitions can help you learn to color in the lines on the blank canvas.

1. *Couplet*: two related lines of poetry, which often rhyme.

   True wit is Nature to advantage dressed,
   What oft was thought, but ne'er so well expressed.

   Alexander Pope

2. *Refrain*: a line or a group of lines that are repeated at the end of a poem or song. Refrains serve to reinforce the main point and create musical effects. Folk singer Harry Chapin used a refrain at the end of each verse of his ballad "Cat's Cradle":

   Cat's in the cradle and the silver spoon
   Little boy blue and the man in the moon...

3. *Stanza:* a group of lines in a poem, like a paragraph in prose. Each stanza presents one complete idea. Here's a stanza of poetry from Alexander Pope's *An Essay on Criticism:*

   True ease in writing comes from art, not chance,
   As those move easiest who have learned to dance.
   'Tis not enough no harshness gives offense,
   The sound must seem an echo of the sense.

The March of Time

As conversation has given way to sound bites and facts to factoids, so the style of poetry has changed over the years. What was the creme de la creme of poetry in the past strikes some modern readers as sour milk.

Here's a stanza from an early nineteenth-century poem called "A Tender Lay." The title alone is a hoot.

Be gentle to the new laid egg,
For eggs are brilliant things;
They cannot fly until they're hatched,
And have a pair of wings.

Some modern readers would consider this snippet as sappy as *Miracle on 34th Street* or *It's a Wonderful Life*. It's too mushy for jaded modern literary taste, like marshmallow fluff on white bread.

Mommy Dearest

Now, here's a stanza from an Emily Dickinson poem. Even though Emily lived in the nineteenth century (1830–1886), she went her own way. How similar is this poem to your poetic style?

> What shall I do when the Summer troubles—
> What, when the Rose is ripe—
> What when the Eggs fly off in Music
> From the Maple Keep?

Dickinson's poems do not always rhyme, and her figurative language was too striking for the taste of her time. As a result, of her 1,775 poems, only seven were published during her lifetime—and all anonymously. It wasn't until 1955 that Dickinson's poems were accepted and even appreciated. Now Emily Dickinson is considered the Founding Mother of American Poetry, revered for her concrete imagery, forceful language, and unique style.

Do Your Own Thing

What does this mean for you, an aspiring poet? It means that you can study poems in magazines such as *The New Yorker, The Atlantic Monthly, Poetry, Quarterly West, Prairie Schooner,* and *Harpers* to see what today's poetry editors are buying in the big market magazines. Or, you can write what you wish. You're just as likely to find a publisher—and your poetry will be more honest.

Fortunately, poetry is a matter of individual taste. There is something to suit everyone. Don't let anyone box your muse into a poetic parcel. With poetry, individual voice, wrapped up in craftsmanship, is the whole point. Some people feel that modern poetry can be totally random if it's heartfelt, but in fact, even the most random-seeming language must be carefully crafted if it's to be good poetry.

> **All the Write Stuff**
> One of the most important resources for poets of all stripes is *Poets and Writers Magazine* (Poets and Writers, 72 Spring Street, New York, NY 10012). This journal includes interviews with poets and writers, articles by editors, lists of grants and awards, and ads from publishers seeking poems for magazines, chapbooks, and anthologies.

Remembrance of Flings Past: Poetic Techniques

A good poet has as many tools and strict procedures as any handyman, even though in good poetry that structure may not be forced and obvious. Below is a list of the most useful poetic techniques. Mastering them will teach you why something poetic works on paper—and why it doesn't. You may use all of these techniques all the time, but it's more likely that you'll pick and choose depending on the subject, purpose, and audience in each poem.

Alliteration

Alliteration is the repetition of initial consonant sounds in several words in a sentence or line of poetry. Poets use alliteration to create musical effects, link related ideas, stress certain words, or mimic specific sounds. Here's an example from Dylan Thomas's "Fern Hill": "About the lilting house and happy as the grass was green." The phrase shows alliteration in the repetition of the *h* in *house* and *happy* and the *gr* in *grass* and *green.*

Blank Verse

Blank verse is unrhymed poetry, usually written in iambic pentameter (see the section titled "Meter" for a discussion of iambic pentameter). Many English poets wrote in blank verse because it captures the natural rhythm of speech. Here's an example by William Shakespeare: "Time hath, my Lord, a wallet at his back,/Wherein he puts alms for oblivion."

Bet You Didn't Know

The four Brontë siblings—Anne, Charlotte, Emily, and Branwell—collaborated on an early book of verse, the Gondal poems. Unfortunately, the book sold only two copies—a publishing record that may still stand.

Catalog

The *catalog technique* in poetry predates L.L. Bean and Victoria's Secret—Homer used it around 800 B.C., John Milton in the seventeenth century, and greedy children still use it around Christmas. It's nothing more than a list, but when used with brio, it's as overwhelming as Toys "R" Us on Christmas Eve.

Use Sonnet #43 from Elizabeth Barrett Browning's famous *Sonnets from the Portuguese* as a model of the catalog. The sonnet lists the ways she loves her husband.

> How do I love thee? Let me count the ways.
> I love thee to the depth and breadth and height
> My soul can reach, when feeling out of sight
> For the ends of Being and ideal Grace.

I love thee to the level of everyday's
Most quiet need, by sun and candlelight.
I love thee freely, as men strive for Right;
I love thee purely, as they turn from Praise.
I love thee with the passion put to use
In my old griefs, and with my childhood's faith.
I love thee with a love I seemed to lose
With my lost saints—I love thee with the breath,
Smiles, tears, of all my life!—and, if God choose,
I shall but love thee better after death.

(1845–47)

Bet You Didn't Know

Elizabeth Barrett Browning (1806–1861) was England's most famous female poet during her lifetime. The woman's poetry was smokin'. She's most famous for *Sonnets from the Portuguese*, forty-four sonnets that record her love for husband (and fellow poet) Robert Browning.

Figurative Language

Figurative language consists of words and expressions not meant to be taken literally. Figurative language uses words in fresh, new ways to appeal to the imagination. Figures of speech include *similes, metaphors, extended metaphors, hyperbole,* and *personification.* These were discussed in previous chapters. They're also covered in the "Glossary of Writing Terms."

Images

An *image* is a word that appeals to one or more of our five senses: sight, hearing, taste, touch, or smell. Imagery can be found in all sorts of writing, but it's most common in poetry. The term "imagery" comes from the Imagism movement, which flourished during the early part of the twentieth century.

As sleek and stripped down as Sharon Stone, Imagism hawked radical and original images and hard truths. Shunning rhythm and rhyme, the Imagists depended on the power of the image itself

All the Write Stuff

Want to meet fellow poets? Then consider linking up with the Poetry Society of America (15 Gramercy Park, New York, NY 10003). Membership dues begin at $25 per year for students. The Society sponsors several annual poetry awards.

to arrest attention and convey emotion. Here is a classic Imagist poem by Ezra Pound (1885–1972), who penned some interesting poetry when he wasn't busy being a traitor:

> In a Station of the Metro
>
> The apparition of these faces in the crowd;
> Petals on a wet, black bough.
>
> (1913)

Meter

In life, a meter is an odd-shaped device that demands quarters on a regular basis. In writing, *meter* is a poem's rhythmical pattern.

Bet You Didn't Know

The most common meter in English poetry is called *iambic pentameter*. It is a pattern of five feet, each having one unstressed syllable and one stressed one.

Poetic meter is created by a pattern of stressed and unstressed syllables arranged in metrical *feet*. A poetic *foot* is a group of stressed and unstressed syllables in a line of poetry. A foot is composed of either two or three syllables, such that the nature of the foot is determined by the placement of the accent. There are six basic types of metrical feet in English. The first four are very common; the last two are as rare as a really bad hair day:

Poetic foot	Symbol	Definition
iamb	∪ ´	1 unstressed, 1 stressed syllable
anapest	∪ ∪ ´	2 unstressed, 1 stressed syllable
trochee	´ ∪	1 stressed, 1 unstressed syllable
dactyl	´ ∪ ∪	1 stressed, 2 unstressed syllables
spondee	´ ´	2 stressed syllables
pyrrhic	∪ ∪	2 unstressed syllables

Here are some examples:

Iamb	I taste/a liq/uor/nev/er brewed
Anapest	The Assyr/ian came down/like the wolf/on the fold
Trochee	Earth, re/ceive an/honored/guest
Dactyl	Out of the/cradle/endlessly/ rocking

All the Write Stuff
To *scan* a poem is to figure out its meter—its pattern of stressed and unstressed syllables.

Onomatopoeia

Onomatopoeia is the use of words to imitate the sounds they describe. Here are three examples: *crack, hiss,* and *buzz*. Onomatopoeia is used to create musical effects and to reinforce meaning. Contemporary Irish poet Seamus Heaney uses onomatopoeia in his poem "Churning Day" to suggest the sounds of butter-making:

> My mother took turn first, set up rhythms
> that slugged and thumped for hours. Arms ached.
> Hands blistered. Cheeks and clothes were splattered
> with flabbymilk.

Rock Around the Clock: Rhyme

Rhyme is the repetition of sounds at the end of words. Rhyming the last line of poems creates "end rhyme"; rhyming words in the middle of lines creates "internal rhyme." Here is an example of internal rhyme: "Each narrow cell in which we dwell." *Cell* and *dwell* have internal rhyme because they share the same sound and one of the words is set in the middle of the line. The *rhyme scheme* in a poem is a regular pattern of words that end with the same sound.

Here's some nifty end rhyme for you, courtesy of our old buddy William Blake:

> I was angry with my friend:
> I told my wrath, my wrath did end.
> I was angry with my foe:
> I told it not, my wrath did grow.

Friend rhymes with *end*; *foe* rhymes with *grow*.

Poets use rhyme to create a musical sound, meaning, and structure. Nowadays, except for Hallmark™ cards, rhyme is as out as John Denver, Crisco™, and laugh lines. But there are those of us who like John Denver, Crisco, and laugh lines. To thine own self be true; there's nothing wrong with sticking by your style—even if it's out of style at the moment. Who knows what tomorrow will bring?

Groovin' to the Beat: Rhythm

Rhythm is the pattern of stressed and unstressed words that create a beat, as in music. Rhythm is created by poetic meter. When you write a poem, use the punctuation and capitalization in each line to help your reader decide where to pause and what words to stress to make the rhythm clear. Traditional poetry follows a regular rhythmical pattern; much of modern poetry does not.

Bet You Didn't Know

Prose, as well as poetry, has rhythm. The artful arrangement of words creates a graceful, seemingly artless flow of ideas. Read your favorite novel out loud to see if you can sense the writer's rhythm.

31 Flavors and 57 Varieties

Poetry takes all life as its realm. Its main concern is not with beauty, moral truth, or persuasion, but with experience. Beauty and truth are parts of experience, and so poetry often interprets them. But poetry as a whole is concerned with all types of experience— the good and the bad, the beautiful and the ugly, the strange and the common.

To embrace all these themes, poetry must take a variety of different forms. While some famous poets have become closely linked to specific forms (Shakespeare and the sonnet, Dylan Thomas and the villanelle, Robert Frost and the lyric), others experiment with many different forms. I suggest that you do the same. Try 'em all and see which ones suit your style, audience, and purpose.

Ballads

A *ballad* is a story told in song form. Ancient ballads such as "Sir Patrick Spens" were passed down by word of mouth from person to person; as a result, the words are simple and the ballad has a strong beat. Two of the most famous literary ballads are Coleridge's "Rime of the Ancient Mariner" and Keats's "La Belle Dame Sans Merci." They are both way too long to reprint here, but make great models for your own ballads.

Epics

These are long narratives in an elevated style, presenting high-born characters in a series of adventures that depict key events in the history of a nation. Homer's *Iliad* and *Odyssey* are epics. I know you have both of these memorized.

Free Verse

Free verse isn't poetry marked down for a quick sale. Rather, it's poetry without a regular pattern of rhyme and meter. This kind of verse uses a rhythm that reinforces the meaning and sounds of spoken language in lines of different length. Walt Whitman (1819–1892) gets the nod as the inventor of the form. (Noted word slinger Robert Frost, a good ol' boy from Vermont, said that writing free verse is like playing tennis with the net down.) Here's a sample of Whitman's free verse, the opening lines of "Out of the Cradle, Endlessly Rocking." Notice the strong rhythm, uneven lines, repetition, and alliteration:

> Out of the cradle, endlessly rocking,
> Out of the mocking-bird's throat, the musical shuttle,
> Out of the Ninth-month midnight,
> Over the sterile sands and the fields beyond where the child leaving his bed wandered alone, bareheaded, barefoot…

Haiku

Haiku is a Japanese poetic form that uses three lines for a total of seventeen syllables. The first and third lines have five syllables each; the second line has seven syllables. Haiku creates a distinct emotion and suggests a spiritual insight, often through images from nature. Use the following two samples as models. They were written by the Japanese poet Moritake (1452–1540).

> The falling flower
> I saw drift back to the branch
> Was a butterfly.

> Fallen flowers rise
> back to the branch—I watch:
> oh…butterflies!

Hooked on Sonnets

A *sonnet* is a lyric poem of fourteen lines written in iambic pentameter (a rhythm with five accents in each line.) Originated by Italian poets during the thirteenth century, the form reached perfection a century later in the works of Petrarch and came to be known as the "Petrarchan" or "Italian" sonnet.

To scan the rhyme, assign a letter to each new sound. For example, if line #1 ends with "oe'r," give it the letter *a*. If line #2 ends with "bed," assign the letter *b*. If line #3 ends with "led," assign *b*, because "bed" and "led" have the same sound. And so on.

The first eight lines, called the "octave," rhyme a-b-b-a, a-b-b-a, and present the problem; the concluding six lines, called the "sestet," rhyme c-d-e, c-d-e, and resolve the problem.

Here's a Petrarchan sonnet by Henry Wadsworth Longfellow you can use to learn the form. You might wish to scan the rhyme by assigning a letter to each end sound.

Nature

As a fond mother, when the day is o'er,
Leads by the hand her little child to bed,
Half willing, half reluctant to be led,
And leave his broken playthings on the floor,
Still gazing at them through the open door,
Nor wholly reassured and comforted
By promises of others in their stead,
Which, though more splendid, may not please him more;
So Nature deals with us, and takes away
Our playthings one by one, and by the hand
Leads us to rest so gently, that we go
Scarce knowing if we wish to go or stay,
Being too full of sleep to understand
How far the unknown transcends the what we know.

See how "Nature" uses these features of the Petrarchan sonnet:

➤ Structure: The octave presents the problem—an unwillingness to let go of life. The sestet resolves the problem—death is not to be feared because of the unimaginable glories of heaven.

➤ Length: There are 14 lines.

➤ Rhythm: The sonnet is iambic pentameter because it has five accents in each line and uses the unstressed/stressed pattern.

➤ Rhyme: Here is the rhyme scheme:

Word	Rhyme
o'er	a
bed	b
led	b
floor	a
door	a
comforted	b
stead	b
more	a
away	c
hand	d
go	e
stay	c
understand	d
know	e

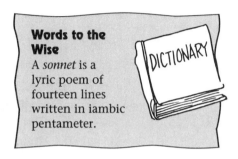

Words to the Wise
A *sonnet* is a lyric poem of fourteen lines written in iambic pentameter.

Sixteenth-century English poets swiped the sonnet format but changed the rhyme to a-b-a-b, c-d-c-d, e-f-e-f, g-g. With the "Elizabethan" (or "Shakespearean") sonnet, the poet describes the problem in the first twelve lines and resolves it in the final couplet. Shakespeare pounced on the form and succeeded in doing for the love sonnet what Godiva did for chocolate.

Here's an English sonnet by Edna St. Vincent Millay that will help you learn this poetic form:

Pity Me Not

Pity me not because the light of day
At close of day no longer walks the sky;
Pity me not for beauties passed away
From field and thicket as the year goes by;
Pity me not the waning of the moon,
Nor that the ebbing tide goes out to sea,
Nor that a man's desire is hushed so soon,
And you no longer look with love on me.
This I have known always: Love is no more
Than the wide blossom which the wind assails,
Than the great tide that treads the shifting shore,
Strewing fresh wreckage gathered in the gales;
Pity me that the heart is slow to learn
What the swift mind beholds at every turn.

Let's analyze the form so you can make it your own:

➤ Structure: The first twelve lines describe the situation—the poet is growing older and her lover no longer desires her. The final couplet resolves the problem—At last, I understand what is happening in my life with my heart as well as with my mind.

➤ Length: There are 14 lines.

➤ Rhythm: The sonnet is iambic pentameter because it has five accents in each line and uses the unstressed/stressed pattern.

➤ Rhyme: Here is the rhyme scheme:

Word	Rhyme
day	a
sky	b
away	a
by	b
moon	c
sea	d
soon	c
me	d
more	e
assails	f
shore	e
gales	f
learn	g
turn	g

Limerick

A *limerick* is a type of humorous poetry. Limericks have five lines, a strong rhyme, and a set rhythm—*aabba*. The first, second, and fifth lines rhyme with each other, and the third and fourth rhyme with each other. The rhyming words are sometimes misspelled to create humor. Most limericks are bawdy; the clean ones usually don't involve buckets and girls from Nantucket. I had to look far and wide to find a limerick clean enough to reprint that didn't involve buckets and Nantucket:

> There was a young lady of Lynn
> Who was so uncommonly thin
> That when she essayed
> To drink lemonade
> She slipped through the straw and fell in.

Nearly all limericks are anonymous. If not written anonymously, they soon become so, because of repeated oral transmission and reprinting without credit. This is unfortunate for the glory of their hard-working writers—people like you.

Lyric Poetry

Poet Emily Dickinson, who made the Phantom of the Opera look like a party animal, was a champ at writing lyric poems. These are brief, musical poems that present a speaker's feelings. In the distant past, before Spandex and Pez, people sang lyrics as they played string-like instruments called "lyres." This is where we get the word "lyric."

Narrative Poetry

Narrative poetry tells a story, either through a narrative storyline told objectively or through a dramatized situation. Examples of narrative story lines include Alfred Noye's "The Highwayman" and Robert Browning's "The Pied Piper of Hamelin." An example of the dramatized situation is Robert Frost's poem "The Death of the Hired Man."

A special form of the dramatized situation is the *dramatic monologue*, in which a character speaks, using the first person point of view. We don't hear the other character's responses, but we can infer them from hints in the poem. It's like listening to one end of a phone conversation. Use Robert Browning's "My Last Duchess" as a model.

> **All the Write Stuff**
> For a good, general poetry collection, try the Norton anthologies (W.W. Norton, New York, NY). Norton has a whole series of nifty books, including *The Norton Anthology of American Literature, The Norton Anthology of English Literature,* and *The Norton Anthology of World Masterpieces.* They're all available in paperback editions.

Give It a Shot

You've read enough; it's time to flex your poetic muscles and do some heavy word lifting. Use the following guidelines to write a poem about yourself. Then feel free to adapt the format to create other poems.

Line 1: Your first name _____

Line 2: Four traits that describe you _____

Line 3: Relative of..._____

continues

continued

Line 4: Lover of..._____(3 people or ideas)

Line 5: Who feels _____(3 responses)

Line 6: Who needs _____(3 responses)

Line 7: Who gives _____(3 responses)

Line 8: Who fears _____(3 responses)

Line 9: Who would like to see _____(3 responses)

Line 10: Resident of _____(city, etc.)

Line 11: Your last name _____

The Least You Need to Know

➤ Everyone defines poetry a different way: take it as "a type of literature in which words are selected for their beauty, sound, and power to express emotion."

➤ There is a wide variety of poetic forms and styles; feel free to express yourself—but learn the techniques and forms.

➤ As Archibald MacLeish said in his poem "Ars Poetica,"

A poem should not mean
But be.

Part 3
Nonfiction

"I don't care what's written about me as long as it isn't true," 1930s wit Dorothy Parker claimed. We'll stick pretty close to the truth here, Ms. Parker—after all, nonfiction is writing that describes real people and events.

Nonfiction can take many forms: biographies, autobiographies, textbooks, articles, instruction, inspiration, newspaper articles, and letters. Each form has its own structural requirements, but their basis is the same: writing that sets up a proposition, defends it, and proves it. That's what you'll learn here…and a whole lot more!

Chapter 10

Whose Life Is It, Anyway? Writing Biographies and Autobiographies

In This Chapter

➤ Define biography and autobiography

➤ Learn what writing elements biography and autobiography share with their cousin, fiction

➤ Write a biography and autobiography step-by-step

➤ Research to get the background facts you need

"The business of the biographer," Samuel Johnson said, "is to lead the thoughts into domestic privacies and display the minute details of daily life." Johnson's own biographer, James Boswell, wanted his readers to see the subject "live and live o'er each scene with him, as he actually advanced through the several stages of his life." The biographer's aim is still the same today.

In this chapter, you'll first learn what biography and autobiography are. Then I'll show you what elements of fiction creative biographers and autobiographers have appropriated for their own—and why. Then comes a discussion of the problems and pitfalls of writing a bio of a living person. Next I'll show you how to get started on your manuscript.

Finally, I'll take you step-by-step through the research process, so you can get what you need to make your subject a living, breathing presence on the page.

Peeping Toms

Right now, biography and autobiography are so hot they're *smokin'*. According to a recent survey conducted by the Library of Congress, more people have read a biography in the past six months than any other kind of book. What makes biography (and autobiography) so popular? Here are some possibilities to consider:

➤ We're a nation of shameless voyeurs, insatiably curious about other people's lives.

➤ A well-written biography or autobiography is a work of art.

➤ A good biography or autobiography is basically an adventure story, and everyone likes those.

➤ Biography and autobiography create a prism of history through which an age is refracted.

➤ Biography and autobiography make us feel the subject's struggles, successes, and failures as though they were our own.

Laying the Foundation

The word *biography* comes from two Greek words, *bio* ("life") and *graphies* ("writing"). A *biography* is a true story about a person's life written by another person. Effective biographies paint a complete picture of the person, telling about his or her flaws as well as admirable traits. In so doing, you'll also present your own interpretations of these facts, explaining both the reasons for your subjects' actions and the meaning of their lives.

Invasion of the Body Snatchers: Biography

Biographies are often written about well-known, important people, such as world leaders, scientists, movie stars, and athletes. Fortunately, for every bio of Socks the First Cat, Dr. Death, and Dennis Rodman, we get a volume on Eleanor Roosevelt, Martin Luther King Jr., and Albert Einstein.

Bios can be written about minor public figures as well, those among us who have had a less obvious but still weighty influence on the world. These subjects range from the writer's parents, children, and assorted relatives to local figures of interest. There have even been bios on legendary, mythical, and fictitious subjects: for example, Grendel the Monster in the Old English epic *Beowulf* had his fifteen minutes of print fame in a wonderful "biography" by John Gardner.

Letting It All Hang Out: Autobiographies

An autobiography, in contrast, is a person's own story of his or her life. It tells the writer's feelings and thoughts about the people, places, and things that are important in his or her life. Writers of autobiographies often share their thoughts and feelings and the effect of certain events on their lives. This allows readers to share closely in the life of the subject.

Autobiography is supposed to be a type of nonfiction, but there is often considerable latitude between how the subject sees his or her life and how others see it. Some people call this "artistic license"; others call it "spin doctoring." I call it dramatic and desirable. Who wants to read a dull story?

Which Biography Is for You?

Before we go any further, it's important to distinguish among the different kinds of biographies—*critical biographies, scholarly biographies,* and *general biographies*. That's the one that's fun to read.

Let's Get Critical: Critical Biography

In this type of biography, the writer analyzes his or her subject. The tone is detached and even skeptical. These bios are intellectual, not emotional; psychoanalytical, not popular. The subject does not spring to life, for that's not the writer's purpose. Rather, with this type of bio, the writer seeks to create a critical discussion, not art.

Cracking the Books: Scholarly Biography

The scholarly bio is a straightforward compilation of facts. The tone is usually detached and even-handed, often as dry as sawdust. These bios offer piles of information about their subjects, but rarely a powerful story.

Words to the Wise
A biography is a true story about a person's life written by another person. An autobiography is a person's own story of his or her life.

All the Write Stuff
How close should you, as the biographer, get to your subject? Some biographers call for detachment and distance; others stump for compassion and even love. It's your call, depending on your subject and intended audience.

Bet You Didn't Know

There's a subcategory: a definitive biography. It includes everything possible to know about the subject. Definitive bios are usually the result of a lifetime of study. Examples include Leon Edel's five-volume biography of Henry James and Carl Sandburg's massive work on Abraham Lincoln.

Bio R You

A pure biography or autobiography—what you'll be writing as soon as you finish this chapter—tells a person's life story. It's a re-creation of a person's life and times. Kitty Kelly did a nice job with Ol' Blue Eyes, Frank Sinatra; Robert Caro's prize-winning bio of power broker Robert Moses was masterful. Check out the recent bio on Harry Truman, too. It's a real requiem for a heavyweight.

All the Write Stuff

As you write your biography or autobiography, you'll also use revealing quotations and dramatic narration to give the reader a sense of a life unfolding.

You will give your subject center stage, with just enough historical context to set the scene. While you will have to provide some psychological insights to flesh out the bones of your narrative, you'll be careful not to lapse into critical commentary or psychobabble. It boils down to the business of telling a story. You'll aim to engage your readers' hearts as well as their minds, to draw your readers into the subject's life. By the end of the story, your readers should feel they know your subject intimately. They may even feel a sense of loss at his or her death.

The Fab Five

As a biographer or autobiographer, your job is to elicit, from the coldness of paper, the warmth of a life being lived. How can you do this? Effective biography and autobiography employ fictional techniques you learned in Chapters 7 and 8—*characterization, detail, order, point of view,* and *tone*—without resorting to fiction itself. You'll tread a fine line between nonfiction and fiction, reality and storytelling.

Getting to Know You: Characterization

Characterization is the way a writer presents the characters. As a biographer or autobiographer, you will use many of the same methods short story and novel writers do to make their subjects come to life. Here are two such methods: *direct* and *indirect characterization*.

➤ *Direct characterization* takes place when you tell how the character looks, acts, and thinks. You state it outright, about as subtle as Madonna but not nearly as firm.

➤ *Indirect characterization* takes place when you let your readers draw their own conclusions about a character. For example, you might show how other characters react to this person.

Details, Details, Details

Detail provides pieces of information. Writers of biography and autobiography use details to give the actual facts about a person's life. These details come from many sources:

➤ Letters

➤ Interviews

➤ The subject's own writings

➤ Diaries

Biographies do more than just relate details, however. The details that you choose, arrange, and examine help communicate your own opinions and character as well as those of your subject.

All the Write Stuff
Our top twentieth-century biographers include Carl Sandburg (biographer of Abraham Lincoln), Justin Kaplan (Mark Twain), Leon Edel (Henry James), Mark Schorer (D. H. Lawrence), and Barbara Tuchman (two-time Pulitzer Prize winner for bio).

Read their work and use it as a model for your own.

Order in the Book!

Order is the arrangement of events in a work of literature. Most biographies and autobiographies use *chronological order*, the order of time. In a comprehensive biography, you list the major events of the subject's life from birth to death in chronological order. However, bios and autobios may use *flashbacks* to help fill in missing information, explain the characters' actions, and advance the story.

Point of View

Point of view is the standpoint from which a story is told. Nearly all biographies are told from the *third-person point of view*. With this point of view:

➤ The narrator is not a character in the biography.

➤ You will use the pronouns *he, she,* and *they.*

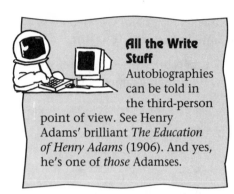

All the Write Stuff
Autobiographies can be told in the third-person point of view. See Henry Adams' brilliant *The Education of Henry Adams* (1906). And yes, he's one of *those* Adamses.

Autobiographies, in contrast, are usually told from the *first-person point of view:*

➤ Here, the narrator is one of the characters in the story.

➤ The narrator explains the events through his or her own eyes, using the pronouns *I, me,* and *mine.* Readers know only what the writer remembered, felt, and saw through his or her own experiences.

Tone

Tone is the writer's attitude toward his or her subject matter. For example, the tone of a biography can be admiring or critical, fawning or hostile. Many biographers start with a reverential attitude toward their subject, become antagonistic as the work bogs down, and end on a worshipful note. Keep an even tone as you write.

Here's part of an autobiography that a ghostwriter wrote about actor and body-builder Arnold Schwarzenegger's early life. As you read it, analyze the uplifting tone. Doesn't it make you want to run out and bench press 300 pounds?

First, call me Arnold.

I was born in a little Austrian town, outside Graz. It was a 300-year-old house.

When I was ten years old, I had the dream of being the best in the world in something. When I was fifteen, I had a dream that I wanted to be the best body builder in the world and the most muscular man. It was not only a dream I dreamed at night. It was also a daydream. It was so much in my mind that I felt it had to become a reality. It took me five years of hard work. Five years later, I turned this dream into reality and became Mr. Universe, the best-built man in the world....

When I was a small boy, my dream was not to be big physically, but big in a way that everybody listens to me when I talk, that I'm a very important person, that people recognize me and see me as someone special. I had a big need for being singled out.

Role Model

He received me very courteously; but it must be confessed that his apartment, and furniture, and morning dress, were sufficiently uncouth. His brown suit of clothes looked very rusty; he had on a little old shriveled unpowdered wig, which was too small for his head; his shirt neck and knees of his breeches were loose; his black worsted stockings ill drawn up; and he had a pair of unbuckled shoes by way of slippers. But all these slovenly particulars were forgotten the moment that he began to talk.

Published in 1791, James Boswell's *The Life of Samuel Johnson, LL.D.* is still the greatest biography in English. Boswell is to biographers what Mickey is to mice: the *sine qua non*.

With Boswell's bio, don't look for a storyline. Instead, think of the book as a late-night talk show with an especially entertaining guest and an interviewer who knows enough to shut up and listen.

Boswell's bio is so lively that you'll feel you're being whisked from commercial to commercial without time for a beer. Johnson is drawn so convincingly that you'll think you've spent a month in the country together. And you'll wish you had. Boswell's characterization and tone are rarely equaled, never surpassed.

Now, part of Boswell's genius was picking the right subject for his life's work; Johnson was a lot more literate than our modern wits: Ren and Stimpy, Bill and Ted, Beavis and Butt-head. Johnson was not only a great conversationalist but the author of the *Dictionary of the English Language*—which he wrote, alone, over eight years—after reading every important piece of English literature from the sixteenth century to his own day. Boswell's prodigious memory, diligence, and style catapulted biography from sleepy backwater form to a major player.

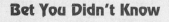

Bet You Didn't Know

Here's a classic bit of Johnsonese from Boswell's bio that applies to the writer as well as the libertine: "Were it not for imagination, sir, a man would be as happy in the arms of a chambermaid as a duchess."

Magical Misery Tour

There is a living hell inhabited by biographers who dare to write about famous people who are neither consenting or dead. The economics of publishing today has put pressure on biographers to select living subjects in place of the nice safe dead ones. The problem is that living ones tend to say no, early and often. They swear their friends to secrecy, too. Trying to write about these subjects, people like Woody Allen and J.D. Salinger, is a demoralizing and difficult process—with no sure pay-off in the end. This can make the biographer's life less than peachy.

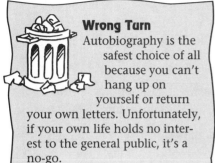

Wrong Turn
Autobiography is the safest choice of all because you can't hang up on yourself or return your own letters. Unfortunately, if your own life holds no interest to the general public, it's a no-go.

All the Write Stuff
Some biographers argue that only by retracing the subject's steps can you make the person come alive. It worked for me when I wrote on Laura Ingalls Wilder. I trekked across the midwest to visit every Wilder home, planted new apple trees, made some bread, and thanked my lucky stars my father was an engineer rather than a homesteader.

Why would anyone do this? First off, no one ever expects this kind of hell. Many of these biographers sincerely admire their subjects, which include movie star Woody Allen and writers Eudora Welty and Doris Lessing. Who imagines that a source will hang up when biographers call and grovel? Who imagines subjects will return fawning letters—unopened? Subjects also cut off all access to their papers, refuse rights to quote from their own writings, and invoke copyright laws.

Let this be a warning to you: Think very carefully when you select a subject for your biography. You'll be spending three or four years "living" with this person. A famous dead person is a safer choice; after all, the dead can't sue you. You'll only have to contend with their heirs and estate.

Don't Go There

Boswell stated that his aim in writing a biography of Johnson was "to write, not his panegyric, which must be all praise, but his Life; which, great and good as he was, must not be supposed to be entirely perfect...in every picture there should be shade as well as light." All well and good, because Boswell is long dead. But for those of us still kicking, where does a celebrity's private life end and his or her public life begin? What kinds of questions—if any...should a biographer avoid?

We're seeing an enormous rise in the brazenness of many modern celebrity biographers and their comrades-in-arms, the paparazzi kamikaze photographers. This dynamic duo have been known to rifle through a celebrity's garbage, scale their security walls, and swipe their mail from the mailbox. Don't people, even famous and ridiculously gorgeous people, have the right to privacy?

But biography and autobiography are essentially about exposure. Subjects often create images of themselves and then project their images as fact and history. We can argue that the public has a right—and the biographer the obligation—to reveal the truth. It's a line only you as the writer can draw for yourself. Take heart from what writer and wit Dorothy Parker said to her future biographers: "I don't care what's written about me as long as it isn't true."

Desire, Dedication, Determination

Remember this silly joke: "How do you eat an elephant?" Answer: "One bite at a time." That's the best way to go about writing your biography or autobiography. You can get it all done if you take it slowly. Here are a few points to keep in mind:

➤ Start by deciding on your subject. This is easier said than done. Think very carefully, because you're probably going to have to live with this person longer than you lived with your last mate.

As Johnson once thundered to Boswell: "You have but two subjects, yourself and me. I am sick of both."

➤ Find out what access you can get to the person (if living) and to his or her letters, diaries, and friends. *No one* can write a credible biography without information.

➤ I recommend that you gather all the information you need *before* you start writing. This method can help prevent you from getting a year or two into the project and then discovering that you can't get the information that you need. It can also prevent you from drawing the wrong conclusions or taking the wrong focus in your writing because you didn't have all the facts early on.

➤ Organize your material into a working *outline*. This will help you decide on a method of organization, probably chronological. Then plug in the facts.

➤ Make sure your material is stored in a safe place. Keep back-up disks and copies of everything in another location. Backup material can be crucial for legal verification in case you're sued for libel.

> **All the Write Stuff**
> Check *Books in Print* (available in print and online) to see who has been biographized and by whom. Do you really want to spring one more bio of Marilyn Monroe or Elvis Presley on the unsuspecting world? Look for fresh blood.

> **All the Write Stuff**
> Biographer Jay Martin began his life of writer Nathaniel West with the moment of West's death. Rather than starting with your subject's birth (unless it occurred in a manger or log cabin), consider starting with a dramatic event, like his or her death.

> **All the Write Stuff**
> Many serious biographers place an advertisement in the Book Review section of *The New York Times*, soliciting correspondence and personal recollections about their subjects.

Ready to write your biography? Use this checklist to get cooking.

_____ 1. I picked an interesting subject.

_____ 2. I decided whether I wanted to write an authorized (with permission) or unauthorized (without permission) biography.

_____ 3. I researched my subject through primary sources: interviews, letters, diaries, journals.

_____ 4. I researched my subject through secondary sources: books, articles.

_____ 5. I have all the materials I need.

_____ 6. I organized my notes on my subject.

_____ 7. I decided what my *tone* will be in the book.

_____ 8. I know what information and incidents to include and what to discard.

_____ 9. I have a working outline.

_____ 10. I promise to refrain from using psychobabble.

My Life, and Welcome to It

Writing an autobiography is essentially the same as writing a biography, except that the subject has already been chosen for you and you know you'll have pretty free access. Gather materials for an autobiography the same way you did for a biography. Naturally, you can use all these methods when you're researching a biographical subject as well.

Here are sources to consider:

➤ Birth certificates

➤ Marriage certificates

➤ Death certificates

➤ Baptism certificates

➤ Birth announcements

➤ Wedding announcements

➤ Wedding invitations

➤ Letters

➤ Family Bibles

➤ Journals

➤ Diaries

➤ Wills

➤ Military records

➤ Photographs

➤ Deeds

➤ Genealogical records

- ➤ Genealogical charts
- ➤ Census records
- ➤ Lineage societies
- ➤ Government records
- ➤ Newspapers
- ➤ Family organizations
- ➤ Passenger lists

Begin with an *oral genealogy*, which simply means people's memories. Talk to friends and relatives. Even longtime neighbors can add bits of information you may have forgotten or never known. How trustworthy is the information people give you? Memories can be faulty, and sometimes people have specific reasons for wanting to withhold or finesse the past. Verify all information in print sources, such as genealogical records, if possible.

All the Write Stuff
Consider using a tape recorder when you create oral histories. This technique enables you to get all the details down and quote from them later.

A Branch on the Family Tree

You can find genealogical records in libraries, archives, houses of worship, cemeteries, courthouses, and other facilities. *Vital records* are specifically created to record births, marriages, or deaths. You can find out more about your past by sending for "Where to Write for Vital Records," a pamphlet issued by the U.S. Government (Consumer Information Center, P.O. Box 100, Pueblo, CO 81002).

Words to the Wise
Vital records are specifically created to record births, marriages, or deaths.

The Mormons

The Genealogical Department of the Church of Jesus Christ of Latter-Day Saints (the Mormons) is creating a major genealogical index. Called the International Genealogical Index, or IGI, it contains more than 88 million individual records from more than 100 countries. The IGI is arranged by major locality (such as the state where a person was born) and then alphabetically by name. It's based in The Genealogical Library in Salt Lake City, Utah (35 North West Temple Street, Salt Lake City, UT 84150).

Take a Letter, Maria

Here are four other useful sources you can use to find information for your autobiography:

1. For government census records, military records, passenger lists, and many other government records:

   National Archives and Records Administration (NARA)
   8th and Pennsylvania Avenue, NW
   Washington, DC 20408

2. The National Genealogical Society is the focal point for genealogical activities on a national level.

   National Genealogical Society
   4527 Seventeenth Street North
   Arlington, VA 22207-2363

3. The New England Historic Genealogical Society is the oldest American organization created for collecting, studying, and preserving family and local history for genealogical research. Their services include an international liaison service, members' ancestor charts files, and Bible record collection.

   New England Historic Genealogical Society
   101 Newbury Street
   Boston, MA 02116

4. Founded in 1977, the Afro-American Historical and Genealogical Society encourages research in Afro-American history and genealogy.

   Afro-American Historical and Genealogical Society
   P.O. Box 73086
   Washington, DC 20056

All the Write Stuff
When writing your autobiography, you can start by thinking about a turning point in your life.

As you research, be confident—your life is a lot more interesting than you think. Remember that until relatively late in their lives, Abraham Lincoln and Ronald Reagan could have thought they were too poor or average to ever have anyone interested in their lives.

And even if you never become famous, wouldn't you like your descendants to be able to read the story of your life? Here are two other reasons to consider writing your autobiography:

➤ By writing the story of your life, you help preserve the history of our nation.

➤ If you connect yourself with the past, you can help fashion a better future.

The Least You Need to Know

➤ A *biography* is a true story about a person's life written by another person. An *autobiography* is a person's own story of his or her life.

➤ Effective biography and autobiography use many techniques from fiction, including characterization, plot, conflict, tone, and point of view.

➤ Research facts carefully.

➤ A biographer and autobiographer create life on the page. What could be more fun? (Don't answer that!)

Chapter 11

You Could Look It Up: Textbooks and Reference Books

In This Chapter

➤ Break into the textbook and reference book markets

➤ Get the skills you need

➤ Discover how to write text and trade book proposals that *work*

America's readers aren't fools; they know what they want. As the runaway success of the *Complete Idiot's Guide* series demonstrates, people want quick and easy books that help them learn new skills and polish their existing abilities. They demand "how-to" reference books that will help them get ahead in their private and public lives. No matter what the topic, successful reference books have these qualities in common:

➤ Good writing   ➤ Solid facts

➤ Useful illustrations   ➤ Helpful diagrams

➤ Friendly advice   ➤ Valuable tips

In this chapter, you'll learn how to use your creativity to write practical books that help millions of readers lead more fulfilling lives. I'll teach you the basics of writing reference books alone and in teams.

See Dick and Jane Write! Dick and Jane Can Write Text and Trade!

There are two kinds of reference books: textbooks and trade reference books. These two kinds of creative writing endeavors are like Patty and Cathy, those perky identical cousins that Patty Duke created in her first life. Reference books and textbooks walk alike and talk alike, but there are some big differences between them. Unless you understand them, you could lose your mind.

How can you tell a textbook from a trade reference book? Study this handy chart.

Textbooks	Reference books
Group writers	Usually individual writers
Can take at least a year to write	Written quickly
Relatively conservative	Timely
Sold by reps	Mostly sold in bookstores

Bet You Didn't Know

Most computer books these days are written by groups of writers and sold by reps to corporate clients as well as through bookstores. These books are so timely that 1,000-page books are sometimes written in only thirty days.

Here's some more information on text and trade to throw into the hopper.

Text Time

Textbooks comprise at least half of all the books published in America. When I say "text," think "school books." And stop that shuddering; school's out for us, bubba. We're finally the grown-ups.

Almost all texts written today are the joint product of an established scholar, a phalanx of freelance writers, and the editors at the textbook publishing company. As a result, breaking into this field is about as easy as breaching the Dallas Cowboys' defensive line. I'd be lying if I said that it's not difficult for a novice writer to publish a textbook—but it's not impossible. After all, I did it. (And I lived to tell the tale.)

Textbooks are sold by representatives ("reps") from the textbook publishers. Reps prowl school corridors, waylay innocent department heads, ply them with free lunch—and unleash their sales spiels. Textbook marketing serfs also endure educational trade shows, such as the annual conventions of the National Council of English Teachers, The National Council of Mathematics Teachers, and the National Council of Barefoot Aluminum Foil Dancing Teachers. The reps set up booths larger and noisier than the Magic Kingdom, give out pencils and other tschoches, and take orders for books the size of backhoes.

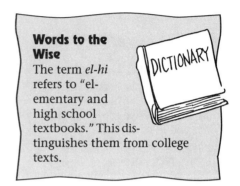

Words to the Wise
The term *el-hi* refers to "elementary and high school textbooks." This distinguishes them from college texts.

The Age of Specialization

Like gourmet coffee, textbooks have fallen under the spell of specialization. This is great news for you, the writer, because it makes it more likely that you'll find your personal area of expertise.

Here's a sampling of textbooks for just one course: freshman college composition. I culled this list from the spankin' new catalogue I received from one of the world's largest textbook publishers. Check out the categories and subcategories. Which ones interest you the most?

➤ *Handbooks:* Comprehensive, Brief, Multimedia

➤ *How-To Books*: Modes, Purposes, Writing with Computers, Writing from Sources/ Research, Argument

➤ *Readers (anthologies of short fiction and nonfiction)*: Purposes, Thematic, Multicultural, Cultural Studies, Argument, Writing Across the Disciplines, Environmental, Language, Technology, Life Writing

These books require the same writing skills but different ones require different areas of specialization. They show you what you can do with a little tweak of your writing skills.

Not Free to Be You and Me

According to a new study, the surest indicator of success on the job isn't a ritzy college education, intelligence, or even productivity. The employees most likely to make the cut in these lean and mean times are the workers who are team players. The winners submerge their egos and get along with others. They play nice and share their toys.

Nowhere is this more evident than in team textbook writing. You must submerge your individual voice and ego to work effectively in a textbook team. As the textbook writer, you're on the bottom of the food chain. In this situation, it's not a bad place to be. It leaves you relatively alone to write your heart out.

All the Write Stuff
Although no writer is an island, you can expect to have more autonomy if you're writing your own textbook. Writing as a team, however, enables you to learn much more about the field of textbook writing.

Below is a sample chain of command for a major textbook project. Expect variations depending on the size of the company and the size of the project. The larger the company and the larger the project, the more layers there will be and the more brass will be involved. For example, if you're writing part of a series of literature books for grades 6–12, expect scores of staffers and as many as hundreds of freelancers to have a finger in the pie. But with a small project, such as a textbook revision, there might be only three layers.

Publisher
⇓
Senior Editor or Executive Editor
⇓
Project Supervisor
⇓
Editor
⇓
Writer (that's *you!*)

A Lid for Every Pot: Reference Books

Now, "reference books" are the books you find in the reference section of the library, the books sold in bookstores and through mail-order catalogues. Reference texts can be as dry as Steven Segal or as juicy as Sharon Stone. The *Complete Idiot's Guides* books are classified as reference texts. The *Complete Idiot's Guides* are clearly some of the juicy ones.

Reference books are a great entry way for the beginning writer. Just about anyone who has useful information that people want can find a publisher. Although it may seem that there are already piles of books on every imaginable self-help topic, from ant-removal to zebra breeding, every year hundreds of new how-to books are published. Part of the reason for this boom is that every year new fields open up or old ones expand.

Here are just a few hot reference areas you can consider writing for:

➤ Travel   ➤ Pets

➤ Child care   ➤ Sports

➤ Food   ➤ Fitness

➤ Drink   ➤ Health

➤ Hobbies   ➤ Gardening

➤ Languages   ➤ Self-improvement

➤ Computers   ➤ The Internet

Geek Lit

Technocrat and technobrat alert—good technology writers are the splice of life. They can be as hard to find as the stuff a girl's dreams are made of.

Proficient technology writers can make complex and confusing information useful and understandable. They can clarify the effect of technology on the reader's life. Dumbed-down prose insults readers no matter what the subject. When you write techno textbooks, you want to put important issues into context and help readers think through their questions intelligently.

Does this job description fit you? If so, consider writing a textbook that tells me how to make my computer respect me in the morning.

All the Write Stuff
Learn how to RAM your ROM, hard-wire your Mom, and call the White House (president@whithouse.gov.) You'll make a name for yourself. Yahoo!

Top of Your Game

The reference market is not restricted to trendy new topics like risotto on a stick du jour. Every year, stacks of new how-to books are published on topics like traditional crafts, diets, and collecting antiques. The key is the usefulness of the information and the clarity of its presentation.

How can you publish a reference book? Here are two ironclad requirements:

1. Make yourself a leading expert in your field.

2. Present what you know in a logical fashion.

And that leads to the creative writing skills you need to produce winning text and reference books. Read on to discover what it takes to make it in this market.

Making the Grade

How is writing a textbook or reference book different from writing a novel, short story, play, or poem? They're more different than you might think. Successful textbook and reference book writers have these Big Three Creative Writing skills:

1. A strong sense of organization

2. A good background in learning theory

3. The ability to define jargon effectively

A surprising number of novelists, poets, dramatists, and essayists support themselves writing textbooks and reference books. By day, they toil in text and trade; at night, they take up their pens for their fiction. You can use all the skills you'll learn in this section in other kinds of writing, too. So let's take a closer look at each creative writing skill. By the end of this chapter, you'll be ready to hit the Text and Trade Trifecta!

Organization

Do you know where you put the faux snakeskin cowboy boots you couldn't live another moment without? Can you give clear directions to the kinfolk lost on the parkway? Are you able to get the party invitations out before the night of the party? If so, you've got the organizational skills you need to convey information to others effectively.

One of the keys to writing a textbook or reference book is organizing the material to match the subject and audience. Here are eight different methods of organization used to arrange information logically:

1. Chronological order: the order of time

2. Spatial order: the relationship of objects to each other in space (above, below, next to, etc.)

3. Order of importance: from least to most important, most to least important, and so on

4. Thematically: by subject or category

5. Comparison and contrast: how the topics are alike and different

6. Cause and effect: the reason something happened and the result

7. Example: a specific instance of something

8. Problem/solution: an issue and possible resolutions

When you write a novel, short story, or play, you almost always use chronological order, recounting events from beginning to end (with the occasional flashback). When you write a poem, in contrast, you might use thematic organization or spatial order. But when you write a textbook or a reference book, you select the method that communicates the book's message most clearly and effectively based on these two considerations:

➤ Subject matter (your topic)

➤ Audience (your readers)

If U Cn Rd This...Learning Theory

Back in the good old days when dinosaurs roamed the earth and I was very, very innocent, intelligence was a simple matter: you either had it or you didn't. It was denoted by the cabalistic symbols "IQ" and measured by a nasty test. I was considered intelligent by this measure, even though I cannot balance my checkbook, do a somersault, or drive more than a block without getting lost. I once misplaced my car at a rest stop on the Jersey Turnpike. Honest.

It was not until the 1980s that Howard Gardner, a Harvard psychologist, proposed that intelligence is not such a simple matter. Gardner went so far as to claim that there are seven (7!) different types of intelligence, not just one. Most people have more than one intelligence. An understanding of how people learn directs the way you write a reference book. You need to learn how people absorb knowledge to understand in what order and format to present it. Here's the breakdown of the Seven Intelligences:

> **All the Write Stuff**
> An element of rhythmic repetition enters here. As a result, people with musical intelligence often learn better with tools like "In 1492 Columbus sailed the ocean blue."

Intelligence	Characteristic
Linguistic	Verbal; thinks in words. Highly developed auditory skills; likes to read and write. If you like to write, you've got a seat here.
Logical-Mathematical	Logical; thinks conceptually. Capable of highly abstract thinking and reasoning. Mr. Spock (and the rest of the Vulcans) fit here.
Spatial	Artistic; thinks in visual images. Skilled at drawing, building, inventing. This is for people whose clothes always match, not those among us who wear two different color shoes...and think nothing's wrong.

continues

continued

Intelligence	Characteristic
Musical	Rhythmic; sensitive to music and sounds. Moves to music. If you sing in the shower *in tune,* you may have musical intelligence.
Bodily-Kinesthetic	Athletic; has excellent fine-motor coordination. Processes knowledge through bodily sensations. Often communicates through body language. Do you assemble the VCR to see how it works rather than reading the manual? Then you have bodily-kinesthetic intelligence.
Interpersonal	Organized; socializes smoothly. If you can work the crowd and schmooze like a pro, you are an interpersonal learner.
Intrapersonal	Solitary; prefers to work alone. Intuitive, independent, private, self-motivated. Monks fall into this category.

Further, Gardner claimed that we don't all learn the same way. We absorb information most effectively, Gardner says, when it's presented to us in a way that we can master. As a result, the same teaching method is not equally effective with all students.

Bet You Didn't Know

Gardner's theory got a big boost when subsequent research indicated that each intelligence is located in a different part of the brain. Since the different parts of the brain cooperate with each other (except on Monday mornings), it appears the seven different intelligences interact.

When you write a textbook or a reference book, you use this learning theory and other new developments to convey information to your readers in the most effective way. For example, pictures and illustrations help spatial learners absorb the text; diagrams and theorems help logical-mathematical learners get the message.

Teach the Lingo

Microcomputer, microprocessor, and *modem.* A decade ago, few of us had any idea what these terms meant. But thanks to top-notch reference book writers, we can sling these words around with aplomb—or at least a reasonable assurance that we won't make complete fools of ourselves.

As a textbook and reference book writer, you've also got to be able to take the jargon of the field and make it understandable to your readers. Nowhere is this more obvious than in the field of computers. There's so much jargon—and it's growing so fast—that skillful writers need to know how to make the difficult seem easy. It takes creativity to make material like this interesting and accessible. Here are some methods you can use:

➤ Use a light tone to make the subject less scary.

➤ Use italics and boldface type to make the text easier to read.

➤ Define each acronym.

➤ Break the information into small, easy-to-digest bits.

➤ Use numbered steps.

➤ Consider a glossary of terms.

➤ Include side elements for useful but less main-stream information—like the sidebars in this book.

➤ Try visuals, too.

➤ Link new facts to familiar terms.

➤ Include useful and *interesting* information.

> **Words to the Wise**
>
> Here are some of the important terms you're most likely to encounter as you write a textbook:
>
> | | |
> |---|---|
> | PE, SE | pupil's edition, student edition |
> | TE | teacher's edition |
> | ATE | annotated teacher's edition |
> | Ancillaries | extra goodies: videos, test packets, CD-ROMs, etc. |

Following is part of a chapter I wrote about computer terminology. See how I used each of these methods to make it easier for readers to grasp the information.

Light tone—— The latest government study on computers found that nearly ten years after their introduction, almost one-third of all Americans use a computer at work or at home. In 1984, eight percent of all households owned a computer; a decade later, the figure had doubled. Since it's plain that computers are here to stay, you better learn the lingo! This chapter can help make you computer literate.

Boldface —— **Hardware**   Let's start by looking at the physical and mechanical components of a
type   computer system—the electronic circuitry, chips, screens, disk drives, keyboards, and printers. All these components of a computer are called the *hardware*. How many of these words have you heard—and wondered about?

Computer Terms: Nuts and Bolts

Italics —— *acoustic coupler*   A portable device for connecting two compatible computers via a telephone line; a modem.

Define —— acronyms   *CD-ROM*   Compact Disk Read-Only Memory. A peripheral system that uses a CD-ROM laser disk and CD-ROM reader connected to the computer. A single disk can hold a tremendous amount of text, such as an entire set of encyclopedias.

chip   Tiny wafer of silicon containing miniature electronic circuits which can store millions of bits of information.

New facts — linked to familiar term; CPU = brains   *CPU*   Central Processing Unit: The part of the computer where all incoming information is controlled; the computer's "brains."

disk   Flexible mylar plastic wafers used to store information. Also called *floppy disks,* even though they don't flop anymore.

Information— in bite-size pieces   *laptop, notebook*   Small, lightweight, portable battery-powered computers with a thin, flat, liquid crystal display screen.

TechnoSmarts   Once you have learned the terms on the following chart, you'll feel a lot more comfortable around a computer. If possible, link each word with its function by sitting at your keyboard as you learn these terms.

access   To store and retrieve data from a disk.

authorization code   A password that enables a person to gain access to a computer system.

back up   To copy a file.

boot   To start a computer by turning it on.

bug   A mistake in a computer program...

Useful and — interesting information   **Surf the Net**   Have you "driven" on the information superhighway yet? The "information superhighway"—the *Internet*—links people though computer terminals and telephone lines in a web of software and networks in *cyberspace. Cyberspace* is a series of computer networks and bulletin boards in which on-line communication takes place. According to current estimates, about 15 million people in America and 25 million people around the world regularly "surf the net"—as accessing information on the Internet is called. Originally created by the Pentagon, the Internet is now subsidized by the National Science Foundation.

148

Follow the Leader

When you write a novel, play, poem, or script, you can use all the pages your little heart desires. Your finished work can be as short—or long—as you want. I've read some novels that could double as doorstops or anvils; I sat through eight hours of *Nicholas Nickleby* when it played on Broadway.

But textbooks and reference books are a different kettle of fish entirely. There's only so much space in a textbook or reference book—even though some of them seem as big as the national debt. How can publishers be sure that what you write will be the right length for the number of pages you've been allocated? How can you be sure your manuscript won't come up short (or long)?

To ensure your manuscript will be the right format, you will get a set of formatting guidelines. These "specs" (specifications) describe how the manuscript should be formatted. It explains what font (typeface) to use, how many spaces to leave, how wide your margins should be, and how many lines fit on a page. The guidelines may also include spacing, tabbing, and other style considerations.

> **Wrong Turn**
> Different books have different guidelines. Be sure you have the right set of guidelines. It's almost never possible to reuse guidelines, unless you're writing two or more books in the same series.

> **All the Write Stuff**
> Increasingly, guidelines are being sent on disk rather than hard copy. If this applies to your book, be sure to tell your editor whether you work in a Macintosh or IBM environment. In many cases, submissions to publishers are required on disk.

Make a Commitment

So you want to write your own, individual reference book all by your lonesome? You mean I haven't scared you off yet? Then let's get down to the business of proposing your book. Down on one knee, please.

But before you declare your intentions, get the publisher's guidelines. I've mentioned this in previous chapters; now it's time to take a closer look. These guidelines explain what the publisher is seeking in new submissions.

For example, a proposal for a book in the *Complete Idiot's Guide* series must consist of the following elements: (1) Proposal Matter, (2) Author Bio, (3) Complete Book Outline, (4) Preliminary Sidebar List and Samples, and (5) Sample Chapter.

Write Me

Here's what I had write to sell this book (and the others I've done in the series) to the acquisitions editor:

1. Proposal Matter

   ➤ General description of the book.

   ➤ Rationale: Why does the world need this book?

   ➤ Market: Who will buy this book?

   ➤ Competition: What other books are already out there that will compete with this book?

   ➤ Organization: How will the book be laid out?

   ➤ Style: Can I write a clear, concise, readable, and slightly cheeky text?

   ➤ Delivery: What word processing package do I use?

   ➤ Foreword: Whom do I know who will endorse the book?

   ➤ Publicity and Promotion: What I can offer to the book in terms of promotion and publicity?

2. Author Bio

   ➤ Why am I the right person to write this book?

   ➤ What makes me an authority in this field?

   ➤ What are my notable book credits?

   ➤ What awards have I won in this field?

3. Complete Book Outline

4. Preliminary Sidebar List and Samples

5. Sample Chapter

Sample Proposal

Here's part of the proposal I wrote for another book in the *Complete Idiot's Guide* series, *The Complete Idiot's Guide to Grammar and Style*. I selected this example because it is typical of what you'll have to do to propose a textbook or a reference book.

As you read through it, notice how I matched form to function. By using the "clear, concise, readable, and slightly cheeky" tone I show that I can write the way the publisher wants. A proposal for a science text, in contrast, would have a much more serious tone.

Introduction

At first blush, it would seem that the world needs another grammar guidebook as much as Custer needed more Native Americans, Michael Jackson needs more plastic surgery, or Joey Buttafuco needs more attitude. *Books in Print* reveals that there is no shortage of writing style guides; I counted over fifty such volumes cluttering the shelves. Fortunately for my purposes here, virtually all these books are expensive, cumbersome, and as dull as watching paint flake.

Rationale

With all those guidebooks clamoring for attention, why write still another grammar and usage guide? Here's why—adults are looking for a truly useful, concise, and *interesting* guide to the grammar and usage dilemmas they face in their professional and private lives.

No one in the real world is losing sleep over the old grammar canards: better not split an infinitive, don't end a sentence with a preposition, and never confuse *who* and *whom.* Generations of school kids got their knuckles rapped over that last one— but they don't care. Dick and Jane grew up and got jobs in corporate America. They're sitting in cubicles and around conference tables, where their language concerns are very different. Today's savvy consumers want to master hands-on grammar, usage, and mechanics issues so they can write with assurance in all business and personal situations.

These everyday real-world grammar conundrums include such problems as how to:

➤ select the appropriate level of diction

➤ punctuate sentences logically

➤ determine the tense of verbs

➤ avoid sexist language

➤ distinguish between homonyms

➤ construct logical sentences

Market

The Complete Idiot's Guide to Grammar and Style is targeted at adults interested in filling in the embarrassing gaps in their education. The book is aimed at the literate mid-level workers who realize they slept through 10th grade English and now wish that Miss Schkeleweiss had been just a little more interesting.

All the Write Stuff
See Chapter 16 for sample query letters and a step-by-step procedure for making first contact with publishers.

In *The Complete Idiot's Guide to Grammar and Style,* I will show that there is a way of using language that is better—clearer, more precise, and more elegant. I'll guide readers to appreciate and master the language of educated people, the language that gets you ahead in the business world. That's what our readers want.

There's more, but you get the idea by now.

You Can't Tell the Players Without a Scorecard

So who publishes all these textbooks and reference books? Below is a partial list of some of the country's most active reference book publishers. Look in *Literary Market Place* or the *Writer's Market* for each company's address. Before you send off that query letter, be sure to get the name of the current editor—and double-check it with a phone call.

➤ Addison Wesley

➤ Allyn and Bacon

➤ AMSCO

➤ Barron's Education Series

➤ Cambridge University Press

➤ Garland

➤ Glencoe

➤ Harcourt Brace Jovanovich

➤ Harper & Row

➤ Heath

➤ Random House

➤ Routledge, Chapman & Hall

➤ Scott Foresman

➤ Holt Rinehart Winston

➤ Houghton Mifflin

➤ Longman

➤ MacDougal, Littell and Company

➤ Macmillan

➤ McGraw Hill

➤ Mayfield

➤ Modern Curriculum Press

➤ National Textbook

➤ Prentice-Hall

➤ Silver, Burdett and Ginn

➤ St. Martin's Press

➤ W.W. Norton

Publishers typically specialize in certain types of textbooks or reference books. Addison Wesley (now merged with Scott Foresman) for example, is a leader in math. Target your efforts where you know they'll pay off. Check *Literary Market Place* to see which publishers excel in which areas.

Bet You Didn't Know

Sometimes you have to find the right division within a company: Addison Wesley, for example, has a computer book division, but if you send in the greatest idea ever for a computer book to the math division, it might end up in the wastebasket.

Sometimes, publishers develop book topics and then seek authors to write the books. So even if you don't have an idea or know the market inside and out, you can approach a publisher with your expertise and find a match with a title they've already got on their list—but with no author yet signed. This is quite different from traditional fiction publishing, where titles are author-driven.

The Least You Need to Know

➤ Textbooks are generally sold to schools and universities; reference books are sold to the general public.

➤ To write textbooks and reference books, you need a strong sense of organization, knowledge of learning theory, and the ability to define jargon well.

➤ All textbooks and reference books are written to specific guidelines to make sure the copy fits.

➤ At least half the books published in America are textbooks and reference books. This is a monster market, baby.

Wrong Turn
Publishing companies change hands more quickly than poker chips at a hot game. Before you mail a proposal, check carefully to see who owns whom this week. For example, Allyn and Bacon, Modern Curriculum Press, and Prentice-Hall are all divisions of the same parent company.

Chapter 12

Glossies 101: Writing Magazine Articles

> **In This Chapter**
>
> ➤ Discover today's sizzlin' sellers
>
> ➤ Craft lively *leads*
>
> ➤ Practice different methods of organizing the body of your article
>
> ➤ Learn how to write the most salable articles

Word Alert! There's a magazine that needs your article right now. Why? Because you're a creative writer and magazines of all types and categories flourish in the United States. People may not make time to read books, but they sure are reading 'zines. According to the *World Almanac*, the best-selling magazine in 1996, the *NRTA/AARP Bulletin*, has a circulation of 21,875,436 readers. The number 2 best seller, *Modern Maturity*, boasts 21,716,727 readers. *Reader's Digest*? 15 million readers. *TV Guide* has sales of over 14 million.

In this chapter, you'll first learn to write a magazine article, from top to toe, lead to conclusion. Then I focus on the most popular types of magazine articles and show you how to write each one. Next I describe different ways to develop your articles. You'll learn methods that apply to virtually every magazine article you write.

The Hit Parade

Here are the current 25 top-selling magazines. Based on this list, what trends do you see? How many of these magazines and trends match your writing style and interests?

1. *NRTA/AARP Bulletin*
2. *Modern Maturity*
3. *Reader's Digest*
4. *TV Guide*
5. *The Condé Nast Select*
6. *National Geographic*
7. *Better Homes and Gardens*
8. *Good Housekeeping*
9. *Ladies' Home Journal*
10. *Family Circle*
11. *Women's Day*
12. *McCall's*
13. *Time*
14. *Prevention*
15. *AAA World*
16. *People*
17. *Redbook*
18. *Playboy*
19. *Sports Illustrated*
20. *Newsweek*
21. *National Enquirer*
22. *American Legion*
23. *Star*
24. *Cosmopolitan*
25. *Southern Living*

Leader of the Pack

Inquiring Minds want to know—what *are* Americans reading in all these magazines? According to a comprehensive survey, the top ten most popular topics for magazine articles are:

1. How-to articles (including self-help)
2. Interviews
3. Informational pieces
4. Inspirational pieces
5. Consumer awareness articles
6. Entertainment
7. Opinion pieces
8. Humor articles

9. As-told-to (articles that retell harrowing experiences, such as members of the Donner Party eating each other)

10. Fillers (short, sometimes humorous fiction)

How can you get in on the writing? I'll teach you the nuts-and-bolts of writing magazine articles so you can craft your own lively and informative pieces. As Julie Andrews trilled in *The Sound of Music*, let's start at the very beginning, with the *lead*.

Take the Lead

The *lead* is the first paragraph or two of your article. It's the teaser. One or two paragraphs are all most readers are going to sample before they decide to stay with the article or do more exciting things like clean the lint from their navels. The lead fulfills a dual function:

1. It lets your reader know what the article will be about.

2. It entices your audience to read on.

Your lead is an audition. However, it has to do more than convince your reader that you can impart important facts or entertaining banter. Your lead must convince your readers that you're not taking their interest for granted, that you respect their investment of time, and that you're going to do everything in your power to repay their trust.

Leads follow three main formats: *startling statements, brief stories,* and *controversial statements*. Below are some samples of each kind. Match the method you select to the Big Three: Topic, Audience, and Purpose. For example, don't use a startling statement about lowering the drinking age to start an article for Mothers Against Drunk Driving.

Startling statement:

The War Against Pornography

Of all the devices known to pornography—whips, chains, ropes, candles, razors, handcuffs, trusses, and objects too gross to describe here—of all these devices of debauchery, none, for the moment, is as important to the future of smut in America as a crisp, seven-page proposal now before the Los Angeles County Board of Supervisors.

Brief story:

The Mother of Kiddie Porn?

Tall, trim Catherine Wilson radiated wealth and style. She lived in a triplex home in a ritzy Los Angeles neighborhood and kept a small fleet of luxury cars. She took dutiful care of her children, personally driving them to their posh private schools every day. To all outward appearances, she was a pillar of the community—but, say L.A. police, a pillar erected on the muck and mire of child pornography. Working from a list of 5,000 names nationwide, Wilson allegedly built a $5,000,000-a-year mail-order business dealing in kiddie porn.

All the Write Stuff
Read the major feature magazines (or the magazines that you want to write for) and study their leads. Then adapt their techniques to your own writing style.

Controversial statement:

Pornography Through the Looking Glass

Television ushered in the new year by cracking what is breathlessly billed as "the last taboo": incest.

Leads often use the reporter's questions introduced in Part 1 of this book. Here are the questions: *Who? What? When? Where? Why? How?* Some leads answer all the questions; other times, the lead addresses only the questions most important to the article. Read the following lead and then find the five W's:

An Offer We Couldn't Refuse

An important discovery I made recently about my uncle was that he introduced the mob to my family. This is important because my family came from Italy without any money and now we control most of Long Island. My Uncle Luigi gave us money, power, and control.

Who?_____

What?_____

When?_____

Where?_____

Why?_____

Did you get these answers?

Who?	The writer
What?	An important discovery about his uncle
When?	Recently
Where?	On Long Island
Why?	To gain power, money, and control

Next, we'll look closely at some specific types of magazine articles. You can match your writing style and interests with the requirements of each form. Then I'll show you some other writing methods you can use with many different types of articles.

Help Me, Rhonda: Writing Self-Help Articles

This publication cycle, self-help articles rule the pages. We're becoming a nation of wussies, and we need help from our magazine writers (that's you, baby). Today's hottest of the hot topics include:

➤ Personal creativity

➤ Mood management

➤ Staying young

➤ Healing

➤ Mind/body integration

➤ Time management

➤ Relationship management

➤ Community building

➤ Being rooted

➤ Spirituality

It's not enough to jump on the bandwagon, however. You've got to see the wagon comin' down the road and hop on it *before* it starts careening down publisher's row. Anticipate tomorrow's trends today if you want to write articles that sell.

Self-help articles follow a specific format:

➤ State the topic in a catchy way.

➤ Provide the information, the meat-and-potatoes.

➤ Conclude with general information/review the basics/offer a recommendation.

Depending on your topic, you may also want to include inspirational concepts, motivational tips, anecdotes, interviews, statistics, and recommendations. Here's the beginning of a how-to article on America's latest obsession: dieting.

Sin Food: A Fake Revival?

State the —
topic in a
catchy way.
It was just a few years ago that food makers promised that fake fats would create a new world of guilt-free chocolate cake and french fries. They haven't delivered yet, but that hasn't stopped the industry from continuing its crusade. Here's an update from the front:

Provide the information, the meat-and-potatoes. — Salatrim: Nabisco claims it's more like real fat than the others. In other words, the reduced-calorie product re-creates the texture of fat and has a better "mouth feel."

Olestra: Hundreds of millions of dollars later, Proctor & Gamble finally got the Feds to approve their fake fat, which the company is now using in fried snack foods such as potato chips. Good thing P & G hurried—Olestra's patents were almost running out.

Simplesse: Earlier this year, NutraSweet gave up its version of ice cream called "Simple Pleasures." Lousy mouth feel? Perhaps, but the fake stuff is still used in diet cheese and reduced-calorie mayonnaise.

Now, write the conclusion to this brief article. In a single paragraph, sum up with general information, review the basics, or offer a recommendation.

Getting to Know You: Interviews and Profiles

An interview is nothing more than a conversation, hopefully with someone who is a lot richer, prettier, and sexier than you are. Otherwise, who would want to read your article?

All the Write Stuff

Regardless of your topic and tone, always follow the cardinal rule of interviews and profiles: get your facts correct. Check and double check all data.

Seriously, an interview with an everyday person can be just as interesting—and salable—as an interview with a super-star. Like interviews, *profiles* are short biographies, normally addressing one facet of the person's life. A piece in *People* magazine, for example, might focus on a star's new film, while an interview in a local or regional magazine like *South Beach* could focus on a business person's latest venture. Whether your interview is funny or serious depends on your audience and writing style.

Here are ten suggestions for conducting sure-fire interviews.

1. Always prepare your questions ahead of time. Write the questions out.

2. Prepare twice as many questions as you think you will need. You never know.

3. Bring a tape recorder, cassette tapes, and a spare set of batteries.

4. Never tape record a person without securing his or her prior approval, preferably in writing.

5. Write to the person to set up the interview.

6. Follow up with a telephone call to make all the arrangements.

7. Call the day before the interview to confirm the time and place.

8. Dress like a professional.

9. Be polite and business-like.

10. Send a follow-up thank-you letter.

From Famine to Gamin: Consumer Info

Consumer information pieces follow the same format as how-to articles. Sometimes referred to as "service pieces," these articles provide information and make readers aware of important issues. The trick to these articles is hooking the reader right away. You have about five seconds before that page gets turned. In addition, you better provide a sound conclusion or your readers will be left feeling cheated and muttering in their soup. Check the articles in such magazines as *Reader's Digest, Consumer's Digest,* and *Ladies' Home Journal* for examples.

> **All the Write Stuff**
> Less Pain, More Gain: To get double duty out of your ground work, write two (or more!) articles from one research session or interview. Then recycle one article into another.

Basic Instinct

Now, let's take a look at some basic ways you can structure your articles: *problem/solution, cause/effect, comparison/contrast,* and *spatial order*. These patterns work with a wide variety of articles.

The structural problem you face in writing articles is how to include the basic information you have to supply. Otherwise, readers unfamiliar with the subject won't know what you're talking about. The following methods can help you solve this dilemma.

> **All the Write Stuff**
> Several prestigious universities, including the University of California at Berkeley, New York University, and Columbia University, now offer graduate courses in magazine journalism. *The Complete Idiot's Guide to Creative Writing* is a whole lot cheaper.

From Belle du Jour to Bellevue: Problem/Solution

In these articles, writers state a problem and give one or more solutions. In most cases, the solutions will be arranged from least to most effective.

Here's the opening to a problem/solution article. As you read it, look for the problem and try to predict possible solutions.

All the Write Stuff
Research to find the facts you need. In addition to the old standbys such as *The Readers Guide to Periodical Literature*, *The New York Times* index, and the almanac, try some of the new on-line indices and search engines on the World Wide Web.

The deadline for filing federal income tax returns is less than two weeks away, triggering the familiar taxpayer laments about owing too much to the tax collector. The wealthiest taxpayers are as likely to complain as the less well-off—and sometimes more so, as the wealthy are more likely to owe the government money, while the poor are more likely to receive a refund. But everyone gripes about high taxes. And not without reason: Taxes *are* higher; each year the government takes more money out of our collective pockets. It's no surprise that the tax burden is distributed unfairly. How can the burden be redistributed to be more equitable?

The problem: How to make the tax burden more equitable.

The solution? That's your job. See what you can come up with. (Hey, I'm busy solving the problem of cellulite.)

Cause/Effect

In these articles, you set up a situation and describe the results. In most cases, you will trace multiple causes and effects, even within a situation that seems relatively simple. To make your argument easier to follow, telegraph causes and effects with specific *transitions*. Here are the most common transitions used to show cause and effect:

➤ Because	➤ Since
➤ So	➤ For
➤ So that	➤ For that reason
➤ Then	➤ Due to
➤ Consequently	➤ As a result
➤ Thus	➤ Therefore

Here's part of an article developed by cause/effect. See how many causes and effects you can find. Check out some of the transition words, too.

That Lite Stuff

Diet foods aren't new, but the past few years have seen a striking upsurge in their popularity. Health-conscious Americans seem ready for foods that weigh less heavily on their consciences, and food manufacturers are eager to comply. Many products are marketed as "light" or "lite" versions of regular foods—that is, they contain less of such substances as fat, sugar, or alcohol (in the case of beer and wine) and they are usually lower in calories. The whole idea is so palatable that light foods and beverages are one of the fastest growing segments of the American food industry.

FDA Guidelines

Because consumers wonder whether those streamlined foods really do cut back on the calories, the Food and Drug Administration requires products claiming low or reduced calories to meet specific limits on calorie content. This helps consumers shopping with weight control in mind to choose products that represent genuine calorie reductions.

Under FDA guidelines, a food can be labeled "low calorie" only if a serving supplies no more than 40 calories and contains no more than 0.4 calories per gram (28.4 grams = 1 ounce). To be labeled "reduced calorie," a food must be at least one-third lower in calorie content than a similar food in which calories are not reduced, and it must not be nutritionally inferior to the unmodified food.

Food that is labeled low or reduced calorie must also bear nutrition labeling so consumers are not misled. Along with nutrients such as vitamins and minerals, the labels must also give the calories per serving and the serving size to which the figures relate, expressed in identifiable units of measurement such as a cup, slice, teaspoon, or fluid ounce.

Bet You Didn't Know

John McPhee accumulated fifteen years of *New Yorker* rejections before the magazine began buying his articles.

Some Like It Hot: Comparison/Contrast

When you write a comparison/contrast article, you show how two people, places, things, or ideas are the same (comparison) or different (contrast). With this type of article, you can present your material in two ways:

1. Method A	2. Method B
Introduction/Lead	Introduction/Lead
All of topic A	First aspect of topic A
All of topic B	First aspect of topic B
Conclusion	Second aspect of topic A
	Second aspect of topic B
	Conclusion

As with other types of organization, writers of comparison/contrast magazine articles often use transitions to alert readers to key parts of the argument. Here are the transitions you can use as you write these types of articles:

Signal Words that Show Comparison

➤ Still

➤ In comparison

➤ Similarly

➤ Likewise

➤ Like

➤ In the same way

➤ At the same time

➤ In the same manner

All the Write Stuff
Barely one percent of all magazines sold in America appear on newsstands. The vast majority are sold through subscriptions. Research these special interest magazines in *Literary Market Place*.

Signal Words that Show Contrast

➤ But

➤ Nevertheless

➤ However

➤ Yet

➤ Nonetheless

➤ Conversely

➤ Rather

➤ In contrast

➤ On the contrary

➤ On the other hand

Lost in Space: Spatial Order

In this method, you arrange all the events in the article from a single reference point. Events can be arranged from top to bottom, bottom to top, inside to outside, outside to inside, point A to point B, and so on. You will probably use this method most often for descriptive articles, such as travelogues and descriptions of homes.

Here's part of an article whose details are arranged in spatial order. As you read the excerpt, try to see how the writer has arranged the details.

> Nameless, Tennessee, was a town of maybe ninety people if you pushed it, a dozen houses along the road, a couple of barns, same number of churches, a general merchandise store selling Fire Chief gasoline, and a community center with a lighted volleyball court. Behind the center was an open-roof, rusting metal privy with PAINT ME on the door; in the hollow of a nearby oak lay a full pint of Jack Daniel's Black Label.

Did you find that the writer followed the arrangement of stores along the main street?

The Least You Need to Know

➤ How-to articles, (including self-help), interviews, and information articles, are today's best sellers.

➤ Effective openings—*leads*—grab the reader's attention and reel 'em in fast.

➤ Use *transitions* to link related ideas and make it easier for readers to follow your logic.

➤ All things being equal, it's easier to publish a magazine article than a book.

Part 4
Drama, Scripts, and Screenplays

He's as nervous as a badly abused laboratory animal, first kept awake for too long, periodically electrocuted, then given large doses of dangerous drugs and placed in a maze with no exit. In short, he's a script writer.

OK, every job has some stress, but writing a script doesn't have to be as painful as root canal, an IRS audit, or an elementary school orchestra concert. In this section, I'll show you how to write dramatic literature—plays and scripts—without becoming a wreck. The process may not be as easy as programming your VCR or as peaceful as the pit of the Chicago Board of Trade, but we'll have a glorious time anyway.

Chapter 13

Finding the Shakespeare in You: Writing Drama

In This Chapter

➤ Learn dramatic terms

➤ Survey the different forms drama can take

➤ Create structure, conflict, and dialogue in your plays

➤ Revise and edit your plays

➤ Package and present the play

Ever since Zog returned to the cave and put on a show about the size of the saber-toothed tiger that got away, people have delighted in theater. Although we don't have Zog's complete script, we do know from cave paintings and various artifacts such as primitive masks, wigs, and costumes, that men and women since prehistoric times have enjoyed the spectacle of theater.

This chapter opens with a survey of dramatic terms. Then comes a discussion of the different types of drama, so you'll be able to pick the dramatic form that suits your talent and creativity. I'll teach you how to structure dramatic plots, invent exciting conflicts, and create realistic dialogue. Next, you'll revise and edit your dramatic writing. Finally, it's time to package and present the play. Let's raise the curtain.

Aside from that, Mrs. Lincoln, How Did You Like the Play?

Drama is literature written to be performed in front of an audience. The elements of drama are similar to the other forms of fiction you've learned in this part of *The Complete Idiot's Guide to Creative Writing*, such as novels and short stories, but in drama, actors play the parts of characters and tell the story through their interpretation of your words.

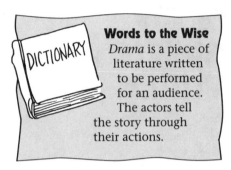

Words to the Wise
Drama is a piece of literature written to be performed for an audience. The actors tell the story through their actions.

Like novels and short stories, plays follow a defined format. For example, you've learned that short stories are a specific length and deal with one main character, conflict, and setting. Plays follow an equally specific set of conventions. These conventions bring up some drama-specific concepts and terms. Here are the Top Ten Playwriting Terms you need to know to write with assurance.

1. *Acts.* Plays consist of one or more *acts*, the main divisions in the action.

2. *Cast of Characters.* Most scripts begin with a list of all the characters in the play. Sometimes each character is described briefly, and these descriptions often show the relationships among characters. The characters are generally listed in the order in which they appear on stage.

   Here's part of the Cast of Characters from George Bernard Shaw's play *Major Barbara:*

   SIR ANDREW UNDERSHAFT

   LADY BRITOMART UNDERSHAFT, *his wife*

   BARBARA, *his elder daughter, a Major in the Salvation Army*

   SARAH, *his younger daughter*

   STEPHEN, *his son*

   ADOLPHUS CUSINS, *a professor of Greek, in love with Barbara*

   CHARLES LOMAX, *a young-man-about-town engaged to Barbara*

3. *Dialogue.* Plays are written almost entirely in *dialogue*, conversation between two or more actors.

   In novels and short stories, dialogue is set off with quotation marks. This is rarely the case in a play. In plays, the characters' names are capitalized and the dialogue follows without any quotation marks. Start a new paragraph for each speaker's words. Here's an example:

STEPHEN: Not at all, mother.

LADY BRITOMART: Don't make excuses, Stephen.

4. *Playwright*. A playwright is a person who writes a play. From now on, that's you.

5. *Props*. Props are objects that the actors need to perform the play, such as books, knives, and bowls.

6. *Scenes*. Acts may be further divided into scenes.

7. *Scenery*. These are the decorations on stage that help show the play's setting.

8. *Script*. The script is the written form of a drama.

All the Write Stuff

Before the dawn of the Politically Correct Age (around 1970), female performers were called *actresses* and male performers were called *actors*. Today, all performers, regardless of gender, are called *actors*. And that's *Ms.* Rozakis, to you, fella.

9. *Stage Directions*. Stage directions are instructions to the actors, producer, and director telling them how to perform the play and set the stage. Stage directions are included in the text of the play, written in parenthesis or italics. They can describe how actors should speak, what they should wear, and what scenery should be used, for example.

Here's a sample from Shaw's *Major Barbara*. The stage directions are easy to spot because they are in italics and parentheses.

LADY BRITOMART: Bring me my cushion. *(He takes the cushion from the chair at the desk and arranges it for her as she sits down on the settee.)* Sit down. *(He sits down and fingers his tie nervously.)* Don't fiddle with your tie, Stephen: there is nothing the matter with it.

10. *Soliloquy*. A soliloquy is a speech one character speaks while alone on the stage. Sometimes there will be other characters present. If this is the case, they seem to become instantly deaf. In the soliloquy, the character often voices his or her deepest thoughts or concerns. Hamlet's "To be or not to be" soliloquy is an example.

Bet You Didn't Know

The first dramas in England were the miracle plays and morality plays of the Middle Ages. Miracle plays told Biblical stories; morality plays, such as *Everyman*, personified key virtues and vices.

171

All the World's a Stage

Playwriting has come a long way since Zog and his saber-toothed tiger. In the last century alone, "play" writing has come to include works not only for the stage but for the screen as well. Since writing for television and the movies is such a fast-growing field, I treat it separately in chapters 14 and 15. In this chapter, we're going to concentrate on the characteristics of stage plays.

Works for the stage fall into three categories:

1. Full-length plays

   ➤ A full-length play is often a two-act play with one intermission or a ninety-minute play with no intermission. Very few three-act plays are produced any more because many producers feel that audiences have developed a shorter attention span. The script for an average full-length play is 85 to 90 pages long.

2. One-act plays

   ➤ One-act plays usually feature five to seven characters and one or two locations. The script runs about 30–40 pages.

3. Musicals

   ➤ Musicals use songs to advance the plot, develop the characters, and create the mood and tone. The length of their scripts depends on whether they are full-length or one-act plays.

Bet You Didn't Know

Watching a play, said Famous Poet and Critic Samuel Taylor Coleridge, involves a tacit agreement between actors and audience to enter into a "willing suspension of disbelief." If not, you've got a gobbler on your hands.

The chocolate and vanilla of drama are *comedy* and *tragedy*. A traditional subdivision of comedy is *farce*. But in these wild and wacky days, we get hybrid dramatic forms of all kinds. Some work well, but others seem about as successful as chicken-fat ripple ice cream.

Below is a list of the different types of drama being written today. Use this list to decide which type or types suit your style, purpose, topic, and audience.

➤ *Absurdism.* Plays that show that the human condition is irrational and silly. In *Rhinoceros,* for example, a rhinoceros runs through the center of town. *Waiting for Godot* (Samuel Beckett) is another boffo example.

➤ *Black Comedies.* Bad things happen to the characters, but the events are so horrible that they're funny. *M*A*S*H,* for instance, shows the horrors of war through comedy.

➤ *Comedy.* A *comedy* is a humorous play that has a happy ending. *A Funny Thing Happened on the Way to the Forum* comes to mind.

➤ *Docudramas.* Plays (and television shows) with a realistic, documentary tone are called docudramas. Steven Spielberg's award-winning story of the Holocaust, *Schindler's List,* is a docudrama.

➤ *Dramadies.* A happy/sad combo, the hog and heifer of theater. Neil Simon has penned a few of these.

➤ *Farce.* A *farce* is a humorous play that is based on a silly plot, ridiculous situations, and comic dialogue. The characters are usually one-dimensional stereotypical figures. They often find themselves in situations that start out normally but turn absurd. Often, humor is created through an identity switch and the other characters' reaction to it. Moliere's *The Doctor in Spite of Himself,* Chekhov's *The Bear,* and W.S. Gilbert's plays are farces.

➤ *Naturalism.* Characters are closely analyzed in a kind of artistic dissection. Humans are at the mercy of the forces of nature. Clifford Odets' *Awake and Sing* is a naturalistic drama.

➤ *Satires.* The vices of a person, society, or civilization are held up to ridicule. Check out Moliere's *The Misanthrope.*

➤ *Surrealism.* Plays that interpret the unconsciousness. Harold Pinter (*The Dumb Waiter*) and Edward Albee (*The Zoo Story*) are famous for these.

➤ *Tragedy.* The leading character has some fatal flaw or weakness that brings about his or her downfall. This results in a disastrous ending, usually death. The most common flaw is overwhelming pride. Arthur Miller's *Death of a Salesman* is likely the most outstanding contemporary American tragedy.

Days of Whine and Poses: Structuring Your Play

About 2,300 years ago, Aristotle pointed out in the first great piece of dramatic criticism, *The Poetics,* that the most important element of theater is the *plot.* Aristotle actually called it the *fable,* and some people call it the *story.* Whatever you call it, there can be little

All the Write Stuff

How can you find the right place to start—and create a logical, believable story line? Start writing your play at the beginning of the story—then throw away the first ten or twenty pages. Now you have your beginning.

argument that what goes on and how it happens is the single most important consideration for the dramatist.

In the past, audiences strolled into the theater, sat down, and listened to one or more characters introduce the other characters, setting, and action. The character might have spoken into a telephone or addressed a minor character. The ancient Greeks used a chorus to accomplish the same thing. It was the classic beginning, middle, and end structure you learned in Chapter 8. Not in today's theater.

Today, an effective play starts with action. The action serves to define the main character, suck in the audience, and propel the play forward. No more leisurely exposition in these frantic days.

Remember the plot diagram you learned in Chapter 8, "The Long and Short of It: Short Stories"? You use the same structure when you build a play, with a few variations:

Action/Exposition — Rising Action — Conflict — Climax — Falling Action — Transformation

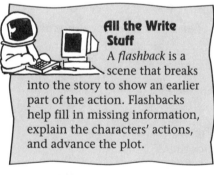

All the Write Stuff

A *flashback* is a scene that breaks into the story to show an earlier part of the action. Flashbacks help fill in missing information, explain the characters' actions, and advance the plot.

➤ *Structuring a Full-length Play*. If you're writing a full-length play, use the diagram twice. Build a climax at the end of Act One and provide a *hook*, a thread of unfinished action that will set off the action in Act Two. Then repeat the diagram and build to a full climax at the end of Act Two.

➤ *Structuring a One-Act Play*. With a one-act play, use a compressed version of the plot structure. There will be fewer conflicts and only one climax.

Why Can't a Woman Be More Like a Man? Conflict

Regardless of the structure you ultimately select for your action, a play without conflict is like freeze-dried kelp made of recycled Styrofoam: empty and tasteless. You'll recall that *conflict* in literature is a struggle or fight. Conflict makes a play interesting because readers want to find out the outcome.

There are two kinds of conflict. In an *external conflict*, characters struggle against a force outside themselves. In Tennessee Williams' steamy drama *A Streetcar Named Desire*, Blanche DuBois has an external conflict with her hunky brother-in-law, Stanley Kowalski.

In an *internal conflict*, characters battle a force within themselves, as Biff Loman does in Miller's *Death of a Salesman*. Plays, as with novels and short stories, often contain both external and internal conflicts. This is true in Arthur Miller's *The Crucible,* for example, as John Proctor battles with Abigail Williams and his own conscience.

Bet You Didn't Know

Read in a theater review: "His performance is so wooden you want to spray him with Liquid Pledge™." No matter how well you write, with your words a play is at the mercy of an actor's performance.

PC or Not PC: Dialogue

Since plays use speech to develop action and character, dialogue is the linchpin of successful drama. Great dialogue can make your play; aimless prattle can break it. Dialogue is not just talk.

Here are some hints for creating realistic, effective dialogue in your plays:

➤ Think of each character's speech as a fingerprint: unique. Match the level of diction to the character's personality. Think how Archie Bunker's use of slang and non-PC language conveyed his character.

➤ Make sure there is an active motive behind what your characters say. Everything they say must be linked to a specific action or feeling.

➤ Use fragments. People rarely speak in complete sentences. Using too many complete sentences can make your characters sound stilted and artificial.

➤ Create a rhythm in each character's speech. Listen to everyday speech patterns to capture these beats.

All the Write Stuff

To create effective, realistic dialogue, read what you've written into a tape recorder. Then play it back and see if each character emerges as an individual.

Good Help Is Hard to Find: Revising and Editing

Revising and editing are vital steps in writing any creative literature, but they can be as baffling as a mosquito in a nudist colony. So much to do! Where to start? Use the following checklist to focus your work. Make photocopies and use a new sheet each time you go back over your play.

1. Structure

   _____Is the opening exciting?

   _____Is there adequate character development?

   _____Is there conflict and action?

   _____Is the plot clear and unified?

   _____Does the play fall within a recognizable category and follow the conventions of that form?

2. Characters

   _____Is each character clearly defined?

   _____Are the characters consistent?

   _____Are the main characters fully developed?

   _____Are the minor characters important enough in the plot to be included?

3. Conflict

   _____Is the conflict introduced in a believable manner?

   _____Is the conflict dramatic and exciting?

   _____Is the conflict resolved in a logical way?

   _____Is the play something that *you* would enjoy seeing?

4. Dialogue

   _____Is each character's speech recognizable and unique to that character?

   _____Is each character's motive clear and logical?

   _____Is dialogue used to advance the plot as well as reveal character?

   _____Have you created realistic dialogue through the use of fragments, diction, and slang?

   _____Does the dialogue follow the rhythms of everyday speech?

5. Script

   _____Is the script in the correct format?

   _____Does the script have a title?

   _____Is the work neatly typed?

   _____Are the pages numbered?

The Moment of Truth: Presenting the Script

You've got a rough draft and a really bad case of nerves. Now you're ready for a *cold reading*. That's when you gather a group of friends to read your play through. A reading is just that: you read the play, sitting around a table, without performing any actions or moves at all. Tape record the cold reading and solicit responses. See what works—and what doesn't—for you and for others.

After you make any necessary revisions to your script, it's time to pass it on to professionals to read. Then comes a *workshop performance*, in which actors perform the play. The input from a real audience helps you gather more information about how the play is working.

> ➤ Do lunch with theater-types and hit the theater party circuit, too.

> ➤ Play nice. We all want to be famous, but remember that the people you meet on the way up will be the same people you'll meet on the way down.

Wrong Turn

An *anachronism is* a chronological error that places a person, event, or object in an impossible historical context— like a character in a Shakespearean tragedy wearing a Timex. Check for anachronisms as you revise and edit.

Words to the Wise

A *cold reading* is an unrehearsed reading of your script.

That's a Wrap: Packaging the Script

"It's all in the packaging," a friend of mine once said. He was right up to a point. The play's package has to conform to the conventions of the genre: no plot summaries spelled out in pepperoni on a pizza, please. Below are guidelines for presenting your script.

Name of the Game: Title Page

Place the following information on the title page:

1. The title of the play, centered in the middle of the page

2. Your name, under the title

3. Copyright statement in the lower left corner

4. Contact information in the lower right corner (including your telephone number). If you have an agent, his or her number goes there instead of yours.

```
                          TITLE OF PLAY
                               BY
                          YOUR NAME



                                        Your Name
                                        Your Address
                                        Your telephone number

 © copyright (current year)
 by (your name)
```

Bet You Didn't Know

A critic is a man who knows the way but can't drive the car. As Disraeli said, "You know who the critics are? The men who have failed in literature and art."

Cast List

The cast list appears on the second page. Here's what it contains:

1. A list of all the cast members and a brief description of each one.

2. The cast size and gender breakdown.

3. The setting (time and place of the action).

4. Length (three acts, one act).

5. Other information (date of the draft, production history of readings, any awards the play has received).

It's a Hard Knock Life

In the long run, it really is *what* you know, not *who* you know—but it doesn't hurt to know people who can help your play get produced. Get a lot of face-time with the theater movers and shakers by following these suggestions:

➤ Network: Get to know the playwrights, producers, directors, and actors in your area.

➤ Attend every possible workshop and play in town—at least twice.

➤ After the play, speak with the playwright, producers, directors, and actors.

➤ Join (or establish) a playwriting group.

➤ Sign up for the local theater groups.

```
                              TITLE OF PLAY




  CAST:

  NAME OF CHARACTER                        Brief description
  NAME OF CHARACTER                        Brief description
  NAME OF CHARACTER                        Brief description
  NAME OF CHARACTER                        Brief description


  Cast Size:  Four Men
  Time: The play begins in 1992 and spans three months.
  Place: Armpit, Idaho
  Length: A play in two acts; one intermission

  Third draft revision:  7/20/97


  TITLE OF PLAY - History of readings and awards


  1996 Winner, Hobart Award
  Arena Stage Theatre Reading, April 1996
```

Pit Bulls and Alarm Systems: Protecting Your Work

Of course you'll have back-up disks and spare copies of your play. But what about the risk of plagiarism? What's to stop someone in a cold reading or workshop from stealing your idea? The law, that's what.

The best way to protect your play from literary theft is to copyright it. To do so, write to the Library of Congress, Register of Copyrights, Washington, DC 20559. Ask them to send you copies of the copyright forms and the information you need to fill them out correctly. Mail back the forms, fee, and a copy of your play. Save the copyright certificate forever. Put it in a safe place, such as a bank vault or under your teenager's bed. No one would *ever* dare go there.

You can also contact the Dramatists Guild (234 West 44th Street, New York, NY 10036, 212-398-9366). They provide a newsletter that lists contests, awards, and the latest marketing and legal news. They also provide quarterly listings of theaters and contacts.

Bet You Didn't Know

When you write a drama, you're working in a long and noble tradition. The ancient Greeks developed drama into a sophisticated art and created such dramatic forms as tragedy and comedy.

The Least You Need to Know

➤ *Drama* is literature written to be performed in front of an audience.

➤ *Comedy* and *tragedy* are the two main types of plays, but there are a slew of hybrid forms nowadays.

➤ Effective plays have zippy action, exciting conflict, and realistic dialogue.

➤ There's a specific way to package, present, and protect your play.

➤ Hell is a half-filled theater.

Chapter 14

California Dreamin': Writing Your Screenplay

In This Chapter

➤ Learn about the different film *genres*

➤ Toon into animated films

➤ Write soap operas

➤ Discover the biggest markets for script writers

Gone with the Wind, Nightmare on Elm Street, Love Story, Dune, Die Hard, 101 Dalmatians, The English Patient, Evita, The Big Chill—movies offer something for everyone. As a scriptwriter, you are in the enviable position of being able to craft a movie that people are really going to want to see. That's what this chapter is all about.

First, I'll take you on a survey of the different types of movies so you can learn the basics of each variety. Then you'll focus on writing animated films, a.k.a "cartoons." Next, ever think about writing for daytime television—the soaps? I've included a section on this type of scripting as well. Then you'll explore the largest markets for script writers and discover what you need to write these types of films. Finally, we'll survey computer software that can make it easier for you to generate and format your scripts.

Can't Tell the Players Without a Scorecard: Feature Films

Before you start to write your script, you have to figure out what kind of movie you're writing. The success of many scripts hinges on whether the structure is appropriate to the genre. You learned in Part 2 that a *genre* is a major literary category. In literature, the major genres are *prose* (novels and short stories), *drama* (plays), and *poetry*. Here are the most common movie genres:

➤ Comedy (farce, parody, slapstick, screwball)

➤ Action/adventure

➤ Thriller

➤ Horror

➤ Romance

➤ Westerns

➤ Science fiction

➤ Drama

➤ Children's

➤ Mystery

➤ Historical

➤ Epics

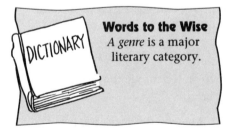

Words to the Wise
A *genre* is a major literary category.

Few screenplays fall neatly into one genre. Many are a mix of genres—a thriller with some romance and comedy, for example. Feel free to combine complementary genres, as long as you understand the boundaries of each one. Let's take a closer look at some of the most popular movie genres—comedy, action, thrillers, and horror—so you can pick the one that's right for you.

Laugh Riot

Here's the basic rule for writing comedy: "A comedy needs to be funny." I know, I know, that's so *obvious*, but if it's so obvious, why do we have so many embarrassingly unfunny flops?

A successful comedy is either funny or it's not funny. There's no middle ground. Being a little funny is like being a little pregnant: not possible. In addition, comedy is a very unforgiving genre. If you're working on a love story and the third act is a little weak, the script can be doctored up a bit here and there. But if a comedy isn't funny, it just isn't funny.

Before you write your script, study the hit comedies. Look at the classics—movies like *Bringing Up Baby, Desk Set, Adam's Rib, A Night at the Opera, Duck Soup*—as well as flicks by Mel Brooks, Albert Brooks, and Woody Allen. See what devices the writers use to create humor. Here are some techniques to watch for:

➤ Dialogue

➤ Sight gags

➤ Characterization

➤ Physical comedy

➤ Silly, absurd plot turns

Non-Stop Action

Die Hard, Lethal Weapon, Rumble in the Bronx, Rocky, Predator, 48 Hours, Rambo. When they make it, action movies make it big. Why? Well, it's clear that many theatergoers enjoy a well-done escapist piece (including yours truly and her hubby), but an action movie needs more than mad car chases to be a blockbuster. Action movies hinge on these five qualities:

➤ Admirable heroes

➤ Villains worth fighting

➤ Emotional depth

➤ Universal themes (freedom, patriotism, justice, love, family, destruction of evil)

➤ A fresh take, not a stale rehash

All the Write Stuff
Pay attention to what the general public seems to be into at the moment: see what kinds of trends there are in the marketplace and write to that, if you can.

Thrills and Chills

Successful thrillers are driven by edge-of-your seat suspense and a gripping plot that accelerates like a commuter about to miss the last bus. These movies sweep us into the emotional maelstrom of the characters and situation by creating genuine suspense and mounting tension. To work, the plots have to hang together logically; no holes large enough to drive a Buick through, please.

Here are some ways that you can make your thrillers really thrilling:

➤ To heighten the terror and suspense, create a terrifying villain.

➤ The villain must have a very strong motive. It is often revenge.

➤ Make the villain (as well as the hero) a three-dimensional, complex character.

➤ Have the hero completely deceived by the villain at first.

➤ Isolate your hero from his or her support system.

Again, watch the winners over and over to see how it's done. Anything by Alfred Hitchcock is ideal, especially *Psycho, Rear Window, Vertigo,* and *Notorious*. Modern nail-bitters that make good models include *Basic Instinct, The Temp, Fatal Attraction,* and *Silence of the Lambs.*

The Horror! The Horror!

What do *Nightmare on Elm Street, The Hills Have Eyes, Shocker,* and *The People Under the Stairs* all have in common? They were all created by one of the modern masters of shock-a-roonies, Wes Craven. Here are some of Craven's suggestions for crafting a truly horrifying horror film:

1. Write sympathetic central characters.

2. Don't exploit your characters, especially women.

3. Create charismatic, powerful, frightening villains.

4. Craft a clear, compelling storyline.

5. Deal with the forbidden.

6. Tap dreams and daydreams.

7. Hit the areas where there are deep disturbances in our psyches.

Fine Tooning

Come on, you can tell *me* your secret little vice…you watch cartoons, don't you? Okay, so it's *The Simpsons, The Critic,* and *Ren and Stimpy* rather than *Teenage Mutant Ninja Turtles, Rugrats,* and *Beavis and Butthead*—but they're still cartoons. Not to worry; you have plenty of company. Everyone likes cartoons, those delightful moving images known in the business as "animated films." This is one of the most exhilarating and wide-open types of script writing.

Are you child-like but not childish? Do you like videos and comic books? Then you might have a flair for writing cartoons. Cartoon writers need to produce strong visual story-telling, pared-down dialogue, and fast pacing. Tooners must also be able to appeal to children without talking down to them or talking over their heads.

There are many different kinds of animation writing. You're probably most familiar with Saturday morning cartoons, beloved by late-sleeping parents and early-rising tots. But there are also animated feature films (*Who Killed Roger Rabbit?, Toy Story*), *anime* (as fans call Japanese animation), interactive games, computer animation, and animation-as-art films.

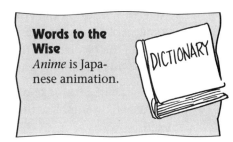

Words to the Wise
Anime is Japanese animation.

Fan Fare

Cartoons can be divided into two categories:

➤ Soft: comedy, fairy-tale cartoons with a soft look, such as *Rainbow Brite*. These are generally targeted at girls and boys ages 3–8. Focus on fun stories that kids can relate to.

➤ Hard: quasi-realistic action/adventure shows, such as *X-Men*. These are generally aimed at older boys, ages 5–12. The tone can be a little harder; the situations a little more sophisticated.

Words to the Wise
Soft cartoons are sometimes called *squishies* by cartoon writers.

Both types of animated features follow the same script format.

Bam! Pow! Zowie!

Scripts for animated features are fraternal twins to scripts for live-action movies. Scripts for toons are different in three major ways:

1. There's more visual description.

2. There's less dialogue.

3. The description is much more specific.

As a result, half-hour cartoon scripts tend to run from 36 to 46 pages, as contrasted to 24-page half-hour live-action scripts. That's because directors of live-action scripts require only guidelines for movement and action. But cartoon artists need to know exactly what to draw and how it will fit in with the whole sequence. In effect, the writer of an animation script is like a director.

Animated films come together in different ways. In some instances, you write a script, it gets bought, the producer hires an animator, and voilà! In other cases, the scriptwriter is also an animator. Some writers seek out an animator to create storyboards for them. The process depends on the writer's reputation and skills.

To learn how to get the visual aspect of animated features, study comic books. Since a comic book doesn't move, the panels function as a kind of shorthand. In effect, you "read between the pictures" to fill in what's missing. In an animated show, the writer has to provide this linking information.

Here's part of a comic-book script. It was written by Bob Rozakis, author of more than 400 comic book stories. Use this sample as a model when you write scripts for animated features.

> Panel 1: Charlie Chipmunk is sitting in his treehouse, looking down, curiously, at a pile of chestnuts on the ground below.
>
> CHARLIE (thought): Hmmm, those look delicious. I wonder who left me a present.
>
> Panel 2: Shooting over the shoulder of Farmer Bill, holding a net in his hands. He's laughing as he sees Charlie in the tree looking down at the nuts.
>
> BILL: Heh heh! That's it, my little chipmunk friend. You just come down and get those nuts—
>
> #2:—and THEN I've got you!!

Toon In

How can you break into this type of screen writing? Getting your finger in this pie is easier than writing feature films or television scripts because the money is much less. In cartoons, the writer is paid once, unlike writers of live-action features. Because the writers' fees are lower, producers risk much less money when they hire a novice writer. There is also a lot less competition. Follow these steps to become a Tooner:

1. Pick a cartoon show you like.

2. Focus on a syndicated show; they do more episodes and consequently need more writers.

3. Call or write Local 839 (4729 Lankershim Blvd., North Hollywood, CA 91602-1864, telephone 818-766-7191) and ask for a Studio List. It's free and lists all the union companies.

4. There are non-union companies as well. You can get these from the lists of animation producers in trade magazines, such as *Daily Variety* and *The Hollywood Reporter*.

5. As you write, use the model of the comic book panel here.

That's all, folks.

Daze of Our Lives

Will upright Bernie bed Bridget, that slut? Is Harriet homosexual, bisexual, or asexual? When will Brittany admit that she really loves the reformed alcoholic Colin (her first boss, second cousin, and third husband)—and not that reprehensible rake William?

Call it melodrama, voyeurism, or real life. Whatever you call it, soap operas ("daytime TV" in the industry) are daily fare for millions of viewers. That makes the soaps a rich market for scriptwriters—*you!* Most people in the daytime TV industry agree that a new writer with talent and persistence will eventually get hired.

Here are three terms you have to know to write for the soaps:

➤ *Script*: the dialogue in the form of a 35- to 40-page shooting script.

➤ *Breakdown*: the story outline for a single show in narrative form. Figure 1–12 pages.

➤ *Sample:* a trial script or breakdown.

All the Write Stuff
Try creating a "storyboard" to help you visualize the interplay of characters and action. Make a storyboard by drawing small boxes. Fill in each box to plot the story. The finished product will look like a comic strip.

All the Write Stuff
To write the soaps, read the classics—Dickens, Thackeray, and Austen. The classics deal with timeless human themes like love, revenge, jealousy, and so on, and soaps play on the same heart strings. Soaps are the same classic stories in modern clothing.

Soap Suds

Being a great writer doesn't guarantee success in the soaps, however. The following five qualities are essential:

1. The ability to write for already-existing characters
2. A complete knowledge of the show's plot and style
3. The capacity to tell a great story

All the Write Stuff
To get the dialogue right, turn the show on and close your eyes. You know the characters well enough to write their dialogue if you can distinguish them from their voices and speech patterns alone.

Words to the Wise
A *tag* is the dramatic closing scene in a soap opera, the cliffhanger.

4. The aptitude to interweave plot lines (since each hour show interweaves five to seven story lines)

5. The ability to create realistic dialogue

How can you acquire these skills?

1. Select and study a specific soap opera.

2. Know how many acts "your" show has.

3. Discover which plot is numero uno.

4. See what role humor plays in the show.

5. Study the camera angles. Since soaps are generally videotaped with three cameras, there are limited camera angles.

6. Pay close attention to scene openings.

7. Explore the ending tag, the *punch*.

8. Be able to write *fast*.

Down and Dirty

In Chapter 15, you'll learn the nitty-gritty of writing a script: structure, characters, plot, and dialogue. Here are some specific guidelines for writing a soap script:

Each episode contains 18–24 scenes. The opening segments, called *teasers*, serve to catch the audience's attention. Every 60-minute show has a teaser as well as six acts; each act includes two or three scenes each—labeled A, B, C. Each drama is divided into three stories, ranked according to their importance. The first, or main story, is usually introduced in teaser C and continued in act 1, scene A. Cliffhangers are used to carry the audience through commercial breaks. They are also added at the ends of the teasers in acts 3 and 6.

The script must also follow a specific format. Write the following information on page 1:

➤ The title of the show

➤ The episode number

➤ Tape date and air date

➤ Creator's name

➤ Producer's name

➤ Writer's name

➤ Complete cast list

Write the following information on page 2:

➤ A list of all scenes

➤ The sets in which they play

Typically, freelancers are hired to write dialogue. Most are assigned a 35- to 40-page script each week, which they write at home. For a 60-minute show, the minimum fee for a script is about $2,000; for a breakdown, about half.

All the Write Stuff
Writing undercover? To figure out what pen name you should use if you write a soap opera script, take your middle name plus the street where you grew up.

Not-So-Silver Screen

IBM has solutions for a small planet...and they show it on film. GTE makes good things come to light...and they show it on film. Same with JC Penney, Kodak, Ford, GEICO, Little Caesar's Pizza, Farmers Insurance Group, and heaps of other large and small firms. Then there are corporate and industrial videos. Ever wonder who writes the scripts for industrial and commercial films? That "who" can be you!

Industrial and commercial scripts are a different kettle of film. Each calls for different skills. Most of what follows is about corporate and industrial films. Check with people in the field or in books on the topic for additional information.

Take all the multiplex movies ever produced, add all the television shows, and you're still nowhere near the miles and miles of corporate, industrial, and educational films and videos that have been produced. Scriptwriters with their sights set on Hollywood often overlook this juicy market. It's a great source of income while you learn the ropes for writing a blockbuster film. It can also be a great creative writing career itself.

These films fall into the following main categories:

➤ Education

➤ Business

➤ Motivational

➤ Sales

➤ Training

➤ Safety

➤ Product introductions

All the Write Stuff

The International Television and Video Association (ITVA), which has chapters throughout the United States, is a good way to get leads for writing business and training scripts.

More and more companies are relying on films and video. In some cases, they are even using news videos instead of or in addition to newsletters. Many larger production companies have writers and producers who work on staff, but smaller companies use freelancers. Advertising agencies are another source for this type of film-making. Ad agencies often produce training films and business-related shows.

See Chapter 15, "Tales from the Script," for step-by-step guidelines for writing your script.

Sleepless in Seattle

If you want to write the next *Gone with the Wind,* you'd better be based in Hollywood. Looking to break into television writing? New York is not a bad place to reside. You say you live in Furry Armpit, Nowhereville? That's not a promising locale for someone looking to write a blockbuster script for either the large screen or the small one.

But one of the chief advantages of making educational, training, and sales films is that you don't have to live or work in Hollywood or New York. Companies that make non-feature films are scattered throughout the United States. As a result, it's much easier for you to network and make personal contacts no matter where you live. You don't have to be based in California or the Big Apple.

The rules are the same, however. If you want to break into this creative writing market, you have to market yourself.

Fast Track

Try the following ideas if you're interested in this type of creative writing:

1. If you don't have any track record at all, hook up with a volunteer project, such as a charity. Write a great script. You can even get a friend to produce it.

Bet You Didn't Know

Public access cable allows the community to use its production facilities for free for community-oriented projects.

2. Use this script and video as a sample.

3. Do a sample script on speculation for a company.

4. Send letters.

5. Make phone calls.

6. Join professional organizations.

Once your foot is in the door, get a lot of face time with the brass so they know who to call when they're in crunch time. And be sure to keep up with the latest trends in your field.

A lot of big companies have their own corporate video departments with on-staff producers and directors. There are also small production companies (usually listed as video production facilities or producers) that are hired to do the whole thing but farm out the scripting. Management consulting firms like American Management Association often produce generic skills video courses for sale to corporations.

> **All the Write Stuff**
> The International Television Association and the International Association of Business Communicators focus on business and educational scriptwriting.

> **All the Write Stuff**
> The best preparation for writing scripts is reading scripts. You can find scripts in most libraries and bookstores.

Get with the Program

It seems like there's computer software to aid us in everything we do, from getting a date to writing our wills. But perhaps no aspect of human endeavor is as inundated by software as writing.

Over the past few years, heaps of programs have magically appeared to serve a wide range of writing functions: from sparking creativity to formatting scripts to selling your finished work. Since scriptwriting is so hot, many Bill Gates wannabees have churned out a slew of scriptwriting software. These programs fall into two distinct groups: *story development* software and *formatting* software. And not to worry; there are programs for both Mac and PC users.

> **Wrong Turn**
> Now, just because I'm listing all these computer programs doesn't mean you should throw away your pencils and typewriters. It *does* mean that you might want to check these newfangled programs out to see if they work for you.

191

I know that you're too busy writing your script to crawl the mall, so here's a roundup of the latest and greatest scriptwriting software. But since programmers stay up all night eating donuts and turning out more and more stuff, you'll still have to visit some monster chain computer stores and read computer mags like *PC World* to stay up to speed. Or you could always befriend a computer geek of your very own. It worked for me.

Story Development Software

Sick of staring at a blank piece of paper or an equally blank screen? Then you might want to take a look at some of these programs. Since they focus on the creative side of scriptwriting rather than mechanical concerns such as formatting, they might be able to help you round up the usual suspects: plot, characters, structure.

1. *Plots Unlimited.* As the name suggests, this program can help you develop a storyline. Sold as "a kind of thesaurus of plot fragments," *Plots Unlimited* contains more than 5,000 "Conflict Situations," which you can use as the framework for your film's plot. (Around $400)

All the Write Stuff
Get more bang for your buck: even though these programs are marketed as scriptwriting aids, you can easily use them for writing fiction and drama as well.

2. *StoryLine.* The self-help movement squared: *StoryLine* is a 22-step program to building a film. The breakdown of three hit films lets you see what works and what doesn't. (Around $300)

3. *Collaborator. Collaborator*'s like a small child, asking question after question. The questions become an outline built on the time-honored three-act dramatic structure. There's a detailed analysis of the weepy Christmas perennial, *It's a Wonderful Life,* that's nice for studying dramatic structure. (Around $300)

4. *Dramatica.* Through the Desktop, you can create and analyze your story. The program is unique among the ones I examined because it encourages scriptwriters to create their own format rather than filling-in-the-blanks with a pre-established template. The entire program is very versatile and interesting to use. (Around $300)

Formatting Software

There's a specific format to professional screenplays/scripts. If you send in a script that's not in the proper form, your work will scream "AMATEUR"—and then it's rejection slip time. Your handy-dandy computer and some of the following software can take care of this aspect of writing with surprising ease.

Here's half a dozen of the latest programs designed to make your script look like a script. I've listed them from most-to-least ornate. Inspector Gadget–types will no doubt gravitate toward the first entries; Two-Left-Thumbers should shop closer to the end of the list.

1. *Final Draft.* This program formats scripts to industry standards. This lets you focus on writing without getting stalled on form. Press the return key and the cursor leaps to the next logical script element, such as dialogue or character. This baby even inserts the words *More* and *Continued* at the top and bottom of pages for page breaks. There's a spellcheck, thesaurus, and "A and B" pages that convert submission scripts into production scripts. (Around $350)

2. *Scriptware.* Here we have a DOS-based word processing program that formats screenplays, treatments, outlines, and letters. In addition, it can create two-column formats for audio-visuals, documentaries, and commercials. You can keep a running list of scenes with a feature called "Dialogue Box"; "Scene Shuffle" lets you rearrange scenes to get drama to the max. "Format Types Box" matches your writing to film-submit, film-shooting, TV standard, and TV sitcom format. (Around $150)

3. *Scriptware Lite.* This is the bare bones of TV and film scriptwriting. In addition to being easier to operate, it's cheaper. Current prices run around $130 for *Scriptware Lite*; the full-fat version will set you back $20 more.

4. *PlayWrite ScreenWriter.* This baby also formats scripts, but for a lot less money than *Final Draft* and *Scriptware.* Fewer bells and whistles make this a handy option for writers who don't need production and TV features. (Around $150)

5. *Scriptor.* This is the granddaddy of them all. Born in 1983, *Scriptor* is still the program of choice for many industry pros. Designed by people with brains, it's an add-on to Word and WordPerfect. The "Vocabulate" feature scrutinizes your diction, based on word frequency, uniqueness, and more. You can use this feature to make sure your characters speak with a consistent voice. (Around $300)

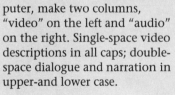

All the Write Stuff
If you don't have a computer, make two columns, "video" on the left and "audio" on the right. Single-space video descriptions in all caps; double-space dialogue and narration in upper-and lower case.

6. *Writing Screenplays.* This is an add-on to Microsoft Word or WordPerfect. It's the cheapest of the lot and gets the job done. ($100)

The Least You Need to Know

➤ There are many different film genres: comedy, action, thrillers, horror, and so on.

➤ Consider writing animated films—cartoons.

➤ Scripting soap operas can provide steady work.

➤ There's a giant market for business and educational films. Jump right in!

➤ Scriptwriting software can make your task easier.

SCENE 1:1
FADE IN...

tap
tap

Chapter 15

Tales from the Script

In This Chapter

➤ Master the script trinity: story, structure, character

➤ Learn how to write a premise

➤ Find out how to create a treatment

➤ Decide if collaborative writing is right for you

"Best picture of the year!" "Two thumbs up!" "Hugely entertaining!" "A blazing triumph!" "A stunning achievement!" "Provocative and entertaining!" The movie is a smash—people are clamoring to see it. Lines stretch around the block; there's even talk of a major award. It's happened to a lot of script writers, even first-timers. It could happen to you.

In this chapter, you'll learn the basics of writing a movie or television script: story, structure, and character. I'll also teach you how to write a *premise*, and explain why you should. Then you'll explore story *treatments*. Finally, I discuss writing in teams so you can decide if collaboration is right for you.

Hot Stuff

If you choose to play the Hollywood game, realize that people who read your script are usually not looking to put their heads in a noose. They want to recommend a script that will make them look good. The burden of proof is on *you* to write that script.

So what are the movie moguls looking for in a winning television or movie script? Here's a checklist you can use:

Concept

____ Is the concept striking and original?

____ Have similar ideas done well in the marketplace?

____ Does the concept have mass appeal?

____ Does it have blockbuster potential?

Story

____ Does the story hook me right away?

____ Might the story offend certain people?

____ Is there a strong emotional pull?

Plot and Structure

____ Is there a clear beginning, middle, and end?

____ Is there strong conflict that engages the audience?

____ Are the scenes logically connected?

Character

____ Is the main character identifiable?

____ Can the main character carry the weight of the role?

____ Are the characters revealed through action?

Dialogue

____ Is the dialogue believable, intelligent, compelling?

____ Does each character have his or her own manner of speaking?

____ Is the dialogue too profane or sexually explicit?

Television and movie producers want a powerful story, sturdy plot , and strong characters. The dialogue must sparkle; the conflict must sizzle like a well-marbled steak on the barbecue. Let's look again at the Big Three: plot, structure, and character, this time as they apply to writing scripts and screenplays.

> **Wrong Turn**
> Hey, careful readers—did you notice that Hollywood wants original ideas but also proven ideas? It's a fine line you tread, bucko.

Story Hour

Story is the tale itself; plot is how the events are arranged. Let's cut to the chase. If your script doesn't ignite by the first few pages, it's nothing more than a heap of wet ashes. Most executives truck home a bundle of scripts every night. If you don't hook these poor overworked, overpaid schnooks from the start, you've earned a one-way ticket to Palookaville. If someone likes what he's reading from the start, he'll keep on reading…and be much more willing to overlook flaws down the line.

Unlike novels and short stories, the internal conflicts in a film script must be made visible. After all, a personal struggle may make a great novel, but nobody's going to sit for two hours and watch someone on screen sitting in a chair and grimacing. Further, the story pacing must be tailored to fit the time (half-hour, two hours, or whatever).

Hook your audience from the get-go. A *hook* (or *teaser*) is a striking incident or action at the opening of a movie that captures your audience's attention. It's most often a bit of dialogue or action, such as a murder, car crash, or sex.

> **Words to the Wise**
> A *hook* (or *teaser*) is a striking incident or action at the opening of a plot that captures your audience's attention.

You know a good story when you see one, hear one, or tell one. A good story has a strong central conflict that can sustain the action over the long haul. Remember that a *conflict* in literature is a struggle or fight. Conflict makes a story interesting because readers want to find out the outcome. Here are some essential conflicts:

➤ Personal conflict (person vs. person)

➤ Inner conflict (person vs. himself or herself)

➤ Extrapersonal conflict (person vs. society)

Film scripts often contain all three kinds of conflicts. For a conflict to be effective, it must be important. The stakes have to be high enough to matter.

Set up the central conflict as early as possible. Ditch the gauzy atmosphere and go for the gusto. Once you've established what's going on, then you can throw in the smoke and mirrors because you've conveyed the core of the story. In movies, you can get rid of a lot of the description and set-up you use in novels and short stories. Since the visual setting in a movie creates immediate atmosphere, you can put leader text on screen to establish time and place quickly. You can also use music and sounds to convey emotions and a change of mood. None of this applies to other forms of fiction.

Build a Better Mousetrap: Plot and Structure

Structure is the arrangement of events in the plot. You've learned in previous chapters that *plot* is the arrangement of events in a work of literature. Plots have a beginning, middle, and end. You arrange the events of the plot to keep the reader's interest and convey the theme. Here's your basic structure:

➤ Act 1: Exposition

➤ Act 2: Rising action

➤ Act 3: Climax and Resolution

All the Write Stuff

Exposition introduces the characters, setting, and conflict. *Rising action* builds the conflict. *Climax* shows the highest point of the action. *Resolution* ties up all the loose ends.

While there's no hard-and-fast rule for script structure, most often the conflict is apparent in the first ten minutes of the film. The rising action builds for most of the movie to create edge-of-your-seat suspense. You'll find the climax and resolution in the last 20 minutes. As you can see, the three acts listed above don't fall into three roughly equal parts.

Set up the conflict in the first act by establishing what the protagonist wants or what he or she is up against. Build the tension in the second act by creating an increasing sense of jeopardy, tension, or urgency. Solve the central conflict in the third act. Tie up all the loose ends in the resolution. Too much can't be left to the audience's imagination. Be sure there's a climax at the end of each act.

The script must move, build, and intensify to hold the audience's attention. There must be a logical connection between scenes. Avoid predictable plotting. The payoff has to be satisfying. Reward the audience for paying attention.

The construction of Sophocles' *Oedipus Rex* and George Bernard Shaw's *Mrs. Warren's Profession* have much in common with the construction of last night's episode of *Frasier* or the movie *Forrest Gump*.

Bet You Didn't Know

British novelist E.M. Forster (*A Passage to India*) described a plot this way: "The king died and then the queen died of grief." Note how one event leads to the other and then builds to a climax and resolution.

Talking Heads: Character

No matter what kind of movie or screenplay you're writing—comedy, drama, musical, bang-bang shoot-'em-up—the characters bring it to life. Create characters who are textured enough that you and your viewers really want to get to know them.

➤ Introduce all your major characters and conflicts as early as you can—preferably in the first 25 pages.

➤ Introduce each character with a brief "sound bite." Short, sweet—and evocative.

➤ Check your dialogue to make sure that every important character sounds unique and can be easily distinguished from every other character.

Words to the Wise
A "sound bite" is a brief description in the form of dialogue.

What the industry also wants is "castable" characters, star roles. Hollywood is a star-driven town, and stars can get movies made. Provide your characters with charisma and depth and the stars will want to play them. There aren't a lot of directors who can make that happen, but there are some stars with the clout. Take the time to create star roles. Make your leading heroes—and villains—unique, powerful, and dynamic.

A sure sign of a novice writer is when character is revealed through dialogue rather than through action. Although dialogue can reveal character, it is limiting. Viewers learn a lot more about characters by what they do.

Film is a visual medium. It's all about revealing characters through behavior.

All the Write Stuff
Characters have a way of developing lives of their own and sometimes the plot has to be shimmied to fit them. Writing is a process of discovery. Stay open to the idea of radical plot shifts.

Bite Me

A word or two about taste. We're all grown-ups here, and we know where the lines are drawn. If a script passes too far over the line, it's going to be bounced. In today's political climate, film executives are definitely concerned with the societal impact of a film and how it will be interpreted.

Here are some boundaries to watch:

➤ Excessive violence

➤ Sexual abuse

➤ Profanity (spare us the Tarantino wannabees, pleeze)

➤ Racism

➤ Sexism

➤ Blasphemy

➤ Mistreatment of animals

Killer Bimbos from Hell Eat *!%#@ *Squirrels*? If you're targeting major studios, you're better off not writing a script that can be easily seen as offensive, degrading, tasteless, or vulgar.

Plot Lite: The Premise

You're sitting all alone, staring at the computer screen. There's a cup of stale java on your right; a half-eaten cookie on your left. Now what? Now you write the *premise*.

A *premise* is a basic idea for a script, what the story will be about. It's the seed for the story, and like a seed, it contains all the elements of the fully grown plant. A premise is *not*

➤ An idea

➤ An area

➤ A concept

A premise *is* your entire story distilled to the fewest possible words. A premise is a summary. As such, it contains your characters, setting, central conflict. Take your time crafting your premise, because it can help you clarify your thinking about the entire story line.

An effective premise accomplishes three main goals. It

➤ Names and describes the main characters

➤ Explains the primary conflict

➤ Hints at the story's resolution

All the Write Stuff
Your *premise* should be no more than two pages long, preferably shorter.

An effective premise, like the plot that develops from it, makes sense. It engages your audience with its emotional tension, humor, or action. Follow these ten steps as you write your premise.

10 Steps to a Foolproof Script Premise

1. Get an idea. Make it a snazzy, fresh one.

2. Expand or contract the idea to fit the length you need: a full-length motion picture, a one-hour television movie, a half-hour television show, and so on.

3. If you're writing an episode for a television series, start with the continuing characters. Fit your story around them.

4. If you're writing a movie, use any characters you wish.

5. Visualize the characters as the premise takes shape. If you can't get a mental image of your characters, neither will the people judging your premise.

6. Create a time and place for the action.

7. Come up with a problem the main character has to solve. The problem must engage the audience, usually through an emotional link.

8. Decide how the problem is solved.

9. Check the characters' motivations to see that everything makes sense.

10. Check your logic. Make sure every action has a logical reason behind it.

Double-check the rough draft of your premise before you make a final copy. Use this checklist.

_____ 1. Does the premise have an interesting "hook" that grabs my attention from the very start?

_____ 2. Do I want to find out more about this idea?

_____ 3. Are the characters realistic and motivated?

_____ 4. Is the central conflict clear and logical?

_____ 5. Is the action intriguing?

_____ 6. Is the ending emotionally satisfying?

_____ 7. Is the overall premise interesting?

_____ 8. Do all the events hang together?

If you answered "yes" to all eight questions, you're ready to move ahead. If not, it's time to retool. Go back over your premise and hone it until it's logical, interesting, and intriguing.

Trick or Treatment

Would you build a nuclear reactor without a blueprint? Does anyone invade a banana republic without a battle plan? You wouldn't even send for an inflatable mate without a detailed list of requirements. Okay, maybe *you* would, but I don't want to know about it. Scriptwriters plan.

Before they actually start to write the screenplay, most professional script writers first map everything out in an outline, called a *treatment*. They go act by act, scene by scene, piece by piece. The treatment is so important, in fact, that many script contracts often include a treatment stage. The executive works closely with the writer to noodle the story, plot, and characters in preparation for the actual screenplay.

Here's a basic outline for your treatment. Expand it to suit your needs. Use your premise (about a paragraph long) to build your treatment. You should have about two pages.

Fill in this worksheet to create your story treatment.

ACT ONE

time and place

_____

Scene 1

_____

Scene 2

_____

Scene 3

_____

Scene 4

_____

Scene 5

_____

ACT TWO

time and place

_____

Scene 1

_____

Scene 2

_____

Scene 3

_____

Scene 4

_____

Scene 5

_____

ACT THREE

time and place

_____

Scene 1

_____

Scene 2

_____

Scene 3

_____

Scene 4

_____

Scene 5

_____

All the Write Stuff
You can use your treatment as a sales tool. If you do so, keep it short and sweet. Err on the side of brevity.

Now it's time to flesh out the treatment into a full-fledged script. Use what you learned in Part 2, "Fiction and Poetry," to select a point of view. Then add dialogue, flashbacks, , and characters as you've learned in chapters 7, 8, and 13. With a script, you even get music, sound effects, and special effects!

Love at First Sight

Writing scripts is both a solitary creative act and a collaborative effort, first among writer, editor, and producer, and then among writer, director, and actors during production. In the script biz, there are plenty of people willing to offer direction.

Many scripts are written as a collaboration. Teamwork helps spark ideas, situations, and characters. Most comedy writers, for example, work in teams. They bounce lines off each other as they would an audience. What happens when writers collaborate?

1. Sometimes, one writer sits at the computer while the other (or others!) paces the room. Think Rob Petrie, Buddy Sorrell, and Sally Rogers on *The Dick Van Dyke Show*.

2. In other collaborations, both writers talk into a tape recorder as they develop the premise.

3. Other times, one writer gets a passage down and the partner rewrites it. Back and forth they go.

If you decide to collaborate, try several different methods (and partners) until you find the combination that works for you. Successful script collaboration is like a good marriage. A bit of crockery may get smashed, but you know you're in it for the long haul.

Is collaborative scriptwriting for you? Only you can decide that. If you decide to take the plunge, here are some guidelines to help you make sure you don't drown:

➤ Respect your partner.

➤ Be willing to compromise.

➤ Meld your creativity with your partner's.

➤ Set your ego aside.

Formatting the Script

Using the correct script format can overwhelm beginning screenwriters. But once you get it down, you'll do it without even thinking, like climbing that damned Stairmaster.

Here are some basics:

1. Use standard 8 1/2 by 11" white paper.

2. Start with FADE IN. Every script starts this way; it's like "The Curtain Rises" in a stage play.

3. Two spaces below FADE IN is the first image or *shot*. Each shot is written in capital letters. One or more shots make up a scene. The first shot tells if the scene is inside (INT) or outside (EXT); whether it's day (DAY) or night (NIGHT). You also give the location (APARTMENT—KITCHEN).

4. Two spaces below this is a description of the characters and scene, written in lower-case letters, margin to margin.

5. Capitalize characters' names the first time they are listed.

6. If you describe the characters, be brief. Here's an example: "LOU, a ruggedly handsome man in his early thirties."

7. Write basic shot descriptions. Specify a close shot, CLOSE ON, if you want something in sharp focus; use ANGLE ON if you want a different perspective.

8. Center dialogue on the page. It is written in lower-case letters, single-spaced.

9. Write the name of the character who is speaking in capital letters two spaces below the shot description.

10. Include directions to tell the actors what to do in a scene. If the descriptions are long, write them single-spaced in lower-case letters, margin to margin. If they are short, write them in brackets within a speech.

11. Write CUT TO: or DISSOLVE TO: at the end of a scene. Place the words on the right side of the page.

12. When a character's speech continues to the next page, write MORE on the line under the last sentence, indented to the same margins as the character's name. Then write the character's name and CONTINUED on the top of the next page.

For additional information on formatting your script, you may wish to check *The Complete Guide to Standard Script Formats, Part One, The Screenplay* by Cole and Haag (CMC Publishers).

Learn the Lingo

Here are some other terms you may wish to use in your script:

➤ ESTABLISHING SHOT: wide-angle shot

➤ TIGHT ON: close-up shot

➤ ANOTHER ANGLE: a new viewpoint

➤ CLOSER ANGLE: closer perspective

➤ CLOSE UP: tight shot

➤ CLOSE SHOT: tight shot

➤ POV: point of view

➤ REVERSE ANGLE: opposite of point of view; other person's view

➤ BACK TO: return to POV shot

➤ FAVOR (CHARACTER'S NAME): focus on that character

➤ CUT TO: end of a scene

➤ DISSOLVE: old scene fading out and new scene fading in

➤ FADE OUT: image fades to black

➤ INSERT: text inserted into a scene

➤ AD LIB: off-the-cuff comments

➤ DOLLY: move the camera to or from a subject

206

➤ PAN: camera moves from side to side

➤ VOICE OVER (V.O.): spoken narration

➤ OFFSCREEN (O.S.): character speaks off screen

➤ BEGIN TITLES: when credits start

➤ END TITLES: main credits end

All the Write Stuff
Remember that all directions are written from the camera's point of view.

It's a Lock

Here's a sample page from a script. Use it as a model. And remember: it's easier than it looks at first blush.

TITLE

FADE IN

1 INT. AIRPORT BAR—NIGHT 1

LOUISE and RITA, two attractive women in their late twenties, are sitting at the bar. LOU, a ruggedly handsome man in his early thirties, walks in and takes a seat at a table a few yards away. The room is illuminated only by a few lamps. There is a long bar and half a dozen small tables. Soothing elevator music plays softly in the background.

2 ANGLE ON LOUISE'S FACE 2

LOUISE

Louise , do you remember that man?

RITA (bemused expression)

I should think so, seeing as I was married to him, I think. Or maybe it was his brother.

LOUISE (astonished expression)

Married to him!

RITA (calmly)

It wasn't legal. I've been married to no end of men. No use going into it.

MORE

EXT. AIRPORT GATE—NIGHT

All the Write Stuff
As a rough measure, one page of script equals about 45 seconds of running time, give or take.

Circle the Wagons

By now, you should have hammered out a premise, treatment, and perhaps even a rough script. Keep writing. As you do, remember that less is more. Go light on camera angles and moves. Avoid lengthy descriptions. Let the visuals, music, and sound effects do your work. You're writing a screenplay, not a novel.

Complete this worksheet to make sure you're on track.

---

1. Describe the setting, the location.

    _____

2. Describe the protagonist, the hero.

    _____

3. Describe the antagonist, the villain.

    _____

4. Summarize the plot in 25 words or less.

    _____

5. What problem does the protagonist have to solve?

    _____

6. What is the inciting moment, the event that sets off the plot?

    _____

7. What is the climax, the high point of the action?

    _____

8. How is the conflict resolved?

    _____

9. How do the characters change as a result of their experience?

    _____

A script is long—whether it's for a half-hour sitcom, a one-hour dramatic special, or an hour-and-a-half feature film. Figure at least 100 pages. You'll write, write, and write. You won't get anything else done, other than eat, breathe, and get older. What happens when you've bitten all your fingernails down to the quick and eaten all the super-premium ice-cream in three states? Here are ten tips to keep you going.

1. Keep the action moving. That's why they call it *motion* pictures.

2. Avoid scenes where the characters sit around schmoozing.

3. Even though it seems that every action flick is a remake of *Lethal Weapon* and every comedy is another *48 Hours,* be original. Does the world really need another movie or TV show about buddy cops, drug busts, or damsels in distress?

4. Create a believable world for your characters. Even a sci-fi film has to have an internal logic to be believable.

5. Don't condescend to your audience.

6. Don't plagiarize.

7. Go out on a limb. Remember: You're the only one with the saw.

8. Everything on the screen must have a point and provide information; if not, remove it.

9. Stick with it.

10. Write the movie you want to see when *you* go to the movies.

The Least You Need to Know

➤ Winning scripts have a socko story, a three-part structure, and intriguing characters.

➤ Write a *premise* and a *treatment* to plan your script.

➤ Use the right format to create professional-looking scripts.

➤ Take a body count and keep going. It will be worth it in the end.

Part 5
Selling Your Work

British writer Anthony Trollope was forty-two years old when he earned his first substantial sum from his writing. That money meant so much to him that even at the end of his life he was furious at those people who scorn writing for money. Here's what he said:

"I received my £100, in advance, with profound delight. It was a positive and most welcome increase in my income, and might probably be regarded as the first real step on the road to substantial success."

We write for many different reasons: pleasure, posterity, recognition. Whatever your reason for being a creative writer, let me show you how to support yourself through your labors. In this section, you'll learn how to write query letters, enter writing contests, acquire an agent, and negotiate a contract. I'll explain how winning writing contests and grants can help you make your literary dreams a reality.

Chapter 16

On the Road: Selling Fiction and Poetry

In This Chapter

➤ Learn how to identify the markets for fiction and poetry

➤ Network for fun and profit

➤ Discover how to write a winning query letter

➤ See if electronic publishing is for you

Right now, there are more publishing opportunities than ever before. But nothing's *that* easy. The competition is strong, and it's not just enough to write well—although that is certainly necessary. Sometimes identifying the right markets for your work can take as much time as the writing itself! But you've got to search if you want to publish. That's what this chapter is all about.

Here, you'll learn how to get started publishing your novels, short stories, and poems. I'll show you how to network like a pro and locate the best markets for your work. You'll discover how to write a query letter that works. We'll even talk about publishing on the Web. So lick those stamps and read on.

Don't Shop Till Your Drop: Identifying Your Market

About fifteen years ago, I was a new mother with a long-time job teaching high school English and a burning desire to write. I had earned a Ph.D. so I had read a heap o' books. Books about everything: literature, writing, literature, and more writing. "Write what you know," all the self-help writing books exhorted. What did I know? I knew only one thing: books. So I decided to write a textbook.

Thanks to a casual comment from a colleague in the lunchroom, I came up with an idea for a review text. "What we need is a good review text for Advanced Placement Literature," she had mused over her egg salad. With the bravery born of abject ignorance, I checked the bookstores for an A.P. English review book. There was only one book available and I didn't like it at all. Between spoon-feeding strained pears to my baby and strained grammar to my ninth graders, I wrote up a table of contents, a sample chapter, and set about finding a publisher for my textbook.

Jump Right in...The Water's Fine

I sent the table of contents and sample chapter to every publisher I found in the *Literary Market Place*. My postage bill was larger than the gross national product of a small banana republic. I'd like to say that I promptly forgot about the proposal, but I didn't. Instead, I checked the mail every afternoon as eagerly as a teenage boy searches his chin for new growth.

Sooner than I would have expected, I had a nibble. The nibble turned into an offer, and I published my first book. Of course, the publisher was the first one on the list—ARCO (a division of the same company that is publishing this book!). The moral of the story? Forget mass mailings; target your efforts. That's what the following section is all about.

Let Your Fingers Do the Walking: Literary Market Place

Before you can publish anything, you have to identify your market. Start with the almanac of the U.S. and Canadian publishing industries—*The Literary Market Place*. This book is published every year by Writer's Digest Books. It tells you where and how to sell what you write. You'll get the names, addresses, and publication requirements of all the major publishers. Currently, *LMP* lists more than 30,000 publishers. *Writer's Market* is another excellent source for this info (Writer's Digest Books).

Here's what you can find in these two books:

➤ Advice for making your first sale.

➤ Sections on contracts and agreements.

➤ Your rights as a writer.

➤ Copyrighting information.

➤ Tax information.

➤ Pricing guidelines.

➤ Major book markets.

➤ Small publishers.

➤ Consumer magazines.

➤ Trade, professional, and technical journals.

➤ Scriptwriting information.

➤ Syndicates.

➤ Literary agents and literary agencies.

➤ Writer's contests and awards.

> **All the Write Stuff**
> Get the most recent edition of *The Literary Market Place* or *Writer's Market*. People in publishing change jobs, names, and duties faster than Dennis Rodman changes hair color. Dated reference texts yield dated (read "useless") information.

Finding the Right Strings and Pulling Them: Networking

Sometimes, locating the right market for your writing is enough to make an easy sale—but a little extra push never hurt. That's where networking comes in. It's the same principle behind my mother's classic comment before every one of my dates: "So put on a little lipstick. What could it hurt?"

Networking is making and using connections. For example, if the fit is right, submit your manuscript to the publisher where an old friend is an editor. Then call the friend and ask her to put in a good word for your manuscript. You might "do lunch" with the friend and discuss the outlook in her company for novels on your topic, theme, or genre—before you submit your manuscript.

Here are two other ways you can network to help get your words into print. I use both of these methods all the time.

➤ *Attend writers' conferences.* I have made several very helpful contacts at these conferences. Buttonhole writers and get them to give you the help you need: advice about getting published, the name of their agent, a tip about which publisher is looking for what book. You can find conferences advertised in *Writer's Digest, Poets and Writers*, and the National Council of Teachers of English bulletins and magazines.

➤ *Attend library and bookstore signings of authors you want to meet.* Be brash and convince the authors to look at your work or suggest other people who can help your career. The person most likely to do this is someone who has interests similar to

Wrong Turn

If you attend a writer's conference or book signing to network, be sure to come armed with copies of your writing and a resume. Otherwise, your efforts are likely to be for naught.

those shown in your work. For example, if you write about the glories of war, don't expect a pacifist to come out in your corner.

If the world were a different place, you wouldn't have to do all of this politicking. You could sit home and write and your books would sell themselves. It ain't so, Sam. Very few people get jobs by sending out resumes; they beat the bushes on their own behalf. Networking is not for the faint of heart. Screw up your courage and sally forth.

Can't Tell the Players Without a Scorecard: Who's Who in Fiction and Poetry Publishing

It may seem like you have to wade through a million layers of people to publish your fiction and poetry. Actually, there are only a few rungs on the ladder between you and publication. Let's take a look at the hierarchy.

Start with the *literary agent*, your *exclusive* marketing representative. Your agent can find the right market for your writing, get your book to the right editors, set up meetings with publishers, and negotiate contracts. For these services, the agent takes a percentage of your profits. See Chapter 18 for a complete discussion of what an agent can—and can't—do for your writing career and whether or not you should hire one.

All the Write Stuff

Don't just plop your manuscript in the mail and hope the editor whose name you found in *Literary Market Place* reads it. Always try to make a prior connection, by phone, letter, or a personal meeting.

Next we have the honchos inside a publishing company, the editors. An *editor* deals with your manuscript. There are different kinds of editors. An Acquisitions Editor, for example, is charged with finding writers and signing their books. You can submit your novel directly to an editor, without using an agent. However, keep the following in mind:

➤ If you don't make any prior connections with the editor, you're submitting "over the transom."

➤ Your manuscript then goes into the "slush pile" where it may or may not be read.

See Chapter 21 for a complete survey of editors and their responsibilities.

Ever wonder how editors make up their minds whether to accept or reject a book, story, or poem? How do editors decide which writers have that essential *je ne sais quoi* that ensures publication? Which novels make it to print—and which ones don't? The process involves style, taste, reputation, current needs, and sometimes a secret weapon: readers.

Who does all the reading? A group of people called, amazingly enough, readers. These readers sift through books, manuscripts, and galleys in search of what will please the cultural quirks of readers around the world. They look for books they just can't put down—a nonstop read.

Bet You Didn't Know

Readers are also the eyes and ears to the American market for major international publishers. And international sales can make you beaucoup bucks, baby!

Then come the scouts. *Literary scouts* are people whose business is identifying the next resident of the *New York Times* Best Seller list, a new and improved Tom Clancy, Alice Walker, Robert Ludlum, Stephen King, and Barbara Taylor Bradford. To find hot new writing talent, scouts read the stories in mass market and literary magazines. They also talk to agents, attend writing conferences, and meet with big-name writing teachers. In addition, they hobnob with successful writers to get recommendations for up-and-coming talent. How can you get scouted? We're back to networking. It's an effective way to get your work and name on the map.

Bet You Didn't Know

Movie producers and television producers also rely on scouts—a lot.

Letter Perfect: Writing a Query Letter

A *query letter* is a letter to a publisher or editor to get him or her interested in your writing. There is no great mystery to writing a great query letter. It's simply a matter of presenting an idea that has a shot at piquing the editor's interest and writing the letter well enough to show the editor that you know your way around the language.

Wrong Turn
Be sure all your contact information is completely accurate. Nothing kills a potential sale faster than misspelling the editor's name or screwing up his or her title.

There are four sections to an effective query letter:

➤ Make a connection.

➤ Get the editor interested.

➤ Reel 'em in.

➤ Leave 'em panting for more.

Here's the opening paragraph from a query letter I wrote to an acquaintance about publishing an anthology of short stories. Notice how I built on our connection:

All the Write Stuff
If you send a sample chapter from your novel, pick an excerpt that shows off your writing style to best advantage. Send your most polished poems and short stories, too.

It was good talking to you this week—and thanks for the chance to pitch a few ideas about publishing a short story anthology with your firm. I took your suggestion and toured the local book stores. I also contacted a few friends around the country (via the Internet) and asked them to scout the shops for me. Here's what I came up with:

On the following page is a sample query letter for a novel. I've inserted brackets ([ ]) to show you how you can easily adapt the letter to suit any other type of writing. Notice that the letter is single-spaced.

If luck is on your side, the editor might write back asking for a synopsis, sample chapter, and a resume. Luckily, you already have these on hand as marketing tools.

Book 'Em, Danno: Submitting Your Manuscript to Book Publishers

How many unsolicited novel manuscripts do you think are submitted to publishers every year? About 10,000? Maybe 20,000? As high as 25,000? Guess again.

Words to the Wise
According to international standards, a "book" is a publication with at least 49 pages, not counting the covers.

Every year, *more than 30,000 manuscripts* find their way to publishers' desks, sent over the transom, stuffed under the mat, and whizzed through the U.S. Mail. Only about 2,000 brand new novels are published every year. Don't figure the odds; it's too grim. Besides, most of those novels were solicited by the publishers. Only a handful came from first-time novelists.

Your name
Your address

Date

Acquisitions Editor
Publishing Company
Address

Dear (Acquisitions Editor):

I am a New York writer with a new novel called [*Title of Novel*] that I'd like to submit to your publishing company. It's the engrossing story of four single men who discover the truth about their past. My friend Bob Harris, winner of the 1997 Hobart Prize for fiction, suggested that I contact you because of the success he has had publishing his last three books with your company.

Humorous in tone, with touches of satire, the novel explores the nature of communication—and miscommunication—between men and women. In the opening chapter, [description of exposition]. By Chapter 3, [description of characters and conflict]. At the end of the novel, [description of conclusion].

My previous novel, *Heartbreak Hotel*, received enthusiastic critical reviews. Louie Louie, writing in *The Village Voice*, called *Heartbreak Hotel*, "The best slice of suburban life since 'Leave It To Beaver.'"

Would you like to read [*Title of Novel*]? I would be happy to send you a synopsis and sample chapter. I can be reached at the address listed above, at [area code and phone number], or at [e-mail address].

Thank you for your consideration.

Sincerely,

Your name

Paragraph 1, last line: Make a connection.

Paragraph 2, first half: Get the editor interested.

Paragraph 2, second half: Reel 'em in.

Paragraph 3: Leave 'em panting for more.

Don't throw your computer out the window yet; things aren't as bleak as they seem. Publishers *do* buy the novels of first-time authors. They *are* actively looking for fresh, new writing. It's difficult to get your novel published, but it's not the impossible dream.

To publish, you need the three T's: talent, tenacity, and a tough skin. I *know* you have talent. Stick with me, kid, and you'll acquire tenacity and a tough skin.

Bet You Didn't Know

Jean Auel's first novel, *The Clan of the Cave Bear*, fetched a $130,000 advance from Crown Publishers. Within two years, the novel earned her $675,000 in royalties.

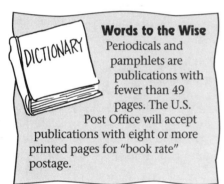

Words to the Wise

Periodicals and pamphlets are publications with fewer than 49 pages. The U.S. Post Office will accept publications with eight or more printed pages for "book rate" postage.

Once your book is finished, you have to decide how to get it into print. Here are your four choices:

➤ A large publisher

➤ A smaller, specialized publisher

➤ A vanity press

➤ Self-publish

The Big Kids on the Block: Large Publishers

The large publishing firms, such as Macmillan and Random House, concentrate on books that will attract huge audiences. They must sell close to 10,000 copies of a hardcover book to break even. Most initial print runs are for 5,000 books. Then the title "remains in print" (available for sale) for one to three years. If the book doesn't sell, it's pulled off the market and "remaindered" (sold at a steep discount) to make room for new titles.

To increase their chances of success, the large publishers spend 80 percent of their effort on the top 20 percent of their books. If you're on the bottom 20 percent, it means you're going to have to beat the bushes yourself before the publisher will throw promotion money your way. Beat away; it worked for me.

Large publishers are right for you if you...

1. Value this type of recognition.

2. Have a personal connection to a large publisher.

3. Are content with the editorial policies and fee structure they offer.

All the Write Stuff
Genre novels—romance, Gothics, and mysteries—are the most lucrative type of fiction.

Mighty Mites: Specialized Publishers

These publishers zero in on certain areas such as regional books, poetry, technical books, and so on. The largest of the small presses often publish only twenty-five or so titles a year; the smallest of the small presses are very small indeed. To find a small press, consult Dustbook's *International Directory of Little Magazines and Small Presses* as well as *Literary Market Place.*

Although smaller publishers can be very pleasant to deal with because they can provide a personal touch, they face the same economic constraints as the big guys. They still have to reckon with the bottom line—rising medical costs, skyrocketing paper costs, and a lack of serious readers.

Specialized publishers are right for you if you...

1. Wrote a book on a very specific topic.

2. Have targeted a niche market.

3. Want to retain more control over your book.

Vanity, Thy Name is Writer: Vanity Publishers

These so-called "vanity publishers" offer regular publishing services—but the author pays the total cost of publishing the book. In return, the author receives 40 percent of the price of the books sold and 80 percent of the subsidiary rights, if sold. Figure on spending between $2,000 and $15,000 to publish your book this way, about $30 per printed page.

Book reviewers tend not to look kindly on books that have been issued by vanity presses. They figure that the book was rejected by large and small publishers. As a result, you're not apt to get any publicity at all if you publish via this route. Since vanity publishers make all their money up front, they have absolutely no incentive to promote your book.

Many of these businesses are advertised in the Yellow Pages of the telephone book under "Publishers." Before you hire one of these firms, consider sending for *Does It Pay to Have It Published?* (*Writer's Digest*, 1507 Dana Avenue, Cincinnati, Ohio, 45207-9988). Also check

All the Write Stuff

If you're thinking of using a vanity publisher, you're better off going to a local printer. This can save you 25 percent to 35 percent over the cost of a vanity press.

out any vanity press you're considering using with the Better Business Bureau before you sign the contract.

Vanity publishing may be right for you if you...

1. Want just a few copies of your book for family and friends.

2. Are not concerned with selling your book.

3. Are not worried about money.

Master of Your Domain: Self-Publish

When you self-publish, you're totally on your own. You take the manuscript to a printer and handle marketing and distribution yourself. But you'll be in good company; self-publishers included Zane Grey, Mark Twain, Edgar Allan Poe, Richard Nixon, James Joyce, and Carl Sandburg.

Words to the Wise

Blurbs are endorsements from well-known people. You want impressive blurbs on your book covers because they can help sell your book. Look for people to endorse your book. (No, Mom doesn't count.)

It takes a great deal of time and effort to self-publish, however. Think it over carefully. While the returns of publishing a book yourself can be greater than the returns from a large publisher, it's also time taken away from your writing. A lot of time.

Self-publish if you feel you...

1. Can afford the investment of time and money.

2. Are willing to promote your book on your own.

3. Want to maintain complete control of your book.

4. Want to start and run a business.

Short Stuff: Short Stories

If you've written several short stories, you can follow the book route. Create an anthology and market it as you would a book. But what happens if you only have one or two stories? In that case, you're more likely to turn toward magazines that publish fiction. Follow these five steps.

1. Look in *Literary Market Place* to find magazines that are most likely to publish your story.

2. Read a few copies of each magazine to make sure you've targeted the right markets.

3. Get each magazine's name, address, telephone number, a contact name, and requirements. Here's a sample entry:

Alfred Hitchcock's Mystery Magazine
Bantam Doubleday Dell
380 Lexington Avenue
New York, NY 10168-0035
editor: Cathleen Jordan
(212) 557-9100

You learn that the magazine pays on acceptance, gives a byline, and buys first serial rights, first anthology rights, and foreign rights. The emphasis is on original and well-written mystery and crime fiction. The story can be no longer than 14,000 words.

4. Send for the writer's guidelines. Be sure to read the guidelines very carefully and follow them exactly. This is no time for creativity. Many editors are very specific about their needs—and they get very annoyed if the manuscript doesn't conform.

5. Submit the story. Keep accurate records of all submissions, noting the names and dates.

Money from the Muse: Publishing Poetry

As with any type of literary publishing, you can't go wrong making your own contacts when you want to publish your poetry. Here are three ways:

➤ Attend poetry readings.

➤ Stage your own poetry readings.

➤ Network with other poets.

Write to the American Poetry Association for a free copy of *Poet's Guide to Getting Published* (P.O. Box 1803-P, Santa Cruz, CA 95061-1803). Here are some other resources to tap:

➤ *The Directory of Poetry Publishers* (Dustbooks, P.O. Box 100, Paradise, CA 95969)

➤ *A Poet's Guide to Freelance Selling* by Kathleen Gilbert (Violetta Books, P.O. Box 15151, Springfield, MA, 01105)

➤ *The Writing Business, A Poets & Writer's Handbook* (Poets & Writers, 72 Spring Street, New York, NY 10012, Telephone 800-666-2268).

On Target

Submit your work like mad. Get your name out there; be in their faces. But you've already learned that sticking a stamp on isn't enough; you have to match your work to the audience. With poetry, match your style of verse to the magazine/journal. Here are some guidelines:

If you write *free verse*, try

➤ *Ascent*

➤ *Poets On*

➤ *Spoon River Poetry Review*

If you write *free and formal verse*, try

➤ *Amelia*

➤ *Blue Unicorn*

➤ *Chariton Review*

➤ *Cincinnati Poetry Review*

➤ *Eclectic Literary Forum*

➤ *Negative Capability*

➤ *Poet* Magazine

➤ *Prairie Schooner*

➤ *Tar River Poetry*

If you write mostly *formal verse*, try

➤ *The Formalist*

➤ *Hellas*

➤ *The Lyric*

➤ *Sparrow*

The Medium is the Message

Let's talk for a second about the appearance of your manuscripts. For novel and short story manuscripts, try to leave a one-and-a-half inch margin all the way around each page. Unless instructed otherwise, be sure to double-space every line. Your pages should be clean.

Penciled-in corrections are acceptable if they are clearly printed and there aren't too many of them on the page. As a rule of thumb, figure no more than two to three penciled-in corrections per page. Be sure to number every page, too.

When you're ready to market your poetry, follow these submission guidelines:

1. If there are no guidelines provided by the publisher, send 3–5 poems, typed single- or double-spaced on good bond paper. Leave at least 1" margins all the way around.

2. Include your name, address, and telephone number on the top left or right-hand corner.

3. Fold your poems in thirds, as you would a letter.

4. Don't staple the pages.

5. Include a cover letter in standard business-letter format. Keep it brief, but be sure to include information about any relevant previous publications.

6. Include a stamped, self-addressed envelope.

Bet You Didn't Know

Publishers' response times tend to be slow in the summer because of vacations. Even at the best of times, expect to wait two to three months for a reply.

Get a Grip

How can you tell if you're ready to submit your work? Fill out this worksheet to assess your progress. And then get the piece in the mail already!

_____ 1. I know the market thoroughly.

_____ 2. For the subject of a novel, I checked *Books in Print* to see what other novels have been published on the subject.

_____ 3. For poems, I checked the poetry journals.

continues

continued

_____ 4. I studied the publisher's requirements.

_____ 5. I have requested writer's guidelines, if they are available.

_____ 6. I checked submission requirements.

_____ 7. I sent only what the publisher wants, a letter, an outline, a proposal, a sample chapter, and so on.

_____ 8. I'm sure my manuscript is in the correct format.

_____ 9. I double-checked all information before mailing my package. I'm sure that I have the correct contact name, and that I spelled it correctly.

_____10. I enclosed a stamped self-addressed envelope with all unsolicited correspondence.

_____11. I made a photocopy of my manuscript.

_____12. I included a good query letter.

_____13. I kept careful records, including photocopies of all submissions and letters.

Electronic Publishing

One of the hottest new ways to publish is on the World Wide Web. You upload your file, post it on an existing electronic bulletin board (or establish your own) and voilà! You're published. Like all of life's simple pleasures, this method has its pros and cons.

Advantages	Disadvantages
It's easy.	You won't earn anything.
There's a massive readership.	You have no copyright.
It's free.	It's not protected.
You don't have to leave your chair.	Only people on-line can read it.
You get feedback—often, quite a bit!	
There's no publisher to deal with.	

> **Bet You Didn't Know**
>
> "Dead tree edition" is cybernaut lingo for the paper version of a newspaper or magazine that also exists in electronic form. Although the term reeks of disdain for a medium viewed as outmoded and environmentally costly, more often than they will admit, cybernauts print their own *dead tree editions* of their favorite Internet fare.

The Least You Need to Know

➤ Be professional.

➤ Target specific markets.

➤ Network, network, and network some more.

➤ Follow up on all submissions; even rejections open the way for acceptances.

Chapter 17

Still on the Road: Selling Nonfiction

In This Chapter

➤ Learn how to sell magazine articles

➤ Discover other markets for your creative nonfiction

➤ Consider KidLit

Now let's turn our attention to getting you some money for your *nonfiction*. You market biographies, autobiographies, textbooks, and reference books as you would a novel. Selling a magazine article requires other approaches, however. In this chapter, you'll get the scoop on publishing short nonfiction. I'll also show you some exciting nonfiction markets you might have never even considered, including greeting cards and kiddie lit.

Articles of Faith

Publishing a magazine article is much more straight-forward than publishing a novel or short story. You can find the editor's name on the masthead of the magazine, send him or her your resume and a brief proposal, and expect a response. If your idea is good

> **All the Write Stuff**
> When you start publishing magazine articles, think small. Consider aiming for a small sidebar piece rather than the cover story.

and the editor likes your style, you may have an assignment, even if you're not a well-known writer. Unfortunately, it's not as simple as writing the article and sending it in.

Doing Hard Time

As you learned with fiction, be sure to analyze the nonfiction market carefully and completely before you even put pen to paper or fingers to keyboard. When it comes to publishing, there's no substitute for doing your homework. Try these ideas.

➤ Using *Literary Market Place,* your local newsstand, or the library's magazine shelves, select a handful of magazines that match your interests.

➤ Read the magazines for several months to familiarize yourself with their format and contents. Get to know what the editors seem to like—and what they seem to hate.

➤ Key into tone. *Reader's Digest* is upbeat and conservative; *GQ* is hip and trendy; *Esquire* is sly and sexy. The more than two million people who bought *V.F.W. Magazine* last year are likely further to the right than Rush. The tone of your article must match the tone of the magazine.

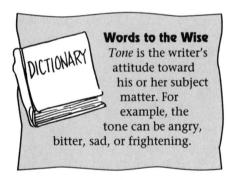

Words to the Wise
Tone is the writer's attitude toward his or her subject matter. For example, the tone can be angry, bitter, sad, or frightening.

All the Write Stuff
If necessary, think about taking less money to publish in a magazine with a large readership. More people will read your work, which will likely lead to more work.

➤ Focus on demographics. Readers of *The New Yorker, Playboy,* and *Condé Nast Traveler* tend to drive Beemers, summer in the South of France, and drink wines I can't pronounce. Readers of *Parents,* in contrast, probably know which Band-Aids stick best and which baby shampoo stings least. Target your articles accordingly. "Sixty Cheap Chicken Crowd Pleasers" won't cut the mustard in *Gourmet* or *Bon Appetite,* but *Women's Day* or *Family Circle* might eat it right up.

➤ Identify the magazine's writers. *National Geographic* writers tend to be world-famous explorers; *U.S. News and World Report* gets some heavy-weight commentators. See where your reputation in a specific area fits with the magazine's reputation.

➤ Check a magazine's publication figures, which are easily available in an almanac. See which magazines are selling best and which ones have filed for bankruptcy. The more copies a magazine sells, the more money it has to pay writers. Of course, this doesn't mean you'll get your share of the pie, especially as a first-time writer.

➤ Check a magazine's schedule. A magazine that comes out once a month will buy fewer articles than one that comes out once a week.

➤ Spot the trends so you can see where the magazine is going with its ideas. For example, a few years back, Scholastic's magazines were jumping on the "Whole Language" movement. Now, however, they are moving back toward phonics. Obviously, today they wouldn't welcome an article trumpeting the glories of Whole Language.

➤ Check the magazine's publishing policy. You will normally sell only first-serial rights—the right to publish the article first in magazine form before its publication elsewhere. This way, any further use brings you more money. Unexpected money is a thing of beauty. See Chapter 19 for a complete discussion of publication rights.

> **Wrong Turn**
> Many publications will not publish articles from writers who accepted "freebies" from their subjects because this creates potential conflicts of interest.

We're in the Money

Payment for short nonfiction articles varies widely. It ranges from less than $1,000 for an article of 3,000–5,000 words to $20,000 or more for a very long, important piece. Few magazines pay more than a dollar a word. It's the rare magazine that pays big bucks. Further, pay for first-time writers is normally at the low end of the scale.

In some cases, the magazine will pay your travel and research expenses. Whether they do or don't ante up for incidentals, be sure to save all your receipts, especially for expenses you incurred on travel articles. You might be able to take these expenses as business deductions on your income tax. Consult your tax preparer.

What happens if the assignment is canceled halfway through? You can usually negotiate a "kill fee" for up to half the payment as compensation for your time if the magazine rejects ("kills") your article.

> **Bet You Didn't Know**
> Writing on "spec" (speculation) is done without any promises from the editor or magazine the article will be purchased or published. Writing on "assignment" is writing with a promise of publication. Novice writers usually begin on spec.

We're in It for the Free Copies

In addition, there are scores and scores of magazines that don't pay any money for your articles. Instead, writers get copies of the magazine in which their work was published.

All the Write Stuff
If the editor came up with the idea for the magazine article, whatever you turn in is at least 75 percent sold.

"What! No money for all my hard work!" you cry in anguish. I share your pain. After all, I received five free copies of *American Transcendental Quarterly* instead of payment for my article on the real woman behind Nathaniel Hawthorne's Hester Prynne. And it was a very nice article.

Still, getting published *is* getting published. And once you're published, it's easier to publish more and more. You can use the free copies as samples to entice more affluent magazines to ante up some bucks.

Watch Out For Hidden Costs

Another issue is permissions and art. Say you want to use a famous poem as the lead to your article. You just can't publish the poem for free; the poet deserves payment for reprinting his or her work. Who pays the permission rights—you or the magazine publisher?

And what happens if you want to include some photographs, illustrations, or other graphics in your article? Who pays the photographer or artist? Good point! Be sure to iron out these issues before you decide where to publish your article. More on this in Chapter 19.

House of Cards: Greeting Cards

Fortunately for creative writers everywhere, most Americans would sooner endure a root canal than pen a personal message. Nonetheless, we all want to reach out and touch

All the Write Stuff
The perfect greeting card message appeals to a mass market, yet makes each buyer feel it was written just for him or her.

someone via print. As a result, greeting cards have become more popular than a one-eyed man in the land of the blind.

Nearly half of all first-class mail consists of greeting cards. Cards are not just for high-visibility holidays anymore; on the contrary, they cover all of life's major—and not so major—events. There are cards for everything from mastering the intricacies of potty training to successfully grooming your pet chinchilla. (If not, you can be sure that someone will write these cards by the time I finish this chapter.) Since people are sending cards for all occasions, greeting card companies are continually searching for *le mot juste*. That's where *you*, the creative nonfiction writer, come in.

When You Care Enough to Send the Very Best

Women still buy most greeting cards, and the three basic categories—contemporary, traditional, and alternative—have held steady for some time. Hallmark, American Greetings, and Gibson Greetings still dominate the market, producing 85 percent of all cards sold.

In general, alternative cards are grabbing a larger slice of the pie. Alternative cards don't refer to lifestyle choices (even though they do exist); in the industry, "alternative cards" are non-occasion cards. Smaller companies have stayed in the running by finding their own market. For instance, Ethnographic produces cards for Mexican-Americans, Asian-Americans, Judaic, and African-Americans. Another small company, Z.I.P., has a line of cards exclusively for adopted children and their birth parents.

Card-Carrying Writer

How can you break into the greeting card biz? Here are five ideas:

1. Keep current on specific company needs.

2. Hang out at the card racks, thumbing through the cards. Try not to crease the corners.

3. Ask retailers which cards are selling best.

4. Read trade magazines such as *Greetings* and *Party and Paper Retailer*.

5. When you find a line of cards that matches your talents and interests, write to the company and request its market list, catalog, and submission guidelines.

When you submit greeting card ideas, be sure to put your most impressive ideas first on the stack. Send five to fifteen ideas at a time, on 3 × 5 cards or 8 1/2 × 11 paper, depending on the specific submission requirements (which you have already sent for, having read the previous paragraph). Most companies pay per idea; a handful pay a small royalty.

> **Wrong Turn**
> Before they even look at your greeting card ideas, many larger companies will make you sign a disclosure agreement, assuring them that your material is original and has not been submitted elsewhere. Be sure you understand the document before you sign.

All the Write Stuff
Some card companies also buy ideas for gift products, including mugs, bumper stickers, buttons, posters, and the like. You can pitch these, too.

Follow these guidelines when you submit greeting card ideas:

➤ Label each sample.

➤ Send a stamped, self-addressed envelope with each submission.

➤ Record when and where you send each sample.

➤ Keep all cards for each company in a batch.

➤ Number each batch.

➤ Write the number on the back of your return stamped self-addressed envelope. This makes your record-keeping much easier.

To Market, to Market

There are many different greeting card companies; the following list is a representative sampling. I selected these companies because most of them buy many submissions from freelancers. The Big Three—Hallmark, American Greetings, and Gibson Greetings—don't cotton much to freelancers, but they *are* the big kids on the block. Consult *Literary Market Place* for additional entries.

1. *Amberely Greeting Card Company,* 11510 Goldcoast Drive, Cincinnati, OH 45249-1695. Phone: (513) 489-2775. *Looking for:* outrageous humor, no seasonal cards.

2. *American Greetings*, Dept. WM, 10500 American Road, Cleveland, OH, 44144. Phone: (216) 252-7300. *Looking for:* conventional mass market verse, prose, humor.

3. *Blue Mountain Arts,* Inc., Dept. WM, PO Box 1007, Boulder, CO 80306. *Looking for:* sensitive writing about love, friendship, families, philosophies.

4. *Gibson Greetings*, 2100 Section Road, Cincinnati, OH 45237. *Looking for:* Won't say, which means they are a tough market to crack.

5. *Hallmark Cards*, PO Box 419580, Mail Drop 216, Kansas City, MO 64141-6580. *Looking for:* "exceptional originality and previous experience in the field." (Translation: Your uncle should be a company VP.)

6. *Imagine*, 21431 Stans Lane, Laguana Beach, CA 92651. Phone: (714) 497-1800. *Looking for:* open to all ideas.

7. *Life Greetings*, Dept. WM, Box 468, Little Compton, RI 02837. Phone: (410) 635-8535. *Looking for:* humorous, inspirational, sensitivity.

8. *Oatmeal Studios*, PO Box 138W3, Rochester VT 05767. Phone: (802) 767-3171. *Looking for:* birthday, friendship, anniversary, get well, holiday cards.

9. *Paramount Cards Inc.*, Dept. WM, 400 Pine Street, Pawtucket, RI 02860. Phone: (401) 726-0800. *Looking for:* all types of conventional verse.

10. *Red Farm Studios*, 1135 Roosevelt Avenue, PO Box 347, Pawtucket, RI 02862-0347. Phone: (401) 728-9300. *Looking for:* conventional, inspirational verse, sensitivity and soft line cards.

> **All the Write Stuff**
> *The Greeting Card Handbook* by Edward J. Hohman and Norma E. Leary (Barnes and Noble Books, a division of Harper and Row, 1981) describes what to write, how to write it, and where to sell it.

KidLit

Writing nonfiction for kids, like raising them, requires a special touch. I suggest you start by concentrating on juvenile and young adult magazines. Read recent issues of the magazines to see which ones match your interests and abilities. Here are some markets to get you started.

For readers ages two to five:

➤ *Chickadee*

➤ *The Friend*

➤ *Humpty Dumpty*

➤ *Stone Soup*

➤ *Story Friends*

➤ *Turtle*

➤ *Crayola Kids*

> **All the Write Stuff**
> *Children's Writer's and Illustrator's Market* (Writer's Digest Books) contains an extensive list of juvenile markets.

For readers ages six to eight:

➤ *Boys' Life*

➤ *Chickadee*

➤ *Children's Playmate*

➤ *Cricket*

➤ *Hopscotch*

➤ *Highlights for Children*

➤ *Jack and Jill*

➤ *Kid City*

➤ *Kid Sports*

➤ *Ranger Rick*

➤ *3-2-1 Contact*

➤ *Sports Illustrated for Kids*

➤ *The Dolphin Log*

➤ *Child Life*

➤ *Math Power*

➤ *Family Fun*

For readers ages nine to twelve:

➤ *Boys' Life*

➤ *Cricket*

➤ *Jack and Jill*

➤ *Highlights for Children*

➤ *Kid City*

➤ *Ranger Rick*

➤ *3-2-1 Contact*

➤ *Sports Illustrated for Kids*

➤ *American Girl*

➤ *Calliope*

➤ *Cobblestone*

➤ *Dynamath*

➤ *Scholastic Math*

➤ *Falcon Magazine*

➤ *Girl's Life*

➤ *Owl*

Puzzle Me This

Want to make your children's articles more fun—and more salable? Try including a puzzle, quiz, craft, recipe, magic trick, or project. Follow these three steps to get started:

All the Write Stuff
Read child development books to help you match the activity to the appropriate age group. I recommend books produced by the Gesell Institute of Child Development series.

1. Target a few magazines.

2. Study several issues.

3. Request writers' guidelines.

Then look for activities that children can complete without adult supervision. The adults will bless you for it, believe me. With crafts, recipes, and science projects, stay away from obscure ingredients and dangerous tools. No plutonium or sabers, please. Since children have short attention spans, keep it simple. List the steps and ingredients in order. Be sure the final product looks good.

Hot Prospects

Here are some children's magazines that buy activities and use them often. To match the right market for the activity, be sure to read several issues of the magazine.

➤ *American Girl*

➤ *Children's Playmate*

➤ *Math Power*

➤ *Scholastic Math*

- ➤ *Boys' Life*
- ➤ *Crayola Kids*
- ➤ *Calliope*
- ➤ *Cobblestone*
- ➤ *Cricket*
- ➤ *Dynamath*

- ➤ *Falcon Magazine*
- ➤ *Girl's Life*
- ➤ *Hopscotch*
- ➤ *Highlights for Children*
- ➤ *Jack and Jill*
- ➤ *Turtle*

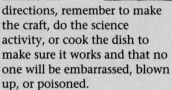

All the Write Stuff
Before you finalize the directions, remember to make the craft, do the science activity, or cook the dish to make sure it works and that no one will be embarrassed, blown up, or poisoned.

The Least You Need to Know

- ➤ Analyze the market carefully before submitting your articles.
- ➤ Payment varies widely—and some magazines pay only with copies, not cash.
- ➤ Consider other outlets for nonfiction, such as greeting cards and children's nonfiction.

I LOVE YA BABE! LOVE YA!

Chapter 18

Secret Agent Man: Literary Agents

In This Chapter

➤ Learn what a literary agent does

➤ See if you need a literary agent

➤ Discover how to select the agent who's right for you

According to legend, a popular writer requested in his will that upon his death, his body be cremated and 10 percent of his ashes thrown in his agent's face.

As this anecdote illustrates, agents tend to spark somewhat ambivalent feelings among their clients. Maybe that's because the author/agent relationship is likely the most significant relationship in publishing.

You've learned something about literary agents in previous chapters. Here's where I concentrate on the nitty-gritty of dealing with agents. First off, we'll see if you really need an agent. I'll take you step-by-step through the advantages and disadvantages of hiring an agent. If you decide that you *do* need an agent, I'll show you how to find the one that's right for you.

Do You Need a Literary Agent?

➤ You've finished half of your first novel. Do you need an agent now?

➤ An editor liked the synopsis and sample chapters from your first novel. Should you start agent shopping now?

➤ Happy day! A publisher wants to buy your novel. Is it time to hire an agent to work the deal?

➤ Maybe you've already sold a few novels on your own but you think you're not making as much money as you could. Do you need an agent?

Words to the Wise
A literary agent is an author's representative.

Literary agents represent writers—at all stages of their careers. An agent is your front man or woman. But *exactly* what does a literary agent do? Here are some of a literary agent's functions.

A literary agent…

1. Is your *exclusive* marketing representative.

2. Finds the right market for your writing.

3. Shops your books, plays, and screenplays around.

4. Gets your book to the right editors.

5. Sets up meetings with publishers.

6. Negotiates contracts.

7. Recommends you for other writing work.

8. Saves you time and money.

9. Collects all advances and royalties due to you.

10. Shelters you from conflicts with editors and publishers.

11. Tracks your publishing accounts.

12. May or may not provide tax information to the IRS.

13. Takes a percentage of your income.

Wrong Turn
If you sign with an agent, it becomes an exclusive deal. This means that anyone who wants to talk about your literary properties must go through your agent.

Wrong Turn
Getting a good agent to represent you can be as difficult as getting a publisher to publish you. You can't just go out and hire an agent like you buy a pot roast.

Say you're a beginning writer, plodding away on your first book. If you've created a strong synopsis for your novel and have several impressive chapters written, odds are you don't need an agent to sell the book. Therefore, at this point in your writing career, it may be premature of you to be thinking about hiring an agent to *sell* your work. Note the emphasis on the word "sell."

If this scenario fits your current situation, I suggest that you first try to publish some excerpts from your novel in literary or mass-market magazines. Once you succeed in this, you'll have the beginnings of a literary track record. This will make it easier for you to publish more fiction and nonfiction, especially longer pieces. It will also encourage an agent to want to represent you, if you decide that's what you want.

> **All the Write Stuff**
> You're least likely to need an agent to sell a mystery, science fiction, or romance novel.

First Night Jitters

Even if you sell your first book on your own, you may wish to have an agent close the deal. That's because a good agent can often help you get better terms than you can get on your own. This paves the way for more lucrative contracts in the future, too.

"Hold the phone!" you say. "I'll have to shell out 10 to 15 percent of my money for the agent's cut. How can I still do better with an agent?" Logic would suggest that you're better off flying solo on this one. But not so fast.

Your first writing contract is important, perhaps the most important one you'll ever get. Mistakes at this point can cost you a great deal of time, money, and aggravation. Losing time and money are bad enough, but having to endure aggravation is simply not acceptable.

> **All the Write Stuff**
> A good agent can earn out his or her percentage—and more— by knowing how to ask for more on subsidiary rights, foreign sales, and so on.

Keep in mind that when you sign a contract with a "publisher," the odds are that you're really entering into an agreement with a multimedia entertainment conglomerate. The days of Mom-and-Pop publishing houses are as long gone as the iceman, 10-cent cigars, and "till death do we part." Even if you and your editor have forged a close personal relationship, your editor is under no obligation to stay with the publishing house forever. If your editor leaves, all you have is that piece of paper you signed with Monster Publishing, Inc. If you're not careful, Monster Publishing will control your novel until the end of time. And you, too.

> **All the Write Stuff**
> Shy writer alert: Agents are especially useful if you're not good at selling your work yourself.

No Windows or Heavy Lifting

You've learned what an agent *will* do for you. Now it's time to see what an agent *won't* do for you:

An agent won't...

1. Act as your editor.

2. Proofread your work.

3. Loan you money.

4. Act as a therapist.

5. Be your travel agent.

6. Be your lawyer (unless this is part of the deal).

7. Do public relations work (again, unless this is part of the deal).

8. Function as a secretary.

9. Be available 24 hours a day, 7 days a week.

10. Be your best friend.

Work it Out

Only you can decide if and when you need an agent to represent you. Fortunately, I can make your choice a little easier for you. To help you make some decisions, I've whipped up a handy-dandy worksheet. Use it now to decide if you should go out shopping for an agent today.

Check each statement that applies to you.

_____ 1. I don't have a completed manuscript yet.

_____ 2. I'm not sure I want to market my book now.

_____ 3. If I do decide to sell my book, I'm tough enough to negotiate with the big kids.

_____ 4. I'm comfortable in business meetings.

_____ 5. I promise to read the contract all the way through.

_____ 6. I understand legal terms, or know how to get their definitions.

_____ 7. I'm not easy to intimidate.

_____ 8. I have a thick skin.

_____ 9. I'm willing to market my book somewhere else if I can't get the deal I want.

_____ 10. I have the time and energy to deal with contract negotiations.

Bonus: Give yourself 10 extra points if you...

(a) Have raised teenagers and lived to tell the tale.

(b) Survived a cab ride in New York City.

(c) Programmed your VCR, assembled a bicycle, or shopped the day after Thanksgiving.

If you answered *yes* to most of these questions, you're likely best off lighting out for the territory ahead of the rest—alone. This may change later in your writing career, so keep reading!

Hide and Seek: Finding an Agent

So you decided that you need an agent. How do you find one? First of all, you can consult *The Literary Market Place*, the writer's reference book described in Chapter 16. It lists several hundred literary agencies and agents.

Here are some other sources to try:

➤ The Society of Authors' Representatives (P.O. Box 650, New York, NY 10113). This group offers a list of agents.

➤ *Guide to Literary Agents & Art/Photo Reps* (Writer's Digest Books). This is an annual directory that provides specific information about agencies.

➤ *Publishers Weekly*. See which agents make the big deals, which ones represent the types of works you write, which ones are looking for clients, and so on.

➤ Genre-specific magazines. Agents often advertise in genre-specific magazines. Check the magazines for the genre you write: for example, *Romantic Times* for romance, *Locus* for science fiction.

I've always been a strong fan of the personal road to finding an agent—recommendations from fellow authors. This is another good reason to join (or create) a writer's group. Fellow writers can help you get in touch with suitable agents. If you don't know anyone who has used an agent, you might chat up writing instructors, booksellers, librarians, and publishers' sales reps. See which agents they know and how they feel about them. You may very well need that personal reference to get a foot in the door.

Dog-and-Pony Shows: Conferences

Many literary agents attend writers' conferences, conventions, seminars, and workshops to find new clients and to represent their existing stable of workhorses. As a result, these events can be great places to shop for an agent. If you decide to go this route, here are some guidelines to follow:

1. Be professional. Dress appropriately, and stash the gum. No distracting body piercing or purple hair, either.

2. Try to arrange a private meeting with the agent.

3. Explain the project you're trying to sell.

4. Don't offer a manuscript; it's tacky.

5. If you decide to use the agent, send a letter reminding the agent where you met and how.

6. If you don't want to use the agent, follow-up with a thank-you letter.

All the Write Stuff
According to *Literary Market Place*, about 40 percent of book agents will not read manuscripts by unpublished authors. Another 15 percent will not even answer query letters from them.

Agent Organizations

Truckers and teachers are teamsters; secretaries are protected by the CSEA. The Association of Authors' Representatives is the professional organization for agents. Among other functions, the AAR distributes a list of members and copies of their ethics canon to all interested parties.

If you're one of those interested parties, send a check or money order for $5 (payable to AAR) and a stamped self-addressed envelope to AAR, 3rd Floor, 10 Astor Place, New York, NY 10003. If you'd like further information, call (212) 353-3709.

Wrong Turn
The Association of Authors' Representatives is not a regulating group. There are many reputable agents who are not members of AAR.

Hand in Glove

As you can surmise from the previous section, finding a literary agent isn't difficult. However, finding the *right* one is. How can you choose a literary agent who is right for you?

Not everyone needs the same thing in a literary agent. Some writers like big agencies; others want small shops. Some writers want a lot of contact with their agent; others don't want a call until the deal is done. Before you start looking for an agent, narrow down your specifications. This will make it easier for you to get the right match. Fill out the following worksheet to clarify your thinking.

Number these items from one to ten to decide what you want in a literary agent.

_____ I want an agent who specializes in a specific area of publishing, such as romance or mysteries.

_____ A general literary agent is better suited to my needs.

_____ A big firm is right for me.

_____ I prefer a very small literary agency.

_____ I want to see every bit of correspondence, even rejection letters.

_____ I only want to be called when the contract is ready.

_____ It's important that my agent really like my writing.

_____ I don't care if my agent likes my writing, as long as I get top-notch representation.

_____ I want an agent to handle all aspects of my business affairs, including taxes, contracts, and any necessary legal representation.

_____ I only need an agent to sell my book and negotiate the contract.

Analyze your answers. What pattern do you see? Use this information as you look for a literary agent who can do what you need and want.

Busting the Charts

Say you want to publish a popular blockbuster novel, à la the Danielle Steele bodice-rippers or Sidney Sheldon airport fiction type of book. Only about twenty literary agents represent 90 percent of America's best-selling novelists. If you're looking to publish a blockbuster, try to hire an agent who handles these kinds of books. The literary types among us who favor poetry and highbrow lit should instead seek out agents who specialize in more serious types of books.

Submissions coming from this select group usually get prompt and serious attention from publishing's highest realms. These agents know what the leading editors and publishers are looking for as a potential best-seller. As a result, they are best equipped to make the big deals and push a book by an unknown author to nose-bleed heights. Here are two conditions that must be met:

➤ Your book should be a gem.

➤ One of these agents must be willing to take you on.

At this point, I know that your novel is a gem, polished and shining. It's just waiting for the right setting: publication. So how can you get one of these agents to get your blockbuster published? Try the following five steps. They're slightly sneaky, but all's fair in love, war, and book publishing.

1. Pick an author you admire whose work is similar to yours.

2. To find out which agent represents this author, go to a large bookstore or library and ask to see the current catalog for the author's publisher. Most publisher's catalogs contain rights information (who controls motion picture rights, translation rights, and so on). Look on the bottom of the page on which the author's latest book is described.

3. If you can't find the name of the agent this way, look up the name of the publisher's Subsidiary Rights Director in *The Literary Market Place*.

4. Call or write to this person and tell him or her that you are interested in acquiring the motion picture rights to the novel.

5. You will then be directed to the agent or literary agency.

Now you have the agent's name. What's next? Top agents are busier than Roseanne's plastic surgeon. Don't be surprised if your first attempt at communication is rebuffed.

1. It's generally a waste of time to telephone. Top agents don't have the time to listen to a song-and-dance act from an unknown writer.

All the Write Stuff

Try to match the agent's track record to the type of book you have written. For example, if you've written a romance novel, look for an agent who sells romance novels—not one who specializes in computer reference books.

2. Write a letter. If you write a bowl-'em-over letter, the agent may feel that your novel is equally impressive.

3. The letter should be no more than a page. Include a few lines about the story and a brief description of your experience as a writer.

4. If possible, enclose a letter of recommendation. The most effective recommendation is a letter from one of the agent's clients. If you can't get one of these, try for a recommendation from a well-known novelist whose work is similar to yours. Then comes an endorsement from a writing teacher—the more famous, the better.

Caveat Emptor

All missions entail a certain risk, and it's true of agent shopping. Here are a few guidelines that can prevent a stay at Heartbreak Hotel.

First, beware of agents who push long-term contracts. Also avoid contracts that can't be broken by either party at any time. This is not to say you should discard agents like Liz Taylor discards husbands. On the contrary; when you find a good agent, stick around. But shun agents who claim that you'll bolt once they've given you the best years of their lives. If the agent is good, of course you'll stay.

Second, there are some so-called "agents" who charge a fee for reading your manuscript and then pay students to do the work. They make their money on these fees, not from placing the manuscripts. Think twice before paying an "agent" a reading fee. If you really feel that you need a professional opinion, hire a person or firm that does nothing else. Or, you may wish to join (or create) a writing group.

Finally, always get a written agreement with your agent. There are some writers who have enjoyed fine relationships with their agents with only a handshake to seal the deal. There are other writers, however, who have gotten badly burned on such deals. Agents can sell their businesses, go bankrupt, decide to raise commissions—and where does that leave you? If you have a good contract, that leaves you just fine.

Here are some other considerations:

1. Will your agent respect the confidentiality of your dealings?

2. Will your agent treat you as a professional?

3. Will your agent remember that he or she works for you, and not the other way around?

4. Will your agent work for you, not the publisher?

5. Is your agent a professional in all areas of his or her dealings?

> **Wrong Turn**
> If your agent comes in with an offer from a publisher for your work, I suggest that you grab it. This is not the time to play the reluctant virgin. You're paying the agent for his or her expert advice. Now take it.

An Educated Consumer Is Our Best Customer

You'll get the most from your relationship with an agent if you are a savvy client. Learn how contracts are put together and what they mean. Not to worry; I'll give you a complete overview of contracts in the following chapter. And no contract phobia, now—terms like "subsidiary rights," "royalties," and "kill fee" only *sound* scary.

Even though you're paying your agent for advice, that doesn't mean that you're the silent partner in this deal. Even if you have an agent, don't stop networking. Keep your ear to the railroad track; you never know when the gravy train is rounding the corner.

Money Makes the World Go 'Round

On average, agents charge between 10 to 15 percent of your writing income for domestic sales; 25 percent commission for foreign sales. So what are you getting for your money? You should be getting someone who

➤ Knows the business well.

➤ Is friendly with as many editors as possible.

➤ Knows the trends in publishing.

➤ Can place your book properly.

➤ Can negotiate contracts.

➤ Collects payment.

➤ Applies pressure if payment isn't forthcoming.

➤ Offers support in an often tough and lonely profession.

In addition, publishers sometimes approach agents with projects. When this happens to your (well-connected) agent, some neat-o work can be thrown your way.

Bet You Didn't Know

Today, some agents are also lawyers, accountants, or public relations specialists. Some agents will even act as your business manager—for a fee.

There are some "hidden" agent-generated charges as well. Your agent should not charge you for normal business expenses, such as domestic telephone calls or bookkeeping. But it's very common for an agent to charge for special expenses, such as daytime overseas calls, photocopying, and book purchases. Carefully negotiate every item on your contract to make sure there are no whopping surprises down the line.

By the by, if you get a hot tip without your agent that leads to a super publishing deal, are you still obligated to fork over 10 percent of the gross take? Yes. That's how the game works. No matter how you came to get the lead, your agent will still close the deal, negotiate the contract, and collect all royalties due to you. Your agent still gets the agreed-upon percentage.

Play Nice

Treat your agent with respect and courtesy. Always tell your agent the truth, especially concerning your progress with a manuscript. If your writing is going slowly and you're going to miss a deadline, say so. Don't wait until the last minute and claim you were taken hostage on a space ship or the dog ate your manuscript.

Here are some other tips for dealing well with literary agents:

1. Never just mail a manuscript cold; always query an agent first.

2. Don't send out material to a heap of agents at the same time. Pick no more than three to survey and interview.

3. Always send your very best writing. Stash the rough drafts in the attic; you can dig them out when you become famous.

4. The manuscript should be letter-perfect, too. No coffee spills or tear stains, please.

5. Make sure the manuscript conforms to industry standards regarding typing, spacing, title pages, and so forth.

6. No two-timing: divorce any previous agent before you start dealing with a new agent. It's a small world after all and word gets around fast.

7. Always enclose a stamped self-addressed envelope. Make life a little bit easier for the agent.

8. Sign the contract with the agent and then stay off the horn. Call when you have something to say, not to whine or nag.

9. Return all messages and phone calls promptly.

10. Remember that this is a professional relationship, not a friendship.

All the Write Stuff

Most agents won't return manuscripts unless you request it and enclose postage and a big envelope.

Breaking Up Is Hard to Do

But it happens. Leaving an agent is like dissolving any important relationship, but it doesn't have to be as painful or protracted as a star's divorce. If things aren't going the way you think they should be with your literary representation, it's time to call your agent and calmly talk about your concerns.

Here are some warning signs that it may be time to find other representation:

1. Your agent hasn't sold your book in what you consider a reasonable time, such as three to six months.

2. Your agent hasn't handed you any writing projects for three months.

3. You suspect your agent isn't working hard enough for you.

4. There's no regular communication from your agent, even if nothing has been sold.

5. You're just not comfortable with your agent anymore.

All the Write Stuff
If you fire your agent, be nice. It's free and it can pay off big. Publishing is a surprisingly small world; what goes around can come around.

If this approach is too confrontational for your style, say it in writing. Sometimes misunderstandings are just that; other times, they signal the beginning of the end.

If you do decide to seek new representation, here's where your contract becomes crucial. Whether you've been with the agent for ten years or ten minutes, if your contract specifies that either side can end the relationship with a certified letter saying that thirty days from the date of the letter your professional association is severed, you're in the clear. If not, your departure could take much longer and require legal intervention.

Who Gets Custody of the Kids?

Leave the relationship gracefully. No door slamming, harsh words, or bluster, please. Aside from getting a reputation as a snit if you pitch a fit, you and your agent may still have those "kids" to deal with—whatever works of yours the agent sold. Any of your books, movies, plays, and so on that your agent sold gives him or her *irrevocable* financial interest in any revenue those works generate. This may include subsidiary rights and revised editions, too, depending on your contract. In this capacity, your former agent will still be getting the following materials:

➤ Royalty statements

➤ Any actual royalties

➤ Related correspondence

As a result, your ex-agent will send royalties and relevant correspondence to you. He or she will still be entitled to 10 percent of these earnings.

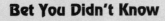

Bet You Didn't Know

If your agent is a member of the Association of Author's Representatives, you have an advantage. According to the group's Code of Ethics, your agent has sixty days to close on outstanding properties. After that, your former agent no longer has any claim on your present or future writings.

Hang in There

Think carefully if you want to dissolve the relationship because the agent you selected is unable to place your work. If a good agent liked your work well enough to spend the time, energy, and money to shop it around, the chances are good that you may be able to publish.

Follow these steps before you consider seeking new representation:

➤ Ask your agent for the publishers' rejections letters.

➤ Read them carefully.

➤ See what revisions they suggest.

➤ Decide if you are willing to make the changes. That's a choice that only you can make.

➤ Decide *why* you want a new agent. Is the problem with the agent, the current economic climate, your work, or a combination of factors?

The Least You Need to Know

➤ Assess your professional situation carefully to decide if you need a literary agent.

➤ If you hire an agent, get a written contract.

➤ Having an agent doesn't mean you don't have to know the business. You still do.

➤ Having no agent is better than having a shoddy one.

Chapter 19

Legal Beagles: Contracts, Fees, and Bookkeeping

> **In This Chapter**
>
> ➤ Learn about publication rights
>
> ➤ Explore contracts
>
> ➤ Keep good books

One size may fit all with tee-shirts and Spandex pants, but not when it comes to selling your writing! Contracts and agreements vary considerably from publisher to publisher. Some editors work only by a handshake agreement, while others have contracts as thick as the phone book. In this chapter, you will learn the basics of the business of getting your writing published.

Know Your Rights!

Some things in life are inflexible, like two-year olds, teenagers, and stale toothpaste. Other things have a little elasticity, like politics and your tax return (we call that "creative accounting").

Fortunately for savvy authors, writing contracts are rarely a take-it-or-leave-it deal. If you suspect that a specific contract is carved in granite, never fear: your editor will let you know up front. At that point, you have the choice of deciding how much you want the assignment and what you are willing to compromise to get it. But most editors are open to some negotiation. Learn to stand up for what you think is important but be willing to bend when it's necessary to make a sale. You may lose a skirmish but you'll win the war.

On the Rights Track

Any time an editor buys a piece or asks permission to publish something, even without offering payment, the editor is asking you for *rights*. In so doing, the editor or publisher is obtaining the right to publish your work. When the rights are not specified, most writers assume that the publisher is buying one-time rights, but that's not always the case. Let me take you on a survey of the different kinds of rights you can sell so you know the score.

1. *First Serial Rights*. Under first serial rights, you grant a newspaper or magazine the right to publish your writing for the first time in any periodical. First serial rights

Words to the Wise
Rights give the publisher legal permission to publish your work.

can be applied to any type of writing: shorter writings such as essays, poems, and short stories as well as excerpts from novels, biographies, and screenplays. Sometimes, even entire books have been first published in magazines when the authors negotiated first serial rights. John Hersey's *Hiroshima* and Truman Capote's *In Cold Blood* are examples.

Under this agreement, all rights to further publication belong to you, the writer.

2. *One-Time Rights*. This is different from first serial rights in that the buyer has no guarantee that he or she will be the first to publish the work. See Simultaneous Rights.

3. *Second Serial (Reprint) Rights*. Under these rights, a newspaper or magazine has the chance to print an article, essay, story, poem, or an excerpt from a longer work after it has already appeared in another periodical.

   Money received from Second Serial Rights to books and book excerpts is often shared fifty-fifty by the author and book publisher. Again, anything is open to negotiation.

4. *All Rights*. A writer who sells something to a magazine or newspaper under these rights cannot use the same material in its present form in any other publication.

   If you think you may want to reuse the article, story, poem (etc.) later on, ask the editor to buy First Rights instead of All Rights. Sometimes, an editor will reassign rights back to a writer after a given period of time, such as one year. Hey, it never hurts to ask!

5. *Simultaneous Rights*. If magazines don't have the same readers, you can often sell the same article to two or more places at the same time. It's a lovely equation: 1 work = 2 sales. For example, a cooking magazine might be willing to buy Simultaneous Rights to a story, even though they know a travel magazine might be using the story as well.

   Always tell everyone involved when you are sending the same piece to different markets simultaneously. Dealing in good faith helps avoid embarrassment as well as possible legal complications down the road.

All the Write Stuff

You can find international markets for your writing in *International Market Place* (R.R. Bowker) and *International Writers' and Artist's Yearbook* (A&C Black Ltd.).

6. *Foreign Serial Rights*. If you sold first U.S. Serial Rights, you are free to resell the same piece abroad. To do so, research magazines and newspapers that buy writing that has already been published in U.S. or North American magazines and newspapers.

7. *Syndication Rights*. Like Serial Rights, Syndication Rights give magazines and newspapers the right to publish your writing. The difference is that your work will appear in many newspapers and/or magazines at the same time. The syndication takes a commission on the sale. The rest of the money is split between you and your publisher.

All the Write Stuff

Try to negotiate a contract that includes all possible rights. Why? Because before you can resell any piece of writing, you must own the rights to it.

8. *Dramatic, Television, and Motion Picture Rights*. These can be crucial rights if it seems even remotely likely that your work will get published in another medium. Therefore, I strongly suggest that you study any contracts carefully for these rights.

   Of course, it depends on the nature of the writing. My contract for this particular book also includes Theme Park Rights. I believe that means I get 25 percent if they make *The Complete Idiot's Guide to Creative Writing* Water Flume Ride. I'm getting a new bathing suit for the event.

9. *Subsidiary Rights*. These include serial rights, dramatic rights, rights relative to revised editions, translation rights, and so on. They are discussed in detail later in this chapter.

10. *Electronic Rights*. The newest of the rights, this territory is as uncharted as Pluto or my attic. Electronic Rights concern any means of electronic transmission, such as

the World Wide Web. This also includes electronic versions of your writing, such as compact discs (CDs). Since even the computer mavens can't predict the spread of the Net, I suggest that you carefully watch how you assign these rights.

Always talk to your editor and read your contract carefully to see what rights you are keeping and which rights you are signing away. Here are three special situations to scrutinize:

➤ If editors or publishers change, the rights may shift as well.

➤ Sometimes endorsing your check signs away rights.

➤ Beware of verbal rights agreements. Get it in writing.

Now, let's compare and contrast the two most common types of writing contracts: a work-for-hire agreement and a royalty structure.

Take the Money and Run: Work-for-Hire

With a work-for-hire agreement, you're a hired hand. As such, you get a flat fee, a one-shot payment. Under this type of contract, you have no claim to what you write; everything belongs to the publisher. The minute you sign the "Work-for-Hire" agreement, you are signing away all future rights to the work.

Bet You Didn't Know

With a work-for-hire agreement, you typically get a little more money up front, and don't have to wait for sales to collect royalties—although the royalties can total more in the end.

A work-for-hire writing arrangement might be right for you if you...

All the Write Stuff
Notice the acceptability clause. If your work isn't acceptable...you may not get paid.

➤ Want a set, guaranteed amount of money

➤ Like short-term jobs with no strings attached

➤ Are looking for a way to support yourself while you write harder-to-sell works such as novels, dramas, and screenplays

➤ Do not want credit for your work—it's rare that your name appears on a work-for-hire job

Below is a sample work-for-hire contract. Read it through carefully to see what protection it does and does not offer to the writer.

WORK-FOR-HIRE AGREEMENT

This agreement between Big Brother Publishing Company, Inc. and <u>writer,</u> an independently established business person, is entered into with respect to <u>Job #000.</u>

 I agree to the following:

1. Any and all materials submitted by me to Big Brother Publishing Company, Inc. is my original work and no materials submitted by me contain libelous or slanderous material. No material submitted by me infringes on any copyright or other person. I further agree to hold Big Brother Publishing Company, Inc. harmless for any infringements or violation of any rights of any other persons arising out of the use and publication of materials submitted by me for publication.

2. I understand that any materials I submit to Big Brother Publishing Company, Inc. are intended for publication. I understand that the copyright in any such materials shall be claimed by Even Bigger Brother Publishing Company, Inc. Accordingly, I agree to assign any title, right, interest in any materials submitted by me which are accepted by Big Brother Publishing Company, Inc. to Even Bigger Brother Publishing Company, Inc., including any rights to renewal of copyrights. I further agree that this assignment shall be binding upon my successors, heirs, and assigns, and that my only right in any of these materials shall be limited to my right to payment as set out in Paragraph 5.

3. I understand that materials I submit to Big Brother Publishing Company, Inc. must be acceptable for publication by both Big Brother Publishing Company, Inc. and Even Bigger Brother Publishing Company, Inc. Final acceptance within the meaning of this agreement shall be evidenced by payment pursuant to Paragraph 5.

4. Big Brother Publishing Company, Inc. may cancel this agreement if work is not deemed acceptable by the company.

5. In consideration of the above agreement, Big Brother Publishing Company, Inc. agrees to pay <u>writer</u> the amount of <u>$$$$</u> upon completion of the following assignment: <u>description of writing assignment.</u>

6. I understand that I will receive from Big Brother Publishing Company, Inc. various instructions and other information to be used by me in the preparation of materials for publication. I understand that these materials were designed for Big Brother Publishing Company, Inc. for projects of a confidential nature. As a result, I agree not to disclose to any other persons any information about these materials nor to copy these materials. I agree to return such materials to Big Brother Publishing Company, Inc. I further agree to hold Big Brother Publishing Company, Inc. harmless for any damage or any breach of this provision by me.

continues

---

continued

7. I understand and agree that I am retained by Big Brother Publishing Company, Inc. for the purposes and to the extent set forth in this Agreement, and my relation to Big Brother Publishing Company, Inc. to be that of Independent Contractor. I shall be free to dispose of such portion of my time, energy, and skill as is not obligated under this Agreement and may do so in such a manner as I see fit and to such persons, firms, and corporations as I deem advisable. I shall not be considered as having employee status or as being entitled to participate in any plans, arrangements, or distributions by Big Brother Publishing Company, Inc. pertaining to or in connection with profit-sharing, or similar benefits for their regular employees. I further understand that as an Independent Contractor I shall be paid in full with no taxes withheld and I am therefore responsible for any federal, state, and local taxes that I may owe.

AGREED   APPROVED

_____   _____

Signature   for Big Brother Publishing Company, Inc.

_____   _____

Social Security #   date

_____

_____

Address

All the Write Stuff
Notice the confidentiality clause. Keeping your mouth zipped about current projects is crucial to establishing your reputation as a writer who can be trusted.

Royal Flush

Royalties are a percentage of the retail price of your book. You receive that percentage as a fee for writing. With certain types of writing, such as novels and biographies, you get royalties instead of a flat fee.

Don't confuse the number of books that have been published with the number of copies that have been sold. A company can publish 100,000 copies of a book...but only sell 5,000 copies. That's what happened to President

Clinton's last book. The publisher was flooded with returned, unsold copies. Someone took a bath on that one.

To protect themselves against this situation, publishers always withhold a certain amount from your royalty check against "returns." It's traditional in paperback publishing to withhold as much as twenty percent from your royalty check against returns.

Words to the Wise
Royalties are a percentage of the retail price received on sales of your book.

Advance Man

An *advance against royalties* is a loan from the publisher to you. The advance is later deducted from how much your book earns in royalties after publication.

An advance is not repayable. Even if only one copy of the book is sold, the advance is yours to keep.

Advances generally range from $100 up. They are generally paid in increments, as follows:

$1,000 on signing the contract;

$1,000 on delivery and acceptance of the manuscript as satisfactory to the publisher;

$2,000 on delivery and acceptance of the completed manuscript as satisfactory to the publisher.

Wrong Turn
Watch out if a contract states that you have to repay an advance. If so, something is definitely not kosher!

Below are general royalty rates. Remember: Everything can be negotiated. Of course, the more books you have published (and sold!) the greater your clout. It's considered bad form in most cases for a first-time writer to demand the sun, moon, and stars. Settle for the sun and moon; get the stars for your second book.

➤ *Hardcover Royalties.* The royalty schedule for hardcover and softcover books is usually different. Traditionally, the publisher pays the author 10 percent of the list (cover) price for each hardcover book sold through regular channels such as wholesalers, libraries, and book stores.

All the Write Stuff
If two people write the book, they sometimes split the royalties equally. Other times, the lead author gets the royalties and the other author(s) gets work-for-hire fees charged against the lead author's royalty account.

Royalties can also be structured differently for the number of books sold. With this payment schedule, the author might receive 10 percent of the net price for the first 5,000 books sold, 12 percent for the next 5,000, and 15 percent on sales over 10,000.

Wrong Turn
I hate to rain on your parade, but *very few* first books earn more than the advance. Also, some books sold at discount (through book clubs or complementary copies) are either credited at a reduced royalty or no royalty at all. Wait until the royalty check clears before you buy that Barbados hideaway.

➤ *Paperback Royalties.* For paperback books, authors usually receive 6 percent for the first 5,000 books sold and 9 percent for any number over 5,000. Here's a sample contract:

10% on the first 40,000 copies sold
12.5% for the next 40,000 copies sold
15% on all copies sold thereafter

➤ *Reference and Textbooks Royalties.* The royalties for reference and textbooks are generally 15 percent of net (the cover price, less 20 to 50 percent). The royalties rise with the number of books sold. Figure around 18 percent as the top, unless you are a very well-established author.

Bet You Didn't Know

Computer books are typically based on 45–50 percent of cover price, with royalties running more around the 5–10 percent range.

Report Cards

Depending on the language of your contract, you'll get a royalty report every month, six months, or once a year. These are comprehensible only to people who can decipher the Rosetta stone. If you are one of these code breakers, a royalty report should tell you the following information:

➤ How many books were printed

➤ How many books were distributed

➤ How many books were returned

➤ How much money you're due

➤ How much money is being withheld against returns

If you can figure out a royalty report, please call or e-mail me at your earliest opportunity. I could use the help with my own.

Subsidiary Rights

There's another way to make money on your book: *subsidiary rights.* Subsidiary rights include the following sales outlets:

➤ Dramatic rights (plays)

➤ Motion picture rights

➤ Theme park rights

➤ Radio rights

➤ Television rights

➤ First periodical rights (magazines, newspapers)

➤ Foreign language rights

Most contracts call for the author and the publisher to split these rights 25 percent author/75 percent publisher, but these can be negotiated as high as 50/50. In some cases, publishers barely break even on the book itself and hope to make big bucks with the subsidiary rights.

Wrong Turn

Any changes you make to the page proofs are called *author's alterations.* Most contracts allow 10 percent "AAs"; anything over that, you have to pay for the changes yourself. Author's alterations do not include errors the publisher or printer made. Some publishers also deduct the cost of indexing from your royalties.

Choices, Choices

So what's it going to be: a work-for-hire contract or royalty? Naturally, each book, magazine article, drama, script, and so on is going to require a separate choice. Further, I'm assuming that you *will* have a choice, which is not always the case. Here are some guidelines you can use to decide which contract is right for you:

Choose work-for-hire if...	Choose royalties if...
You want the money now.	You can wait for the payoff.
The publisher has a mediocre sales force.	The publisher has a fabulous sales force.
You don't anticipate big sales.	You think the piece will fly off the shelves.

Clause and Effect

Let's get real. If your agent sells the book or the publisher sends you a contract, the odds are that you'll be so busy jumping up and down that the last thing you're going to do is read the contract with a magnifying glass. Lord knows I haven't read my contracts carefully enough in the past, and in some cases, I have been badly stung.

"Why bother reading the contract that carefully?" you might say. "After all, there's not much I can do about it. I want to get my book published and these guys are paying me real money." True to a point. There are some clauses that you can't do a thing about. In other cases, however, there are clauses that you can—and should—consider for modification. Below, I've listed the most important ones so you can avoid being burnt.

No, No, Nanette: First Refusal

This clause allows the publisher the first look at your next book. You can keep the clause in if you like the editor, know that she or he will be with the company for a while yet, and plan to write another book in the same genre. If none of these conditions fit, consider having the clause removed from the contract or reworded.

For example, you can have the clause rewritten to state the publisher will have right of first refusal if "your next book is in the same category." Or, that the company must make a decision about your next book within thirty days. This allows you to shop your book around faster.

Termination

Also called a "reversion of rights" clause, this part of the contract is like a divorce. You're no longer a virgin, but at least you're free to get married again.

What happens if your book doesn't sell? Or it sells well in the first few months, but then flatlines? With a reversion clause, you're free to sell your book to some other publisher.

To do so, send a written request for all rights to your book to be reverted to you within a specific time (usually one to six months) or that the publisher reissue your book, generally within six months.

The odds are good that no one is going to want the book now—after all, it isn't selling. But that doesn't stop you from trying again in a few years. And if you come up with a best-selling novel in the meantime, you can bet your booties that your other books will be worth a bundle. But now, the bundle's in your lap.

Performance Anxiety: Date of Performance

Make sure you have this clause: It guarantees that the company will publish your book within a given period of time. If not, the publisher forfeits all rights to your work and you are released from the contract. This frees you to shop your book around elsewhere.

The chances of an established publisher failing to publish your book are less than the chance that Madonna won't change her hair color. But if you're selling your book to a small company, it's a good idea to have this clause included.

Bet You Didn't Know

Many contracts carry a non-compete clause, saying you can't write about that topic for anyone for three years from signing the contract. This could be a killer if you make your living writing similar types of articles or books.

Mission Impossible: Bookkeeping

I doubt you first became a writer so you could practice your bookkeeping skills, but accurate records are a very important part of running a small business—and that's what you're doing as a writer. Here are some things to consider as you contemplate your accounting:

➤ Your earnings

➤ Your expenses

➤ Uncle Sam's bite—your taxes

If you are seriously math-phobic, you can hire someone to do your dirty work for you. But even if you do hire an accountant or have your agent handle your bookkeeping, you'll still have to keep receipts and records.

Fork It Over

What receipts should you save? Any expense you incurred in writing your book (article, essay, poem, play, screenplay) is an income tax deduction if your book (article, essay, poem, play, screenplay) sells. Here's a list of receipts you should squirrel away in shoeboxes:

➤ Business stationery

➤ Office machinery: computers, telephones, copy machines, scanners, fax machines, printers, and so on

➤ Computer disks

➤ Business postage

All the Write Stuff
Try job sharing: do some writing for another small business owner in exchange for bookkeeping and tax assistance.

➤ Business telephone charges

➤ Books, CDs, tapes, and records needed for research

➤ Business entertainment

➤ Pencils, paper, pens, paper clips, etc.

➤ Business travel

➤ Business-related gifts

Spread 'Em

After much trial and error (and enormous help from a husband with a degree in accounting), I developed a great way to keep track of what I spend and what I earn writing. I use a book to track my expenses and a spreadsheet to track my earnings.

Wrong Turn
Don't try to run a writing career from the family phone line. Invest in a separate phone line. You'll thank me for this tip!

Every time I buy something related to my writing career—from a train ticket to meet with a publisher in New York City to a plane ticket to attend a business conference across the continent—I record it in my little journal book. I note the date the expense was incurred, how much I spent, and why. That last column is crucial, for it determines whether or not the IRS will allow your deduction.

Here's what a sample page looks like:

Date	Expense	Reason
5/6	$8.00	Train to meet with Linda Beech at Big Bro Publishing Company re: proposal for scifi story
5/9	$98.00	Cartridge for laser printer
5/11	$6.00	Box of #10 envelopes
5/15	$5.50	Postage to mail mystery short story
5/22	$52.00	Telephone bill (business line)

Now to earnings. You can do what is called "simple single-entry bookkeeping." I don't find anything *simple* about single-entry bookkeeping. Instead, I use a computer spreadsheet to record my earnings. Here's a sample of my spreadsheet:

			1997 Writing		
TOTALS		**BILLED:** $5,562.50			**PAID:**
DATE	COMPANY	CONTACT	JOB DESCRIPTION	AMOUNT	DATE
BILLED				BILLED	PAID
10/10/96	Big Publishing Company	Joe Smith	travel book - signing fee	$2,000.00	1/7/97
1/15/97	Big Publishing Company	Joe Smith	travel book - 1/2 completed	$2,000.00	
3/15/97	Big Publishing Company	Joe Smith	travel book - final sign-off	$1,000.00	
1/1/97	Scribner	Harriet Lewis	Truman Capote bio	$150.00	
2/10/97	Poem Magazine	J.T. Malhotra	Cat: A Sonnet"	$50.00	
2/16/97	Mammoth Publishers	none	royalities on science fiction novel	$327.50	
3/7/97	Poem Quarterly	T'Aysha Moon	Ballad of a Lost Life"	$35.00	

The Least You Need to Know

➤ It's important to learn all about publication rights.

➤ Read your contracts. Then read them again until you understand them.

➤ Carefully record all earnings and expenses.

Chapter 20

We're in the Money: Contests and Grants

In This Chapter

➤ Explore different kinds of writing awards

➤ Learn how to apply for contests and grants

➤ Find the writing contests that are right for you

Ever decide that it takes as long to sell your writing as it does to create it? If so, you're not experiencing one of those 1970s controlled-substance flashbacks. Sometimes it *can* take much, much longer to sell a novel, play, or script than it ever took to write the manuscript in the first place.

What can you do if you just want to write without having to worry about selling your work, but you need enough money to keep the wolf from the door? Consider entering writing contests, applying for writing grants—and winning. That's what this chapter is all about.

You, Too, Could Be a Winner!

Are you a saint or a sinner? *Story*, the most widely circulated literary magazine in America, and *Encyclopedia Britannica* sponsored the 1995 *Story* Seven Deadly Sins Competition. The judges were looking for devilishly good stories based on any of the Seven Deadly sins: anger, avarice, lechery, envy, sloth, gluttony, and pride. Only original unpublished entries of 5,000 words or less were considered; there was a $10 entry fee. The winning manuscripts were published in *Story* for the regular fees. The winners got a nice piece of change *and* a leg up in the business.

Is poetry your passion? Every year, the winner of the Empress Publications Poetry Contest receives $250 and publication in an anthology. Applicants submit original, unpublished poems of up to 25 lines in any form or style. This contest offers great freedom of expression, money, and publication.

Are you a pet lover and a poet? Then the following writing contest is probably right up your alley. Winners of the *Cats, Canines, and Other Critters* Poetry Contest (Anderie Poetry Press) receive publication in an anthology of the same name and $50 (first place), $30 (second place), or $20 (third place). The entry fee is $2 for the first poem; $1 each for every subsequent poem (up to 10 poems). This writing contest offers less pressure, a sweet prize, and publication.

Calling all Type-A writers, those people driven to perfection. Do you thrive on pressure, deadlines, and competition? Then how about going for the cherry on the sundae, a Pulitzer Prize? This organization awards outstanding journalism in American newspapers and outstanding literature, drama, and music by Americans. The deadline for drama is March 1; for literature, July 1 and November 1.

Bet You Didn't Know

Winning an award makes your writing more interesting to publishers. The bigger the award, the greater the interest, too. Be sure to mention awards in query letters you send to publishers.

As this handful of examples illustrates, there are awards for all writers, in all subjects, at all levels of expertise and experience. Let's see how you can go about getting your slice of the pie.

On Your Mark...

Nearly every day, new writing contests and awards are announced in various writer's magazines and publications. I'm not going to fool you; competition for contest money is very keen. To give yourself the winning edge, always send a stamped self-addressed envelope *before* entering any contest to get the information you need. When you get the facts, check and double-check the following details on the brochures, literature, cover letters, and actual applications:

➤ Contest contact names

➤ Addresses

➤ Deadlines

➤ Entry fees (if any)

➤ Rules and requirements for submissions

➤ Guidelines for submission

> **Wrong Turn**
> Get the very latest writing contest information that you can. Some groups lose their funding; some publications fold. Don't waste your time unless you know the contest information is timely and accurate.

Read the guidelines carefully to make sure you don't enter a contest for which you are not qualified. Here are some matters of eligibility to consider:

1. *Writer's age.* Many contests are open only to writers who are specific ages (under 21, over 50, and so on)

2. *Previous publications.* Sometimes you must be a published author; other times, unpublished. Sometimes it doesn't matter whether you've published before or not.

3. *Geographic location.* Where you live can make you eligible for the contest or not.

4. *Type of writing.* Most contests are centered on very specific genres and subgenres, such as sonnets or one-act plays.

5. *Length of work.* Your submission must often conform to very specific word and line counts.

Winning a contest or award is about more than fast cash, however. Snatching the right brass ring on the award merry-go-round has launched many a successful writing career. It can happen to you, too.

Get Set...

To give yourself the winning edge, do a little research before you decide to apply for a specific writing contest or award. Here are some suggestions:

➤ Get a list of previous winners.

➤ Analyze their work. See if you can figure out what qualities in each winning entry appealed to the judges.

➤ Attend the staged reading of an award-winning play. Analyze it.

➤ If you're applying for an award sponsored by a magazine, read several issues of the magazine to familiarize yourself with its style.

All the Write Stuff
When you submit your entry, send only your best work. Make sure it's letter-perfect.

Sometimes, you will have to be nominated for an award. Select prominent, well-connected people to toss your hat into the ring. Be sure to allow them sufficient time to write the letter of nomination. As a courtesy, you may wish to send the person making the nomination a copy of any relevant awards, grants, or other honors you've already snagged. Also include a list of your publications. Keep copies of this information so you can use it again to enter other writing contests.

Go!

Most large public libraries carry lists of funding sources for writers. Increasingly, sources of funding are even listed on the Internet, posted on Web sites and on-line bulletin boards. Here are some resources to check:

➤ *Foundations and Grants to Individuals* (Foundation Center, 79 5th Avenue, New York, NY 10003)

➤ *Grants and Awards Available to American Writers* (PEN American Center, 568 Broadway, New York, NY 10012)

➤ *Poets and Writers* (72 Spring Street, New York, NY 10012)

➤ *Associated Writing Programs Newsletter* (Old Dominion University, Norfolk, VA 23529

➤ *Annual Register of Grant Support* (National Register Publishing Company, 30049 Glenview Road, Wilmette, IL 60091)

You May Already Be a Winner! Grants

Another way to support your writing is to get funding from foundations and agencies. There is a surprising amount of money available; seek and ye shall find. Here are the three most open-handed sources:

➤ Private sources

➤ Service organizations

➤ State agencies

Most of the largest foundations in the United States are headquartered in New York City, but every large city has local foundations that give grants to projects they consider worthy.

Foundations, like banks, invest in worthy projects (that's *you*) and expect a return. Like banks, the first "loan" (grant) is the hardest one to get. I received my first grant in 1986, an Empire State Challenger Fellowship. It was renewed the following year. That was quickly followed by the following grants:

1987	New Faculty Development Award ($750)
1988	Scholarly Research Stipend to research "Laura Ingalls Wilder and the Pioneer Experience" ($3,000)
1989	United University Professor Experienced Faculty Development Award ($500)

I haven't applied for any grants since, as I can now support myself on my writing.

Don't Take It for Granted

"Ah, a foundation would never give me any money," you lament. "There's nothing special I could do." Don't be so sure. What could you do as a writer that would interest a local foundation? Here are some ideas:

➤ Give readings of your work at schools, hospitals, retirement homes, or prisons

➤ Develop a writing program at any one of the above institutions

➤ Write a history of your region

➤ Write a history of the foundation

➤ Write a biography about a famous person in the area or in the foundation

Words to the Wise

A *grant* is a subsidy furnished by an agency to finance a project. There may or may not be strings attached (such as residency requirements, number of publications, age, and so on.) There are usually fewer strings attached to an outright *award*.

Words to the Wise

A *service organization* is a group of people who help others. Notable service organizations include Rotary International, Lions, Kiwannis, Junior League, and the Women's Club.

Wrong Turn

Be sure to include your name, address, and telephone number on all applications. You'd be astonished at how many applications come in incomplete!

Laundry List

Here are some general grants for writers. See which ones match your writing style and personal needs. Then apply, already!

➤ Annual Associateship
Rocky Mountain Women's Institute
7150 Montview Blvd.
Denver, CO 80220
(303) 871-6923

Recipients are provided with a work space, small stipend, support, and services for one year.

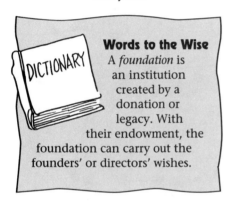

Words to the Wise
A *foundation* is an institution created by a donation or legacy. With their endowment, the foundation can carry out the founders' or directors' wishes.

➤ Annual Grant Award Program
Witter Bynner Foundation for Poetry, Inc.
Suite 118, 105 E. Marcy St.
Santa Fe, NM 87501
(505) 988-3251

Grants for individual poets.

➤ Artist Trust Fellowship
#415, 1402 3rd Ave
Seattle, WA 98101
(206) 467-8734

Grants in playwriting, screenwriting, fiction, and poetry.

➤ Artists Fellowships
Illinois Arts Council
Suite 10-500, 100 W. Randolph
Chicago, IL 60601-3298
(312) 814-6750
(800) 237-6999

Fellowships in fixed amounts of $5,000 and $10,000 to Illinois writers of poetry or prose.

➤ George Bennett Fellowship
Phillips Exeter Academy
Exeter, NH 03833-1104

Annual award of stipend, room, and board to "provide time and freedom from material considerations to a person seriously contemplating or pursuing a career as a writer."

➤ Commonwealth of Pennsylvania Council on the Arts Literature Fellowships
216 Finance Bldg.
Harrisburg, PA 17120
(717) 787-6883

Fellowships for Pennsylvania writers of fiction and poetry.

➤ Fellowships to Assist Research and Artistic Creation
John Simon Guggenheim Memorial Foundation
90 Park Avenue, New York, NY 10016
(212) 687-4470

Highly competitive fellowship to assist writers to engage in any field of knowledge and creation.

➤ GAP (Grants for Artist Projects) Fellowship
Artist Trust, Suite 415, 1402 3rd Avenue
Seattle, WA 98101
(206) 467-8734

The GAP is awarded to about 15 artists and writers every year; it is "no-strings-attached" funding.

$5,000 maximum award.

➤ D.H. Lawrence Fellowship
University of New Mexico
English Department, Humanities 217
Albuquerque, NM 87131-1106
(505) 277-6347

Fellowships for published or unpublished writers of fiction, poetry, or drama.

➤ New York State Writer in Residence Program
New York State Council on the Arts, 915 Broadway
New York, NY 10010
(212) 387-7020

Awards $8,000 for a six-month residency.

Hey, You Never Know: General Awards

Below is an overview of some general writing awards so you can see what's out there. If you decide to apply for any of these funding sources, be sure to get the latest information. You can do so by writing a letter of inquiry or calling the award committee to request the guidelines.

Notice that many of these awards are targeted for specific geographic areas. There are a zillion more writing awards; this is just a very small sampling of what's available so you can do some browsing.

➤ The Christopher Award
The Christophers
12 E 48th Street
New York, NY 10017
(212) 759-4050

Award for outstanding books published during the year that "affirm the highest values of the human spirit."

➤ Editors' Book Award
Pushcart Press
Box 380
Wainscott, NY 11975
(516) 324-9300

Award for unpublished books; must be nominated by an editor in a publishing house.

➤ Louisiana Literary Award
Louisiana Library Association
PO Box 3058
Baton Rouge, LA 70821
(504) 342-4928

Award for published material related to Louisiana.

➤ Minnesota Voices Project Competition
New Rivers Press, #910
420 N 5th Street
Minneapolis, MN 55401
(612) 339-7114

Award for new and emerging writers of poetry, prose, essays, and memoirs from Wisconsin, Minnesota, Iowa, and the Dakotas.

➤ Ohioana Book Awards
Ohioana Library Association
65 S. Front Street, Room 1105
Columbus, OH 43215
(614) 466-3831

Awards for books published within the past year by an Ohioian or about Ohio and Ohioans.

➤ The Carl Sandburg Literary Arts Awards
The Friends of the Chicago Public Library
400 S. State Street, 9S-7
Chicago, IL 60605
(312) 747-4907

Award for Chicago writers of fiction, nonfiction, poetry, and children's literature.

➤ Towson State University Prize for Literature
College of Liberal Arts
Towson State University
Towson, MD 21204-7097
(410) 830-2128

Award for a book written by a Maryland author no older than 40.

➤ Whiting Writers' Awards
Mrs. Giles Whiting Foundation
Room 3500, 30 Rockefeller Plaza
New York, NY 10012

Wrong Turn
Check to see if the contest has an entry fee. Some fees can be very steep, to defray the cost of the contest.

Every year, the Foundation gives $30,000 each to up to ten writers of poetry, fiction, nonfiction, and plays. The awards stress exceptionally promising emerging talent.

Folding Money for Fiction

Can't decide what to do with the trust fund that Grandma Buffy set up for you? Up to your ears in lottery winnings? Need a way to funnel off some stock profits? To get rid of all that extra cash, you can always do what many other well-heeled folks have done: establish literary awards. Some of the awards listed below were started by publishers looking to find good writing, but many were established to honor famous writers, beloved family members, even pets.

Take advantage of someone's generosity and apply for a bunch of these awards today. When you become rich and famous from your writing, you can set up your own awards and give some other struggling writers a leg up on the ladder of success.

➤ AIM Magazine Short Story Contest
PO Box 20554
Chicago, IL 60620-0554
(312) 874-6184

Award for unpublished stories of no more than 4,000 words that "promote brother-hood among people and cultures."

➤ Nelson Algren Short Story Awards
Chicago Tribune
435 N. Michigan Avenue
Chicago, IL 60611

Award for unpublished short stories between 2,500 and 10,000 words by American writers.

➤ Birch Lane Press American Fiction Contest
Birch Lane Press English Department
Springfield College
Springfield, MA 01109
(413) 596-6645

Award for unpublished fiction by established and emerging writers (entry fee; many cash awards).

➤ Robert L. Fish Memorial Award
Mystery Writers of America, Inc.
17 E 47th Street, 6th Floor
New York, NY 10017
(212) 888-8171

Award for the best first mystery or suspense short story.

➤ Ernest Hemingway Foundation Award
PEN American Center
568 Broadway
New York, NY 10012

Award for the first published novel or short story collection by an American author.

➤ Hemingway Short Story Competition
Hemingway Days Festival
PO Box 4045
Key West, FL 33041
(305) 294-4440

Award for unpublished short stories (entry fee; $1,000 first prize).

➤ O. Henry Festival Short Story Contest
O. Henry Festival, Inc.
PO Box 29484
Greensboro, NC 27429

Award for unpublished short fiction (entry fee).

➤ Aga Khan Prize for Fiction
The Paris Review
541 E 72nd Street, Box 5
New York, NY 10021

Award for unpublished fiction of less than 10,000 words.

➤ Minnesota Ink Fiction Contest
Minnesota Ink, Inc.
27 Empire Drive
St. Paul, MN 55103
(612) 225-1306

Award for previously unpublished fiction.

➤ The *Writer's Digest* Self-Published Book Awards
Writer's Digest National Self-Publishing Awards
1507 Dana Avenue
Cincinnati, Ohio 45207

Award for self-published books in all categories ($95 entry fee; $1,000 award).

Bet You Didn't Know

Don't get out much? Then the PEN Writing Award for Prisoners may be just right for you. It's awarded to "the authors of the best poetry, plays, short fiction, and nonfiction received from prison writers in the U.S."

Nonfiction

The Gordon W. Dillon/Richard C. Peterson Memorial Essay Prize awards bucks for essays on orchid culture, orchids in nature, and orchids in use. The Barbara Savage "Miles from Nowhere" Memorial Award forks over a $3,000 prize every year for unpublished books on hiking, mountain climbing, paddle sports, skiing, snowshoeing, bicycling—any adventure travel that doesn't involve public transportation. You can win awards for good writing on behavioral science, European history, biography, and early Spanish history, too. And that's just skimming the surface of the pot.

And you mean to say you haven't won a writing award yet? Let's remedy that situation right now. Read on to see if any of these nonfiction writing contests suits your talents and interests. If not, there's a slew more that you can find in the sources listed in the beginning of this chapter.

➤ George Freedley Memorial Award
Theater Library Association
New York Public Library at Lincoln Center
111 Amsterdam Avenue
New York, NY 10023
(212) 787-3852

Award for books relating to theater.

➤ Joan Kelly Memorial Prize in Women's History
American Historical Association
400 A Street, SE
Washington, DC 20003

Award for writing on women's history and/or feminist theory ($1,000).

➤ Literary Nonfiction Writers' Project Grants
NC Arts Council
Department of Cultural Resources
Raleigh, NC 27601-2807
(919) 733-2111

Annual award to "recognize the literary value of nonfiction and encourage the artistic growth of the state's writers of nonfiction."

➤ Loft Creative Nonfiction Residency Program
The Loft
Pratt Community Center
66 Malcolm Ave, SE
Minneapolis, MN 55414-3551

Award for six creative nonfiction writers and a month-long seminar with a resident writer.

➤ McLemore Prize
Mississippi Historical Society
PO Box 571
Jackson, MS 39205
(601) 359-6850

Award for a book or biography on some aspect of Mississippi history.

➤ The Mayflower Society Cup Competition
North Carolina Literary and Historical Association
109 E Jones Street
Raleigh, NC 27601-2807
(919) 733-7305

Award for previously published nonfiction by a North Carolina resident.

➤ National Jewish Book Award—Autobiography/Memoir
Sandra Brand and Arik Weintraub Award
15 E 26th Street
New York, NY 10010
(212) 532-4949

Award for an autobiography or memoir of the life of a Jewish person.

➤ National Writers Club Articles and Essay Contest
The National Writers Club
Suite 620, 1450 S. Havana
Aurora, CO 80012
(303) 751-7844

Award to "encourage writers in this creative form and to recognize those who excel in nonfiction writing" (entry fee).

➤ National Writers Club Nonfiction Book Proposals Contest
The National Writers Club
Suite 620, 1450 S. Havana
Aurora, CO 80012
(303) 751-7844

Award to "help develop creative skills, to recognize and award outstanding ability, and to increase the opportunity for the marketing and subsequent publication of nonfiction book manuscripts" (entry fee).

All the Write Stuff
There are many awards for children's writers as well. Check *Writer's Market* and magazines for a list.

➤ PEN/Spielvogel-Diamonstein Award
PEN American Center
568 Broadway
New York, NY 10012
(212) 334-1660

Award for the best previously unpublished collection of essays on any subject by an American writer. Prize $5,000.

More Than Pennies for Poetry

For several years now, I've been one of the judges for *The Paumanouk Writer's Award,* given by the university where I teach. Started by Dr. Charles Fishman and the Visiting Writers Committee, the award's large prize and prestige attracts an astonishing variety of poets, from big leaguers to beginners, sophisticated to unworldly.

Bet You Didn't Know

Winning a writing award often leads to many more awards. The last five winners and first runners-up for the Paumanouk Poetry Award, for example, have all gone on to win other prestigious writing awards.

Here's what I've learned about writing contests and awards as a judge and long-standing member of the committee:

1. The more literary contests you enter, the more you learn about the process.

2. The more you learn, the better your next application will be.

3. Entering contests teaches you a lot about your art, too.

4. People who don't win one year may very well win the next cycle.

5. You can't win it if you're not in it.

Here's a list of ten poetry awards and contests, including the one I judge. I selected each of these writing contests for inclusion because they all require previously unpublished poetry.

➤ Annual Poetry Contest
National Federation of State Poetry Societies
3520 State Road 56
Mechanicsburg, OH 43044
(513) 834-2666

There are fifty different awards for previously unpublished poetry.

➤ Arkansas Poetry Award
The University of Arkansas Press
201 Ozark Avenue
Fayetteville, AR 72701
(501) 575-3246

Awards previously unpublished full-length poetry manuscripts.

➤ Gerald Cable Poetry Chapbook Competition
Silverfish Review
PO Box 3541
Eugene, OR 97403
(503) 344-5060

Awards previously unpublished authors; $100 prize and publication.

➤ Cleveland State University Poetry Center Prize
Cleveland State University Poetry Center
Cleveland, OH 44115-2440
(216) 687-3986

Awards book-length unpublished poetry; $1,000 prize and publication.

➤ Compuwrite
The Writer's Alliance
PO Box 2014
Setauket, NY 11733

Awards previously unpublished poems up to 30 lines about writing on a personal computer.

➤ Billee Murray Denny Poetry Contest
Lincoln College
300 Keokuk Street
Lincoln, IL 62656

Awards unpublished poetry.

➤ Discovery/The Nation
The Poetry Center of the 92nd Street YM-YWHA
1395 Lexington Avenue
New York, NY 10128
(212) 415-5760

Open to poets who have not yet published a book of poems.

➤ Milton Dorfman Poetry Prize
Rome Arts & Community Center
308 W Bloomfield Rd
Rome, NY 13440
(315) 336-1040

Offers "amateurs/beginning poets an outlet for their craft. All submissions must be previously unpublished."

➤ Marie Louise D'Esternaux Poetry Contest
Brooklyn Poetry Circle
2550 Independence Avenue, #3U
Bronx, NY 10463

"The purpose of the contest is to encourage young people to study poetry, to write poetry and to enrich themselves and others."

➤ The Paumanouk Writer's Award
The State University College of Technology at Farmingdale
Melville Road
Knapp Hall
Farmingdale, NY 11735
(516) 420-2050

Award for poems, published or unpublished; $1,000 plus travel expenses to receive the award.

Bet You Didn't Know

Prairie Schooner, a literary magazine published by the University of Nebraska, is one of the last magazines to offer a big money prize without requiring an entrance fee. The prize? $4,500 divided among seven different awards. There are prizes for the best work by a beginning writer, best short story, best poem, and more.

Theater Contests and Grants

Most of the contests listed below are for unproduced, unpublished plays. As I mentioned earlier in this chapter, be sure to write for complete guidelines. Contests change a lot, so it's always better to get the most up-to-date information you can.

Contests

I've included only general playwriting contests. Many other playwriting contests are aimed at special interest groups, such as residents of a specific state, members of a specific ethnic group, and so on. Contact *The Dramatists Guild*, 234 W. 44th Street, New York, NY 10036, phone (212) 398-9366 for information on other contests.

➤ Adriatic Award
The International Society of Dramatists
US Fulfillment Center
Box 1310
Miami, FL 33153
(305) 674-1831

Includes full-length plays, translations, musicals.

Award: $250

➤ American College Theater Festival
Michael Kanin Playwriting Awards Program
The John F. Kennedy Center for the Performing Arts
Washington, DC 20566
(202) 254-3437

Student-written plays, produced by universities.

Award: Amount varies.

➤ American Musical Theatre Festival Competition
Box S-3565
Carmel, CA 93921
(408) 625-5828

Full-length musicals.

Award: $2,000 plus production.

➤ *Lucille Ball Festival of New Comedy*
American Vaudeville
Box 2619
Times Square Station
New York, NY 10108
(718) 204-5974

Award: $250, production, expenses.

➤ *Margaret Bartle Playwriting Award*
Community Children's Theater
8021 East 129th Terrace
Grandview, MO 64030
(816) 761-5775

Plays and musicals for young people.

Award: $500

➤ Beverly Hills Theatre Guild—Julie Harris Playwright Award
2815 North Beachwood Drive
Los Angeles, CA 90068
(213) 465-2703

Full-length plays.

Award: $5,000 first prize, plus $2,000 to help finance production in Los Angeles area within one year; $1,000 second prize; $500 third prize.

➤ Susan Smith Blackburn Prize
3239 Avalon Place
Houston, TX 77019
(713) 522-8529

Full-length plays by a female playwright.

Award: $5,000 first prize; $1,000 second-prize.

➤ Bloomington Playwright's Projects Contest
310 West 7th Street
Bloomington, IN 47404
(812) 334-1188

Full-length plays.

Award: $250, production.

➤ Davie Award for Playwriting
GeVa Theatre
75 Woodbury Blvd.
Rochester, NY 14607
(716) 232-1366

Full-length plays.

Award: $5,000 and production.

➤ Dayton Playhouse Playwriting Competition
The Dayton Playhouse
1301 East Siebenthaler Avenue
Dayton, OH 45414
(512) 277-0144

Full-length plays.

Award: $1,000; possible production.

➤ Deep South Writers Conference
c/o English Department
Box 44691
University of Southwestern Louisiana
Lafayette, LA 70504

Three competitions; many awards.

➤ Dubuque Fine Arts Players, National One-Act Playwriting Contest
569 South Grandview Avenue
Dubuque, IA 52001
(319) 582-5558

One-act plays.

Award: $200, $250, $100 and production for all three plays.

➤ Emerging Playwright Award
Playwrights Preview Productions
1160 Fifth Avenue #304
New York, NY 10029
(212) 996-7287

Full-length plays, one-act plays.

Award: $500, production, travel to attend rehearsals.

Manna from Heaven: Grants

Looking for a grant instead of a contest? Then check out the three ideas that follow. Odds are, at least one of my suggestions should send you scurrying to fill out a stamped self-addressed envelope and sing cheery songs!

➤ The National Endowment for the Arts
NEA Theatre Program Fellowship for Playwrights
1100 Pennsylvania Avenue NW
Washington, DC 20506
(202) 682-5425

All the Write Stuff
Get involved in your local or state arts council, through programs and panels. Network to find other sources of funding.

➤ There's state money available as well. Write to find out what your state offers playwrights. Ask them for a list of other foundations in your state that support playwrights. Look in your telephone book for the number.

➤ Finally, write to your local art agency. Let your fingers do the walking through your telephone book to find the arts/cultural commission in your region.

The Least You Need to Know

➤ There's a lot of money out there for writers.

➤ Enter contests to win writing awards.

➤ Apply for grants to get a slice of the pie.

➤ Many prizes include publication as well as money.

Part 6
Common Writing Challenges—and How to Conquer Them!

"We have nothing to fear but fear itself," Franklin Delano Roosevelt claimed. Fear is definitely a major turn-off for most of us. It haunts most writers like the Ghost of Christmas parties past haunts our waistlines every January. Writers are also bedeviled by fear: fear of rejection, fear of offending, fear of running dry. There's even fear of success.

In this part of the book, you'll explore some of these fears in detail and then demystify them. I'll show you how to conquer writer's block and the thousand insecurities and doubts that go with it. You'll discover the pleasures and pitfalls of working with editors. I'll even teach you how to write when you absolutely can't. After all, writing is the hardest work in the world that does not involve heavy lifting. My job is to make it easier for you.

Chapter 21

A Writer's Best Friend: Editors

In This Chapter

➤ Learn what a good editor can do for *you*

➤ Find out how to locate the editor who's right for you

➤ Get the most from the writer-editor relationship

You need criticism—and not the "hurts so bad" variety, either. All writers need educated, specific feedback that will help them improve their work, making it stronger and usually more salable. That's why editors were invented.

In this chapter, you'll learn *why* you need an editor. Then I'll explain exactly what an editor can do for your writing and for you as a writer. Next comes a discussion of editors so you can learn the chain of command in the editor biz. You'll discover how to find the editor who's right for you, through conventional as well as creative channels. Last but not least, you'll learn to get the most from the writer-editor relationship.

Everyone's a Critic

Much as you might think so, it's not true. Everyone can offer criticism, but only a skilled editor can offer targeted comments about your writing that you can really use. Good editors stay on track, too, sticking to the issues at hand rather than chugging down another rail.

Wrong Turn
We all like to think that we can be objective about our own work. But we can't. If editors make strong suggestions, they bear taking seriously. Set aside your ego and weigh the advice carefully.

Is your writing correct according to the accepted rules of English grammar and usage? Is the story provocative, moving, interesting, and entertaining? Effective editors comment on both technique and style. Here are ten big areas that good editors look for when they study a manuscript:

1. Grammar

2. Sentence construction

3. Word choice

4. Plot

5. Character development

6. Pacing and rhythm

7. Theme

8. Conflict

9. The emotions a piece evokes in the reader

10. The issues and ideas in the writing

Bet You Didn't Know

It's often easier for an editor to step back and find suggestions for the material's organization.

Good editors know how to put you on track without demolishing your self-esteem. They are able to encourage your work and career while being brutally honest. They are tactful and honest, never malicious. Often, a good editor will include at least one true, positive point about a manuscript, even if the rest is a total mess. They'll find that glimmer of potential in your work that keeps you going when the going has gotten tough.

Working Nine to Nine

Editors, like one-armed paperhangers, are chronically overworked and just as likely underpaid. What's it like to be a book editor today? Here's a sample of the average book editor's responsibilities:

➤ Field phone calls from authors and agents

➤ Deal with the publicity department

➤ Interface with the marketing people

➤ Conference with the production department

➤ Calculate P & L's (profit and loss) statements

➤ Attend interminable meetings about book covers

➤ Schedule publicity

➤ Work out book deadlines

➤ Hire and fire assistants

➤ Negotiate with management for books they want to acquire

➤ Work out their own pay increases and promotions

➤ Deal with office politics

➤ Manage author temper tantrums (sweet-tempered me, excepted)

What's the result? The average editor barely has time to exhale. Some editors even find themselves doing their actual editing work at night and on weekends, dealing with the avalanche of manuscripts in fits and starts. The bulk of an editor's time ends up being devoted to projects that are signed and sealed, for the publisher has already invested in these books and articles. All this leaves the editor with precious little time to nurture a new author, even if he or she is as marvelous as squid ink Jell-O.

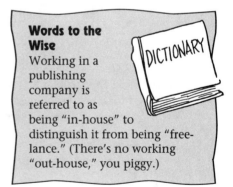

Words to the Wise

Working in a publishing company is referred to as being "in-house" to distinguish it from being "freelance." (There's no working "out-house," you piggy.)

This is not a pity plea for the poor overworked editor. Rather, it's a reality check: You're not the only fish in the publishing pond, baby. That could be why your telephone calls aren't getting returned.

Getting to Know You

A cigar may be just a cigar, but an editor isn't just an editor. There are as many different types of editors as there are books. You usually can't tell the editors apart without a scorecard. Here's the scorecard.

➤ *Executive Editor* (or *Editorial Director*). This is usually the Grand Poobah. Only the Publisher may be higher on the food chain.

All the Write Staff
Want a free lunch? The acquisitions editor is usually the one with the T & E budget (travel and entertainment bucks). I love it when you flash that gold card, baby.

➤ *Editor-in-Chief.* The person responsible for the work flow, the company's future editorial direction, and the bottom-line profit and loss. In large companies, the editor-in-chief is usually an administrator; in smaller firms, the editor-in-chief does hands-on editing as well as crack the whip.

➤ *Acquisitions Editor.* The front man (or woman), the one who usually woos 'em and wins 'em. The duties of the acquisitions editor vary from publisher to publisher. Sometimes they acquire and edit the material; other times, they get the authors on board and then hand them onto someone else to work with text. They may negotiate contracts, too. The acquisitions editor is usually chummy with the agents and has been around the block a few times.

➤ *Senior Editor.* This is often a person with a great deal of experience in publishing. In large firms, there are often several senior editors. The senior editors usually get the better books or bigger bucks because of seniority. They read for the big picture: organization, characters, plot, conflict, and so on.

➤ *Editor.* If there is only one editor in a company, this person is the top banana. If not, these are the people who do the hands-on work on your manuscript. Like senior editors, regular ol' garden-variety editors read for the big picture: organization, characters, plot, conflict, and so on.

➤ *Associate Editor.* One notch below editors, these people are usually waiting to move a rung up the ladder. In the meantime, they slave away on manuscripts.

➤ *Managing Editor.* This person is responsible for making sure the other editors meet their deadlines. He or she oversees schedules. In some companies, the managing editor might be right below the editor-in-chief in terms of power and responsibility.

➤ *Copyeditor.* This is the person responsible for catching and correcting all your errors in grammar, usage, and mechanics. A good copyeditor also catches problems with logic, dates, and names, too. The copyeditor can question the arrangement of your material, but is not authorized to make any editorial changes without consulting the editor.

➤ *Assistant Editor.* The recent college graduate, working for table scraps and still paying off the loans. Eager, earnest, and depressingly perky, these folks get the odd jobs like copying, sending out proofs, and occasional light editing.

Wrong Turn
In the publishing world, titles matter. A lot. Be sure you use the correct title for anyone you contact and work with.

Good Help Isn't That Hard to Find: Finding an Editor

So you've got this manuscript. You've squandered the best years of your life on it, lavishing your energy with abandon. Your best friends say it's the greatest thing since sliced bread; your spouse is bowled over by the beauty of your prose—even your mother-in-law is impressed with your exquisite turns of phrase. Now what?

Don't trust your nearest and dearest. Find an editor to read your work. But, you say, it's easier to find an honest man in New York City, a hot date for New Year's Eve, or a native-English speaking cabby. Not so, I protest. Try the following ideas to locate the editor who is right for you.

First Contact

The first editor you consult doesn't have to work for a publishing company. He or she doesn't even have to be a "real" editor with a fancy editor title. Instead, consider having a local, published writer to act as your first editor.

To find the best published writers in your area, start with the owners or managers of your neighborhood bookstores. They will know the most highly respected local authors in the region. These writers generally come in for signings and readings when their books are published. Local writers also stop by to autograph copies of their books so the booksellers have those fancier copies on hand.

Wrong Turn
Writers-in-residence use their spare time to write books, not read your novel, so this doesn't necessarily make them more accessible.

You can also contact a local university to find out which writers hold "chairs" (special teaching positions) in creative writing. Such distinguished modern writers as Nadine Gordimer, Philip Levine, Alice Walker, James Dickey, Toni Morrison, Robert Lowell, and Bernard Malamud have held university chairs in creative writing. The chairs are often

Wrong Turn
This isn't an easy route to go because most Famous Writers like being pestered by new writers about as much as they like getting a root canal. You might think that everyone agrees that your writing is the most important thing in the world. Not so. Consider getting feedback from a writer's group before you call to see if Mario Puzo has a spare afternoon to read your book.

named after generous benefactors, so look for titles like the "Elmer Fudd Pennypacker IXVII Chair for Poetry" and the "Wilma Wacker Memorial Chair for Distinguished Modern Novelists." These writers-in-residence often have light teaching duties in exchange for the prestige they bring to a university.

Compile a list of all the local writers you can find. Then read their work to see how you react to it. Go for a representative sampling of their writing; one novel or short story won't cut it. Reading several works will help you make sure you have a grasp of the writer's overall career. The last thing you want is a nasty surprise, like finding out the writer's last two books were tawdry pieces of trash.

Be prepared to pay what it takes. You've invested your time, energy, and money in your work. You owe it to yourself to get some useful feedback.

If you hire an independent writer to critique your work, figure on spending about $250–$500 for a first read-through. A detailed edit can run as much as $2,500 to $5,000, depending on the length of your work and the reputation of the author you have approached.

You can use the following worksheet to assess the suitability of a fellow writer's work before you initiate first contact.

Put a check next to every statement you agree with.

_____ 1. Is the work similar to my own in *genre*, so I am comparing apples to apples?

_____ 2. Does the writer get published consistently so I feel he or she is a competent writer?

_____ 3. Are we using similar *themes*?

_____ 4. Do we develop *characters* and *plot* similarly?

_____ 5. Can I sense a clear *voice* in this writing?

_____ 6. Do I like this writer's work?

_____ 7. Do I think I can get a fair reading from this person?

_____ 8. Do I have a snowball's chance in heck of this writer being willing to work with me?

Writing Workshops

Low on cash? Can't find an editor you like? I suggest that you consider forming or joining a writing workshop. Most major universities and big cities have them, but they can also be private and meet in homes, libraries, lodges, and restaurants.

Writer's groups aren't about punch and cookies, sex and scandal. They *are* about members critiquing each other's manuscripts to improve the quality of everyone's work. In an effective writing workshop, the other writers comment on each other's work and make suggestions for revision. Fellow writers can let you know which of your characters are as slimy as Leisure Suit Larry and which parts of your story are as riveting as Rosie. You can then sift through this advice and make your own decisions about which to keep and which to reject.

> **All the Right Stuff**
> Consider getting free feedback and polishing your work before you take your manuscript to someone and fork over hard cash for an opinion.

Another advantage of writing workshops is consensus. An individual editor, no matter how skilled, might be having a bad day, week, or life. He or she might have strong personal feelings for (or against!) you that can influence how the criticism emerges. With a group critique, however, you're canceling out individual preferences.

> **Bet You Didn't Know**
> Critiquing other writers' work is also a good way to build critical faculties in yourself that you can apply to your own writing.

Electronic Life Lines

A new venue has emerged to edit a work-in-progress: the Internet. An increasing number of writers are posting their work on the World Wide Web and soliciting suggestions for revisions.

Like any other method, posting your work for editing on the Web has its good and bad points. It's a great method because it's free and doesn't involve any travel. You can find an editor (or a group of editors) without ever getting up from your comfy swivel chair. This is especially crucial for home-bound writers, those of us constrained by isolated locations, lack of locomotion, or family circumstances. On-line editing also allows you the luxury of getting many different opinions.

All the Right Stuff

Try to get published anywhere you can—the company newsletter or a local writing journal that pays in free eggs. At least you'll be able to see what the editor does to your work and maybe ask him or her a question or two about your writing style in the process. You can also take a local college writing class to get feedback from both teacher and fellow students.

The downside to this new technofad? You have no guarantee that the people reading and editing your work are who they say they are. Any Tom, Dick, or Harry can claim to be any other Tom, Dick, or Harry on the Web. Your on-line reader could be a skilled editor trolling the Web for the next hot writer du jour—or a twelve-year old with too much time and technotraining. Listening to unskilled editors can damage your writing as well as your self-confidence.

Further, once you post your work on the Web it's de facto part of the public domain. Anyone can have it…for free. And, you have no guarantee where it will turn up. Every day, my cyber-friends e-mail me reams and reams of the latest on-line witticisms. These usually include lists of grammatical bloopers, seasonal poems, and extended contemplations on life à la Dave Barry. Who writes these? Got me. This stuff appears on my screen daily and no one ever gets credit—or payment—for his or her writing.

A Match Made in Heaven: Working with Your Editor

So you've signed a contract and you've been assigned an editor like my blessed Nancy Stevenson. Now it's time to get to work. In this situation, good teamwork is essential for success. Follow these ten guidelines to get the most from the writer-editor relationship.

1. Remember that everyone has his or her own taste. How else can we explain the sale of Donnie and Marie Osmond albums? Consider your editor's personal taste when you decide to accept or reject criticism.

2. Be careful of editors who impose their own ideas of what a story should be on your work. There's a subclass of editors who love to write your stories for you—it's easier than writing their own. But even well-meaning people will guide you to write the story *they* want to write. Sift comments carefully.

3. Try to get editors to focus on what is on the page—what works and doesn't work for them. Most important, encourage your editor to articulate the reasons why something is a hit or miss. Ask them to identify these areas:

   ➤ Weak spots

   ➤ Places where there's potential for development

   ➤ Passages that seem to be missing something

   ➤ Errors in logic

4. Remember that every genre generates its own standards of criticism. The criticisms for novels, short stories, poems, screenplays, and essays are all different. For example, the points an editor critiques in a novel (theme, characters, conflict, plot, setting) are different from those an editor critiques in a poem (rhythm, rhyme, tone, and so on).

5. Take all suggestions, but resist the urge to have the editor do the rewriting for you. Do it on your own.

6. Be wary of editors who psychoanalyze the process of writing. These editors tend to say things like, "I think you stopped writing here because you're scared. I *know* there's more, if only you'd delve a little deeper." These editors can be well-meaning, but it's still psychobabble. Also, it can undermine your confidence. Guide the editor to stick to the text.

7. Try to translate unhelpful criticism into direct questions that you can use. If your editor says something is murky, press for more specific information.

All the Write Stuff
Look for recurring issues in your writing in the editor's comments. This can help you identify larger style issues you should work on in your writing in general.

8. You can help prevent miscommunication by rephrasing what your editor said to make sure you understood it. This also gives the editor a chance to correct any misunderstandings that may have occurred.

9. If you can't figure out how to incorporate the feedback into your story, don't get into a lather. Think about it. Let it sit awhile unmolested. If the feedback does indeed contain something important, it will become clear eventually. The important thing is to keep on writing.

10. Above all, don't take any criticism about your writing personally. It's about your book—not you.

Your Momma, Too!

When an editor comments on your work, try to listen quietly and respectfully. Resist the urge to leap back with defenses. I suggest you let the editor's comments sit at least a week before you respond. This will give you the time to process and absorb what has been said about your work. After all, your writing is an extension of yourself, so even the most gentle suggestion might provoke some resentment. Criticism that seemed ludicrous on Monday often makes a lot more sense by Friday.

Here are some more ways to make your work sessions with your editors both smooth and productive.

1. *Check for inferences.* Identify your editor's nonverbal as well as verbal clues. This can help you identify the real (as opposed to the stated) problem with your writing, if there is one. If you're conferencing on the phone (most often the case), check for changes in tone and phrasing.

2. *Keep an open mind.* Don't be quick to leap to conclusions. After all, you've got plenty of time to make unwarranted assumptions.

3. *Check for feelings.* Identify the emotions your editor is stating outright or implying through body language. Gauge the emotional temperature of the conversation to keep it within normal ranges.

4. *Determine how important each criticism is to your editor.* Some comments are minor. Others, however, will matter a great deal more to your editor. This can help you decide where to put the most thought and effort.

5. *Avoid counterattacking.* When we're attacked (or perceive that we're being attacked), our natural reaction is to defend ourselves—perhaps by counterattacking. The counterattack may prompt the editor to strike back, and the conflict will escalate. Feelings get hurt and issues become muddy and difficult to resolve. No matter how much a specific comment may sting, remember that you're a pro. Sit tight and think.

Do You Hear What I Hear?

Often, what someone says is not what we hear. This is not a bad thing when it comes to publishing, for it results in a vast market for *Men are From Mars, Women are From Venus*–type books. But it *can* be a problem during the editing process. So let's talk a little about listening. Listening isn't the same as hearing. Here's a little story to illustrate what I mean.

There's a tale told about the day legendary news reporter Walter Cronkite steered his boat into a Maine port. A keen sailor, Cronkite was pleased to see a small crowd of people on shore waving their arms at him. He could barely hear their excited shouts of "Hello, Walter! Hello, Walter!"

As his boat approached the shore, the crowd grew louder and their greeting more determined. "Hello, Walter! Hello, Walter!" drifted weakly across the bay. Delighted at the reception, Cronkite tipped his sailor hat at the crowd, waved, and even took a bow.

But before he reached the port, Cronkite's boat suddenly jammed aground. The crowd was still. The famous news anchor suddenly realized what the crowd had been shouting:

"Shallow water! Shallow water!" The moral of the story? "Don't let your ego get in the way of hearing the truth."

To receive a message, the listener must first perceive the sound, then decode it, and then interpret it. *Hearing* means perceiving sound. *Listening* means decoding and interpreting sound correctly. Follow these guidelines so you can really listen to what your editor is saying:

➤ Consider the editor's background and experiences. Why are certain points important to the editor? Why did he or she mention them?

➤ Listen for key points, such as answers to your questions.

➤ At the end of the conversation, check your understanding with your editor. Clarify any misconceptions on the spot.

➤ After the conversation, write down key points that affect revisions, deadlines, and so on.

➤ Show that you understand the message by nodding your head, smiling, frowning, or saying "Uh-huh."

Bet You Didn't Know

Research has found important cultural differences in speaking and listening patterns. White Americans, for example, almost always respond nonverbally when they listen closely, but African Americans tend to respond with words rather than nonverbal cues. Keep cultural factors in mind when you work with editors.

Has It Come to This?

What happens if your editor asks you to change something you don't want to change? You might like a particular turn of phrase or a joke that the editor feels falls flatter than yesterday's beer. Can the editor insist on a rewrite or even reject material you favor? The answers depend on your status and your editor's status on the food chain, the importance of the book, your attitude, and outside constraints.

➤ If your editor is well-respected and you're just starting out, the editor is far more likely to be able to make the changes he or she wants.

➤ If the editor has a reputation for being arbitrary and difficult, you may be able to exert effective damage control by calling in others at the publishing company.

Wrong Turn
When you work with an editor in a publishing company, respect the chain of command. Go over an editor's head and you're likely not to get any work at the company again—even if your concerns were valid.

Wrong Turn
Allocate your editorial complaints carefully. Save them, like checkers in the back row, for really important issues.

➤ If the book is very important, the editor is more likely to pull rank, especially if you are a novice.

➤ If you've already made a fuss about a number of other changes, chances are good that the editor will prevail.

➤ If you've been a peach thus far, you'll likely get your way.

➤ If your editor has better taste than you do (I know, amazing though it may seem, writers *have* been wrong), you're probably out of luck when it comes to an editor's insistence on heavy edits.

➤ If the book is already on the schedule and marketing has announced it, chances are you'll be in a position to insist on fewer changes. In this instance, time tends to take precedence over arguments.

What if it's not a marriage made in heaven and you and the editor just don't get along? Is it time for an editorial D-I-V-O-R-C-E?

There *are* times when the writer-editor match just doesn't work. For example, I'm rigid about using correct grammar and usage. Using "impact" as a verb (as in "How does this impact the situation?") or including idiotic nonwords such as "signage" drive me batty. I cannot abide editors who add qualifiers to absolutes, as in "most unique." I even had an editor once who changed my word "facts" to read "true facts." Are there any untrue facts? I can't work with an editor who uses jargon and doesn't know the fundamental rules of grammar and usage.

In some situations, an editor may overstep his or her bounds and change things without your approval. Or, you may have a nasty, rude editor who hurts your feelings without cause. Sometimes you can separate the comment from the person...other times, you can't.

In such an instance, you have several options:

➤ If you're on a work-for-hire contract with other writers, just take your name off the project. That way, no one will think you're the dope. We all like to see our name in print, but not if it will hurt our reputation.

➤ Have a meeting with the editor and calmly share your concerns. If necessary, call in a third party to mediate.

➤ Ask the brass for a new editor. This has happened to me only a few times in my fifteen years as a writer. In each case, I balance the integrity of the project over my personal needs before making a decision.

In his essay "A Qualified Farewell," Raymond Chandler explained how he felt about his writing: "I am a writer, and there comes a time when that which I write belongs to me, has to be written alone and in silence, no one telling me a better way to write it. It doesn't have to be great writing, it doesn't even have to be terribly good. It just has to be mine." Ultimately, the decision to work with a certain editor is yours.

Turnabout Is Fair Play

What happens if you're called on to critique a manuscript? This is especially likely to happen if you are part of a writing group. Once someone in a writing group helps edit your work, it's downright churlish to refuse to return the favor.

Mastering the art of giving as well as accepting criticism is an essential part of becoming a better writer. First, remember that constructive criticism results from a thoughtful, prepared evaluation. After hearing a reading by another writer, take a few minutes to think about the piece and arrange your ideas into a tactful, organized critique that includes the positive as well as the negative.

Comment on the overall picture first. Consider whether the plot is feasible, the characters are staying true to themselves, the events in the story are really pertinent to the plot, and so on. Were you hooked in the beginning? Did the manuscript sustain your interest throughout? Is the dialogue realistic? Do each speaker's words match his or her personality?

Then focus on the more detailed information: Were there any confusing parts? Did you find any unnecessary exposition? Was the point of view clear and consistent? How about too many passive verbs? Finally, address any basic editing errors, specific words that ring false or mislead, and confusing and improper punctuation.

Reality Check

What happens once you sell a book? After you stop cheering, here's the drill:

1. You sell your manuscript.

2. The editor receives it and logs it into his or her files.

3. The editor calls with terms.

4. You talk and agree on terms.

5. The contract is mailed to you. You sign it and return it.

6. Sometime in the future, you receive an executed (counter-signed) copy of the contract.

7. Your editor or an assistant edits the manuscript.

8. You and the editor discuss suggestions and changes.

9. You make any necessary changes.

10. The book is copyedited.

11. Editors get galley proofs. Sometimes you will get a copy to check; if time is short, you won't.

12. The corrected galleys go to production.

13. Editors get advance copies and send copies to you (depending on the terms of the contract).

All the Write Stuff
In the standard contract, authors get 10 free copies of their book. You can negotiate this, if you want more copies.

No matter how wonderful your editor is, once you're done editing, it's all over.

➤ You have no say in a title change.

➤ You will not be consulted about jacket copy.

➤ You will not be consulted on art—even cover art.

➤ You will have no input in the style of your book: the type face and size, paper stock, margins, and so on.

➤ You will not be on national TV (or even local TV) unless your book sells exceptionally well or you arrange the interviews yourself.

The Least You Need to Know

➤ Every writer needs an editor.

➤ Your editor can be a fellow writer or an employee of a publishing company.

➤ Listen carefully to what your editor says, even though you're not obligated to take all of his or her suggestions.

➤ A good editor is more precious than diamonds.

Chapter 22

Writer's Block (or, Just Shoot Me Now)

In This Chapter

➤ Explore the most common fears that writers share

➤ Learn some quick fixes to overcoming writer's block

➤ Resort to stern measures

We live in a stressful world. There's more pressure than ever before: tension on the job, convoluted family situations, less clean water and air, startling new technology. Are you trying to be a writer on top of all of this? If so, you're probably attempting to carve out the time to write in addition to carrying a full-time job. Of course you feel "blocked" at times. And that's just when you have enough energy to realize how exhausted you are.

In this chapter, you will learn what writers fear—and why. You'll soon discover that you're not alone in your concerns. In fact, you've got plenty of company! Then I'll teach you a variety of different ways to overcome writer's block. Best of all, each method is surefire and completely *painless*!

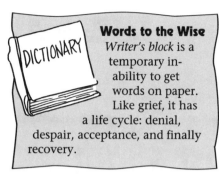

Words to the Wise

Writer's block is a temporary inability to get words on paper. Like grief, it has a life cycle: denial, despair, acceptance, and finally recovery.

The Five Deadly Fears

Milton and the medieval crowd had the Seven Deadly Sins; writers have their own demons. Do you know what bedevils you but you can't quite put it into words? You can use the following list to put a name to your own particular writing demon so you can whip it into submission.

Fear 1: Fear of Failure

This is the one that kicks you in the face. You are afraid that you will toil away for years—and no one will care. Your best shot will fall short of the mark. Your friends, family, neighbors, and co-workers will think you are an idiot for wasting your time. Worst of all, you'll think you've made a horrible mistake by deciding to become a writer.

Fear 2: Fear of Rejection

When you write, you expose yourself. Every time you write, you are revealing your innermost thoughts on paper. You might as well pull your pants down in public and moon the universe. As a result, it's not difficult to feel that if your work is rejected, you are being rejected as well. And rejection stings like the dickens.

Fear 3: Fear of Success

To succeed in something new means that you are breaking with the past. Writing success is virgin territory for you, completely uncharted. If you gain success as a writer, your friends and family might envy you...especially if they have been trying to break into print themselves. You may fear that your friends secretly wish that your success will conveniently vanish as quickly as it came. That way, you won't upset the status quo and be a threat to anyone. Besides, you think, if you succeed once, it was probably just a fluke.

Fear 4: Fear of Offending

What happens if you have too much to say on paper? Suppose a character in your novel makes rude remarks about another character...who just happens to resemble one of your relatives? You have nothing against this person, but your character does. Imagine Auntie Josephina wagging her finger at you during the next family gathering as she says, "You have shamed the family with your nasty writing. We can never hold our heads up in the community again."

Ever consider writing about sex? Can you imagine what your mother or father will say if you write about your first sexual experience and the book gets published and sells a zillion copies? Ouch.

Fear 5: Fear of Running Dry

What if you have nothing to say—or you think that what you say has been said a million times before? What happens if your writing doesn't offer startling new insights? No one will want to read my stuff, you think, because I have nothing new to contribute to the world's storehouse of knowledge. With this fear, you are actually sabotaging the idea of being a writer before you give yourself a chance.

One Step at a Time

Let's look at some of these fears in detail and see if we can demystify them.

Fear #1: *Fear of failure.* You can't win it if you aren't in it. You have the choice between risking the discovery that you were not cut out to be a writer versus spending the rest of your life wondering if you could have done it—if you'd only had the nerve.

Besides, you don't have to shout your intentions from the rooftops. In Part 1, I advised you to tell people that you want to be a writer. If that suits your style, fine. If not, keep your writing to yourself. For what it's worth, the more you want to become a writer, the more likely you are to succeed.

Fear #2: *Fear of rejection.* No matter how the news is delivered—phone, fax, or FedEx—rejection hurts. What's nice about being rejected as a writer, however, is that it's rarely personal. Unless you've dallied with the editor's significant other during the last Christmas party, the rejection is always for your work, not for *you*.

Editors may reject a book because:

➤ They can't take on another project at this time.

➤ They already have a book just like it on their list (this has happened to me twice!).

➤ The publishing company doesn't have enough money in the budget right now to take a chance on a book by a beginning writer.

➤ Books of the type you're proposing aren't selling particularly well right now.

➤ You haven't targeted the right publishing company for your book. This is a very common mistake among novice writers.

➤ The company is undergoing some internal upheavals and you're caught in the cross-fire.

➤ Your book needs a little more polish before it's ready for publication.

Bet You Didn't Know

It took five years for the screenwriter to sell his classic feel-good Christmas movie "It's a Wonderful Life." That's a lot of rejection slips before success!

Keep in mind that there are different levels of rejection. Anything but a preprinted letter of rejection is encouragement to submit again. With each rejection, your novel, story, poem, or script is a step closer to acceptance.

Fear #3: *Fear of success.* It's natural to feel a let-down after any momentous event: graduation, marriage, the birth of a child, winning the lottery, a promotion, and the sale of a book. But after the hoopla dies down, your life is still basically the same: your corns still ache, your middle is still spreading, and your aging pooch still needs to be let out every ten minutes.

There's also the worry that people will treat you differently once you hit the big time. And some will. I have lost one friend who could not accept my success. She had been a professional writer before she started her family and found it difficult to keep up the pace after. She chose other work and is a success at it—but she still resents my success as a writer. That's life. In the grand cosmic balance, I made many wonderful new friends among the writers and editors I have met and worked with. They encourage and support me in countless ways.

Bet You Didn't Know

One of the great anxieties in getting published initially is the fear of running dry: "I have one book in me, but *two*? There's no way I could do this *again*!" And then there's: "When will they realize I'm really no good?"

Fear #4: *Fear of offending.* Writing about alcoholic parents when you have alcoholic parents makes it tricky to face Pater and Mater at the next cocktail hour once the book is published. Yes, you might offend someone when personal revelations hit print. Eventually, they'll get over it. And if they don't, that's something *they* have to deal with. You can't tailor your art to suit individuals. This isn't carte blanche to wound everyone in a twenty-mile radius. It *is* the OK to say what you have to say in print with honesty.

Themes that challenge society's morals or standards might offend entire groups of people, not just family and friends. Some of the world's greatest writing has sparked enormous public controversy. Many books, plays, and essays were so incendiary that they were even banned for a time, including these classics: Lawrence's *Lady Chatterley's Lover,* Twain's *The Adventures of Huckleberry Finn,* Salinger's *The Catcher in the Rye,* Nabokov's *Lolita,* Burrough's *Naked Lunch,* and Joyce's *Ulysses.* And don't forget the furor over virtually every play that George Bernard Shaw wrote!

This doesn't mean that you're going to deliberately set out to offend everyone to ensure your literary immortality. But if you're honest and your work has vision, you might find that your work changes the world. Upton Sinclair's novel *The Jungle* resulted in the passage of the Pure Food and Drug Act; Steinbeck's novel *The Grapes of Wrath* focused attention on the plight of migrant farmers. When seen in this light, what do you care if Aunt Ethel says your book is piggy and has stirred up a peck o' trouble?

Fear #5: *Fear of running dry.* Your life is composed of unique experiences and you see them as no one else can. If you have the desire to write, it's because you have something special and different to say. You can't run dry; there's too much in there. Someone might write it better, but no one will write it exactly the same.

Another great thing about writing is its diversity. If you really can't get started on your second novel, not to worry. Switch gears: try a poem or essay instead. The different types of writing are similar enough to tap the same creativity but different enough to spark new ideas.

Quick and Dirty

Most of the time, blocked writers just need a little jump start to get back to work. Nothing drastic, just a gentle nudge with an electric cattle prod in the right direction. And that's what I have for you here. Below is a series of gentle nudges you can use when the creativity well seems to be running a little low. I suggest that you try 'em all and then pick the nudges that work best for you.

1. Brainstorm, freewrite, web, or use any other pre-writing method to jump start your creative engine. See Part 1 for a step-by-step guide to different prewriting techniques you can use.

2. Redefine the audience. If you're writing for adults, try the same idea as a kids' book instead. And you never know; you might end up creating a better book: *The Little Prince, Alice in Wonderland,* and C.S. Lewis' *Narnia* series can all be read and enjoyed by children and adults.

3. Tell your ideas to a friend. It's often easier to speak to a real audience than to imagine an artificial one.

All the Write Stuff
Too shy to share your writing ideas with a friend? Try "talking" to a tape-recorder.

4. Reexamine your purpose for writing. For example, if you're writing to persuade, try writing to entertain instead. Upton Sinclair's *The Jungle* and Harriet Beecher Stowe's *Uncle Tom's Cabin* both persuade by entertaining. And each accomplished its purpose brilliantly.

5. If a parameter such as line length or word count is holding you back, abandon it—at least for this draft. You can always go back and reshape your writing to fit a specific format.

6. Write the part that's easiest to write. You can fill in the rest later. There's no rule that says you have to start at the very beginning. Start in the middle, start with the conclusion—wherever you want.

7. Briefly do something else that doesn't require thinking, such as laundry, gardening, or washing the dog. (He probably needed it anyway.)

8. Try using a different method of transcription. If you're keyboarding, for example, try writing longhand. If you're writing longhand, try a tape recorder.

9. Draw a picture or a diagram to show what you mean. Use the visual to help you spark ideas and order your thoughts.

10. Change the point of view. Laura Ingalls Wilder wrote the initial draft of the first novel in her *Little House* series from the first-person point of view. Her daughter, a brilliant editor, suggested a switch to the third-person point of view. This gave Wilder the distance she needed to craft her life story into fiction.

11. Develop little rituals or routines that get you in the mood to write. In the winter, I make a cup of hot tea; in the summer, it's iced tea. This goes on the bookshelf to the right of the computer. Then I sharpen two pencils and I'm ready to go. This ritual tells my brain that it had better get ready to write, like it or not. (P.S. I never use the pencils, but they have to be next to the mouse pad and they have to be sharp).

12. Visualize yourself writing. I've lifted this idea from professional athletes, who use visualization all the time. Here's the drill. Close your eyes and sit comfortably. Imagine yourself rereading what you wrote the day before, holding your fingers over the keyboard, and plunging right in. Imagine yourself feeling confident and success-ful. Stick with it, because it can take a few tries to get into the groove.

13. Write your material as a letter. This technique gives you a chance to relax and shoot the breeze on paper without the pressure of "producing." It can also help you develop your unique voice. When you're done, revise the letter into the first draft of your work.

14. Change your personae. Don't write as yourself; write as an entirely different person. If you're a stunning (and modest) female college professor/writer like myself, try writing as a male ice-skating champion, a world-weary diplomat, or a cross-dressing dominatrix. Once you take on a role, you'll feel less inhibited about writing.

15. Picture a scene, sound, taste, or smell. For example, to write a scene in a bakery, imagine the rich yeasty smell wafting through the air, the golden loaves of hot crusty bread emerging from the oven, the satisfying crunch of a buttery warm croissant. Start by describing the sensory feedback and then segue to the plot, characters, setting, or conflict. This method works especially well with poetry or descriptive passages.

Wrong Turn
The same method may not work all the time. If you start to run dry again, vary your attack by trying different methods.

16. Never end a day at the real "end" in the writing. The next day, it's off to the races as you're anxious to finish what you started the previous day. You won't be stuck trying to figure out how to get started, because you'll be busy finishing!

Help! My Brain Is Filled Up!

Sometimes you're just too tired to work. That's not writer's block—that's exhaustion. Learn to tell the difference between burn-out and block. I suggest that you start by giving yourself a good rest. Get enough sleep for a change; eat nourishing food. Let someone else deal with the daily stress for a while. Treat yourself to a massage and some vigorous physical activity. If you still can't write after a few days on my R & R regime, you may really be blocked. If that's the case, we have to take sterner measures.

Stern Measure 1: Punch a Time Clock

Are you stuck? Go back over what you've written. Noodle with it. Play a little here, adjust a little there. This is time well spent; after all, much of creative writing is rethinking and revising.

If this doesn't work, you can establish a strict schedule. This will help you get back into the groove. Try these three steps:

➤ Write for 15 minutes a day—no more.

➤ As you write, don't think or analyze.

➤ Write as fast as you can.

If this goes well, add a few minutes to the schedule at the end of the week. A week later, try to write for half an hour without a break. Keep lengthening the amount of time until you're back into the writing routine.

Bet You Didn't Know

Many writers get blocked when they have to move from planning to actual writing. Once writers get started writing, it's usually smooth sailing.

Stern Measure 2: Work Overtime

Getting desperate? The following unblocking technique is like the total day of beauty regime I subject myself to every six months—a last ditch effort. When things start looking so bad that I just have to do it all—hair, nails, skin, clothes—I bite the bullet and go for it. Same for writer's block. Chomp down.

Set aside a full day—a full day—to write. Plant your butt in the chair *and stay there*. Don't answer the phone, don't putter in the yard. Let the mail go unread and the dishes un-washed. Stock up on junk food to reward yourself for your determination.

The first hour is the hardest—but stick with it. Follow these three steps:

➤ Write anything.

➤ Don't doodle—write sentences.

➤ Stick with it.

Bet You Didn't Know

There is scientific evidence that writer's block exists. See, you're not crazy after all.

Stern Measure 3: Home Alone

Some people can write any place, any time. Some people can also eat White Castle burgers and stay sweet-tempered at the Motor Vehicle bureau. Most of us are not that fortunate; we need real food and people who don't make us crazy. If you fall into this vast majority of sensible folks, this stern measure may be right for you.

All the Write Stuff
Most experienced writers find they can write most easily when they're alone, working without risk of interruption. But, different strokes for different folks.

Keep a log to discover when and where you write best.

On the top of everything you write, note these details:

➤ Where you wrote the piece

➤ When you wrote it

➤ Weather conditions at the time you wrote (sunny, rainy, and so on)

➤ Who, if anyone, was present when you wrote

➤ What music, if any, was playing

➤ Any background noise

➤ Any special circumstances

Photocopy the following worksheet and clip a copy to everything you write for the next month. Fill it in at the end of each writing event.

Place _____
Time _____
Weather conditions _____
People present _____
Music _____
Noise level _____
Special circumstances _____

You might find writing is easiest on the kitchen table at 4 A.M., or on the den floor at midnight. Maybe you have to write on a sunny porch after lunch or in a corner of the living room after everyone has gone to sleep. I like to start writing first thing in the morning and break for lunch at noon. I take a brisk (i.e., punishing) walk after lunch and then I can hammer away until 3:30. After dinner my brain is pretty much fried, so I spend that time doing office work: writing invoices, entering expenses, returning telephone calls, and researching.

Once you figure out when and where you write best, make that place your office. I'm a firm believer in having a room of one's own, a place where a writer can go and be creative unmolested. Maybe it's only a corner of a room, but make it your own, private and respected.

> ### Bet You Didn't Know
>
> Best-selling writer Judith Krantz has a sign on her door that says: DO NOT COME IN. DO NOT KNOCK. DO NOT SAY HELLO. DO NOT SAY I'M LEAVING. DO NOT SAY ANYTHING UNLESS THE HOUSE IS ON FIRE.

Setting aside your own "office" helps your brain know that it's writing time. The crib had a similar effect on my children when they were small. I put them in their cribs only when it was naptime or bedtime—never any other time. As a result, they were accustomed to falling asleep right away when they hit that mattress. Once you find your best writing situation, your brain will get programmed to kick in when you go there.

Stern Measure 4: Get to the Root of the Problem

Occasionally, deep-seated psychological problems can block your ability to write. You may have developed a real fear of writing for some reason you can't fathom. Even though you can't put your finger on the problem, it is very real and it blocks your ability to write.

Take a few minutes to jot down your thoughts about writing. If the thoughts are negative, try to substitute positive ideas. For example, if you're thinking, "I just can't do this," try writing, "I can write. I can write very well." Here are some other positive thoughts you can use to replace the negative ones you may be thinking:

➤ "If I keep working, I can produce something that's good."

➤ "My other writing was great. This shows I can do it—and well."

➤ "I got A's in creative writing in high school."

➤ "I love to write. It gives me great pleasure to put words down on paper."

➤ "Writing is worth the effort it takes."

Stern Measure 5: Define the Problem

Sometimes, you may not be suffering from writer's block at all—you may just have a case of regular old garden-variety procrastination. "Me?" you bluster indignantly. Yes, buckaroo, you may be a procrastinator. If that's the case, some of the techniques for shattering the block won't work for you. Take this simple quiz to diagnose your writing problem.

Circle the situations that apply to you.

You're a Classic Procrastinator if...

1. You're still figuring out if bell bottoms, love beads, and a Nehru jacket are the right look for you.

2. You're just about ready to buy one of those new-fangled TV sets—you know, the ones that show programs in color.

3. You sent for your Woodstock tickets in 1969 and just noticed they haven't arrived yet.

4. You try to pay your bills the very same decade they're due.

5. You can't decide if you should vote for Nixon or Kennedy this year.

You May Have Writer's Block if...

1. A blank sheet of paper makes you even more nauseated than the thought of wearing bell bottoms, love beads, and a Nehru jacket.

2. You're so frustrated that you're ready to pull out your liver through your lungs, chew ground glass, or watch reruns of *Gilligan's Island.*

3. You would spend a week in Woodstock— even in the winter—rather than spend another day trying to write.

4. You find bills reassuring because they show that *someone* can get some writing done.

5. Vote? Make a mark on paper?

> **All the Write Staff**
> Don't be shy about soliciting positive feedback from friends, relatives, and editors. Reread all the good comments you've gotten on your writing.

What can you do if you're really suffering from procrastination rather than writer's block? Setting your work aside for awhile won't help; in fact, it's likely to make the situation worse. Try these ideas instead:

➤ Identify the problem that keeps you from writing. Deal with the problem, and then go back to writing.

➤ Set a regular time to write. Make it the same time every day.

➤ Force yourself to write for the specific amount of time you've set aside, even if you don't think you're producing anything usable. Write for the total time; no fudging!

➤ Keep your goals realistic. Decide to write a paragraph or a page at a time, not an entire chapter.

313

Write On!

Remember that writing is a deliberate act. Don't wait for the muse to come for a cup of tea and a donut. Call that baby in right now. You don't have to stare at a blank page day after day and suffer the torments of the damned. Writing should be pleasurable, not torture. Use the methods I described in this chapter.

If you've gotten this far, you've already gotten lots of good writing down on paper. Keep it up; I know you can do it.

The Least You Need to Know

➤ Even experienced writers sometimes have difficulty getting started.

➤ If you're a procrastinator, give yourself a kick in the pants.

➤ There are many easy and effective ways to overcome writer's block.

Glossary of Writing Terms

Act   An *act* is one of the main divisions in a play. Acts may be further divided into *scenes*.

Active voice   In the *active voice,* the subject performs the action named by the verb.

Adaptation   An *adaptation* is a script based on another work, such as a book or article.

Agent   An *agent* is a person who tries to sell a writer's work, place the writer in the right job, and guide the writer's career.

Alliteration   *Alliteration* is the repetition of initial consonant sounds in several words in a sentence or line of poetry. Use alliteration to create musical effects, link related ideas, stress certain words, or mimic specific sounds.

Allusion   An *allusion* is a reference to a well-known place, event, person, work of art, or other work of literature.

Anecdote   An *anecdote* is a brief story that gets the reader's interest and sheds light on a main idea and theme.

Antagonist   An *antagonist* is the force or person in conflict with the main character in a work of literature. An antagonist can be another character, a force of nature, society, or something within the character.

Article   An *article* is a short work of nonfiction.

Author's purpose   An *author's purpose* is the author's goal in writing a selection. Common purposes include to entertain, instruct, persuade, or describe. A selection may have more than one author's purpose, but often one purpose is the most important.

Autobiography   An *autobiography* is a person's story of his or her own life. An autobiography is nonfiction and describes key events from the person's life.

Ballad   A *ballad* is a story told in song form. Ballads often tell stories about adventure and love.

Biography   A *biography* is a true story about a person's life written by another person.

Blank verse   *Blank verse* is unrhymed poetry, usually written in iambic pentameter. Many poets write in blank verse because it captures the natural rhythm of speech.

Catalog technique   The *catalog technique* is a poetic list.

Character   A *character* is a person or an animal in a story. *Main characters* have important roles in a literary work; *minor characters* have smaller roles.

Characterization   *Characterization* is the act of telling readers about characters. Sometimes, writers tell about characters directly. Other times, writers let readers reach their own decisions by showing the comments, thoughts, and actions of the other characters.

Chronological order   *Chronological order* means arranging the events of a story in order in time from first to last.

Climax   The *climax* of a plot is the highest point in the action. During the climax, the conflict is resolved and the end of the story becomes clear. The climax is also called the *turning point.*

Collaboration   *Collaboration* is cooperation with two or more people in the writing of a script or other work.

Conclusion   A *conclusion* is the end of an article, play, poem, or book.

Conflict   A *conflict* in literature is a struggle or fight. Conflict makes a story interesting because readers want to discover the outcome. There are two kinds of conflict:

- ➤ In an *external conflict*, characters struggle against a force outside themselves.

- ➤ In an *internal conflict*, characters battle a force within themselves.

Stories often contain both external and internal conflicts.

Connotation   *Connotation* is a word's emotional overtones. "Home," for example, suggests warmth and acceptance; "house" carries no such overtones. Compare the connotations of "svelte" and "emaciated" and "thrifty" and "miserly."

Couplet   A *couplet* is made up of two related lines of poetry, which often rhyme.

Creative writing   *Creative writing* is a kind of writing that uses language in imaginative and bold ways.

Denotation   *Denotation* is a word's exact meaning.

Denouement   The *denouement* is the resolution of a story. At the denouement, all the loose ends of the story are woven together.

Description   *Description* is a kind of writing that creates a word picture of what something or someone is like.

Dialect   *Dialect* is the way people speak in a certain region or area. In a dialect, certain words are spelled and pronounced differently. Use dialects to define your characters and setting more fully.

Diction   *Diction* is word choice.

Dialogue   *Dialogue* is conversation in fiction or drama. It is the exact words a character says. In a story or novel, quotation marks are used to indicate dialogue.

Diary   A *diary* is a writer's record of his or her experiences, ideas, and feelings.

Drama   *Drama* is a piece of literature written to be performed in front of an audience. The actors tell the story through their actions and words.

Dramatic monologue   *Dramatic monologue* is a type of poem in which a character speaks, using the first person point of view.

Dramatic poetry   *Dramatic poetry* is a play written in poem form.

Epic   An *epic* is a long narrative in an elevated style, presenting high-born characters in a series of adventures that depict key events in the history of a nation.

Essay   An *essay* is a brief writing on a particular subject or idea.

Exposition   *Exposition* is a type of writing that explains, shows, or tells about a subject. The word can also be used to mean the opening parts of a play or story. During the exposition, the characters, action, and setting are introduced.

Extended metaphor   An *extended metaphor* compares two things at length and in several different ways.

Fable   A *fable* is a short, easy-to-read story that teaches a lesson about people. Fables often feature animals that talk and act like people.

Fantasy   *Fantasy* is a kind of writing that describes events that could not take place in real life. Fantasy has unrealistic characters, settings, and events.

Farce   *Farce* is a humorous play that is based on a silly plot, ridiculous situations, and comic dialogue. The characters are usually one-dimensional stereotypical figures. They often find themselves in situations that start out normally but soon turn absurd.

Fiction   *Fiction* is writing that tells about made-up events and characters. Novels and short stories are examples of fiction.

Figures of speech   *Figures of speech* (or *figurative language*) use words in fresh, new ways to appeal to the imagination. Figures of speech include *similes, metaphors, extended metaphors, hyperbole,* and *personification.*

Flashback   A *flashback* is a scene that breaks into the story to show an earlier part of the action. Flashbacks help fill in missing information, explain the characters' actions, and advance the plot.

Foot   A poetic *foot* is a pattern of stressed and unstressed syllables arranged in metrical *feet*. A foot is composed of either two or three syllables, such that the nature of the foot is determined by the placement of the accent. There are six basic types of metrical feet in English. The first four are very common; the last two are rare.

Foreshadowing   *Foreshadowing* provides clues that hint at what will happen later on in the story. Writers use foreshadowing to create suspense and link related details.

Frame story   A *frame story* is a shorter story within a larger one. Often, the longer story introduces and closes the frame story.

Free verse   *Free verse* is poetry without a regular pattern of rhyme and meter. Walt Whitman's poetry is an example of free verse.

Genre   *Genre* is a major literary category. The three genres are prose, drama, and poetry.

Haiku   *Haiku* is a Japanese poetic form that uses only three lines and a total of seventeen syllables.

Hero/Heroine   *Heroes* or *heroines* are literary characters whom we admire for their noble traits, such as bravery, selflessness, or cleverness. In the past, the term "hero" was used to refer to a male character; the term "heroine" for a female character. Today, "hero" is used for either male or female characters.

Humor   *Humor*—parts of a story that are amusing—can be created through sarcasm, word play, irony, and exaggeration.

Hyperbole   *Hyperbole* is exaggeration used for a literary effect such as emphasis, drama, or humor.

Image   An *image* is a word that appeals to one or more of our five senses: sight, hearing, taste, touch, or smell.

Imagery   See **Image**.

Inciting moment   The *inciting moment* is the beginning of a conflict.

Irony   *Irony* occurs when something happens that is different from what was expected.

➤ In *verbal irony*, there is a contrast between what is stated and what that statement suggests.

➤ In *dramatic irony*, there is a contrast between what a character believes and what the audience knows to be true.

➤ In *irony of situation*, an event reverses what the readers or characters expected.

Limerick   A *limerick* is a type of humorous poetry. Limericks have five lines, a strong rhyme, and a set rhythm. The first, second, and fifth lines rhyme with each other and the third and fourth rhyme with each other—*aabba*.

Lyric poems *Lyric poems* are brief, musical poems that express a speaker's feelings.

Main character The *main character* is the most important figure in a novel, short story, poem, or play.

Memoir A *memoir* is a first-person writing about an event.

Metaphor A *metaphor* is a figure of speech that compares two unlike things. The more familiar thing helps describe the less familiar one. Metaphors do not use the words "like" or "as" to make the comparison. "My heart is a singing bird" is a metaphor.

Meter *Meter* is a poem's rhythmical pattern, created by a pattern of stressed and unstressed syllables. The most common meter in English poetry is called *iambic pentameter*. It is a pattern of five *feet*, each having one unstressed syllable followed by a stressed one.

Minor character A *minor character* is a less important figure in a literary work, who serves as a contrast to the main character or to advance the plot.

Mood The *mood* (or *atmosphere*) is the strong feeling we get from a literary work. The mood is created by characterization, description, images, and dialogue. Some possible moods include terror, horror, tension, calmness, and suspense.

Myth A *myth* is a story from ancient days that explains certain aspects of life and nature.

Narration *Narration* is writing that tells a story. Narrations that tell about real events include biographies and autobiographies. Narrations that deal with fictional events include short stories, myths, narrative poems, and novels.

Narrative poems *Narrative poems* tell a story, either through a narrative storyline told objectively or through a dramatized situation.

Narrator The *narrator* is the person who tells a story. The narrator may also be a character in the work.

Nonfiction *Nonfiction* is a type of writing that deals with real people and events. Essays, biographies, autobiographies, and articles are all examples of nonfiction.

Novel A *novel* is a long work of fiction. The elements of a novel—plot, characterization, setting, and theme—are developed in detail. Novels usually have one main plot and several less important subplots.

Onomatopoeia *Onomatopoeia* is the use of words that imitate the sounds they describe—for example, words like "snap" and "crackle."

Passive voice In *passive voice*, the subject receives the action.

Personification *Personification* means giving human traits to nonhuman things. For example: "The book begged to be read."

Persuasion   *Persuasion* is a type of writing that tries to move an audience to thought or action.

Plot   *Plot* is the arrangement of events in a work of literature. Plots have a beginning, middle, and end. The writer arranges the events of the plot to keep the reader's interest and convey the theme. In many stories and novels, the events of the plot can be divided as follows:

➤ *Exposition*: Introduces the characters, setting, and conflict.

➤ *Rising Action*: Builds the conflict and develops the characters.

➤ *Climax:* Shows the highest point of the action.

➤ *Resolution:* Resolves the story and ties up all the loose ends.

Poetry   *Poetry* is a type of literature in which words are selected for their beauty, sound, and power to express feelings. Traditionally, poems had a specific rhythm and rhyme, but such modern poetry as *free verse* does not have regular beat, rhyme, or line length. Most poems are written in lines, which are arranged together in groups called *stanzas*.

Point of view   *Point of view* is the position from which a story is told. Here are the three different points of view writers use most often:

➤ *First-person point of view:* The narrator is one of the characters in the story. The narrator explains the events through his or her own eyes, using the pronouns *I* and *me.*

➤ *Third-person omniscient point of view:* The narrator is not a character in the story. Instead, the narrator looks through the eyes of all the characters. As a result, the narrator is "all-knowing" (omniscient). The narrator uses the pronouns *he, she,* and *they.*

➤ *Third-person limited point of view:* The narrator tells the story through the eyes of only one character, using the pronouns *he, she,* and *they.*

Prose   *Prose* is all written work that is not poetry, drama, or song. Examples of prose include articles, autobiographies, biographies, novels, essays, and editorials.

Protagonist   The *protagonist* is the most important character in a work of literature. The protagonist is at the center of the conflict and the focus of our attention. See **Main character.**

Purpose   See **Author's purpose.**

Realistic fiction   *Realistic fiction* contains imaginary situations and characters that are very similar to people in real life.

Refrain   A *refrain* is a line or a group of lines that are repeated at the end of a poem of song. Refrains serve to reinforce the main point and create musical effects.

Repetition   *Repetition* is using the same sound, word, phrase, line, or grammatical structure over and over for emphasis.

Resolution   The *resolution* of a plot occurs near the end of a story, when all the remaining strands of the story are woven together.

Rhyme   *Rhyme* is the repeated use of identical or nearly identical sounds. Poets use rhyme to create a musical sound, meaning, and structure.

> ➤ *End rhyme* occurs when words at the ends of lines of poetry have the same sound. Lines that end with the words *bat, cat, sat,* or *rat* would have end rhyme.

> ➤ *Internal rhyme* occurs when words within a sentence share the same sound. For example: "Each narrow cell in which we dwell." *Cell* and *dwell* have internal rhyme because they share the same sound and one of the words is set in the middle of the line.

Rhyme scheme   The *rhyme scheme* in a poem is a regular pattern of words that end with the same sound.

Rhythm   *Rhythm* is the pattern of stressed and unstressed words that create a beat, as in music.

Rituals   *Rituals* are little habits that provide structure to writers.

Scene   A *scene* is a part of a play. Each scene in a play takes place during a set time and in one place.

Science fiction   *Science fiction* (or *scifi*) is fantasy writing that tells about make-believe events that include science or technology.

Sensory language   *Sensory language* are words that appeal to the five senses: sight, hearing, taste, touch, or smell.

Setting   The *setting* of a story is the time and place where the events take place.

Short story   A *short story* is a form of narrative prose fiction that is shorter than a novel; it focuses on a single character and a single event. Most short stories can be read in one sitting and convey a single overall impression.

Simile   A *simile* is a figure of speech that compares two unlike things. Similes use the words "like" or "as" to make a comparison. "A dream put off dries up like a raisin in the sun" is an example of a simile.

Sonnet   A *sonnet* is a lyric poem of fourteen lines written in iambic pentameter.

Speaker   The *speaker* is the personality the writer assumes when telling a story. For example, the writer can tell the story as a young girl, an old man, or a figure from history.

Stage directions   *Stage directions* are instructions to the actors, producer, and director telling how to perform a play. Stage directions are included in the text of a play, written in parenthesis or italics. They describe how actors should speak, what they should wear, and what scenery should be used, among other things.

Stanza   A *stanza* is a group of lines in a poem, like a paragraph in prose. Each stanza presents one complete idea.

Style   *Style* is an author's distinctive way of writing. Style is made up of elements such as word choice, sentence length and structure, figures of speech, and tone. A writer may change his or her style for different kinds of writing and to suit different audiences. In poetry, for example, a writer might use more imagery than he or she would use in prose.

Surprise ending   A *surprise ending* is a conclusion that differs from what the reader expected. In most stories, the ending follows logically from the arrangement of events in the plot. In a surprise ending, however, final events take an unexpected twist.

Suspense   *Suspense* is the feeling of tension or anticipation a writer creates in a work. Writers create suspense by including unexpected plot twists. This keeps readers interested in the story and makes them want to read on to find out what will happen.

Symbol   A *symbol* is a person, place, or object that represents an abstract idea. For example, a dove may symbolize peace or a rose may symbolize love.

Theme   The *theme* of a literary work is its main idea, a general statement about life. The theme can be stated outright in the work, or readers will have to infer it from details about plot, characters, and setting.

Tone   *Tone* is the writer's attitude toward his or her subject matter. For example, the tone can be angry, bitter, sad, or frightening.

Transitions   *Transitions* are words and phrases that give your writing coherence.

Turning point   See **Climax**.

Verse   *Verse* is a stanza in a poem.

Voice   *Voice* is the author's personality as expressed through his or her writing.

Writing   *Writing* is a way of communicating a message to a reader for a purpose.

Index

325

Q-R